Published by The Trevithick Society
for the study of Cornish industrial archaeology and history

Copyright © 2010 The Trevithick Society
and A. J. Clarke

ISBN 978 0 904040 84 5

All rights reserved. No part of this publication may be reproduced, stored in a retrieval system, or transmitted in any form or by any means, electronic, mechanical, photocopying, recording or otherwise, without the prior permission of the Trevithick Society.

Printed and bound in Devon by Short Run Press Ltd.
25 Bittern Road, Sowton Industrial Estate, Exeter EX2 7LW

Typeset by Peninsula Projects, c/o PO Box 62, Camborne TR14 7ZN

Foreword

After 25 years as an (official) Mineral Processing technician with a lifelong passion for the history and intricacies of Cornish mining, I find it difficult to express how excited and privileged I felt when I came across this master work on the mechanical dressing of Cornish tin ores by the (then young and recently graduated) French mining engineer Léon Moissenet in the 'rare books' section of The Cornish Studies Library in Redruth.

Dating as it does from the late 1850s, a time when, unhappily for the researcher, such a superlative mass of material is all too rare, it seems to me to be the very epitome of what such a study should be, yielding a fascinating and detailed insight into the unavoidably laborious and repetitive, but always logical, very highly organized, knowledgeable and capably laid out batch treatment of Cornish tin ores at that time. A study impeccably compiled from first-hand observation, which must have taken many months of painstaking work, and full of the most interesting explanations of what was then current theory and methodology, along with both constructional and operational details for all kinds of apparatus in use at that time.

In addition, he included many excellent diagrams that he drew himself. These were originally inserted as an appendix on thin folded sheets at the end of the volume, and were much creased and very difficult to copy satisfactorily by digital camera. Under these circumstances, the images have cleaned up surprisingly well, though this took more hours than I care to remember, using computer graphics software.

Obviously, a literal translation would be very difficult to read and the relevant information spoilt from the point of view of clear assimilation. Therefore, while attempting at all times to retain the essential meaning and emphasis of the points made and descriptions given, I have taken a few liberties by way of paraphrasing, and interpretation in more modern terminology, simply in order to make the text easily readable. Where I have felt it necessary to add or insert the odd extra word or phrase in order to help achieve this, it has been done in brackets and italics.

Some of the original language and phrasing is remarkably elegant. For instance, in referring to the many assumptions made in the determination of stamps engine 'duty', or useful performance, Moissenet describes the calculations as being 'besmirched with inexactitude'. I have to admit I was sorely tempted to leave this in place purely for its own sake.

Even to an informed and interested party, the sheer mass, variety and complexity of tin ore treatment described is staggering, and a sympathetic heart goes out to those (often underrated and seldom overpaid) men whose job it was to put it into practice, working at the limits of the technology at their disposal.

It only remains for me to express my sincere thanks to Kim Cooper at The Cornish Studies Centre, for permission to undertake this labour, and for the unstinting help of Terry Knight, Neil, Claire and all the staff, past and present, over many other years of research into historical aspects of Cornish mineral dressing technology.

Last, but by no means least, many thanks are due to Pete Joseph for his patience and skill in rearranging and reformatting my initial layout.

Thanks are also due to The ARTFL Project website, for access to various 18th and 19th century French dictionaries – at times, invaluable.

Happy browsing.

Tony Clarke,

Senior Mineral Processing technician,
Camborne School of Mines, 1973 – 1998,
Coombe, Camborne, 2009.

Léon -Vivant Moissenet (1831 – 1906)

Born at Chalon-sur-Saône, 2nd of August 1831, the son of Jean Baptiste Moissenet (wine merchant) and Margaret Thérèse Moissenet, he was brought up and encouraged by his parents and grandparents to develop a strong, open-minded personality.

Along with good grades in college in his home town, he learned more varied practical skills at home, such as basketry and pottery, also studying drawing and stone cutting.

After studying at the Ecole Polytechnique (class of 1851), he entered the prestigious Ecole des Mines in Paris, where he was a student from August 1853 until March 1856, graduating with Honours after being ranked first at the end of each grade, and joined the Corps of Mines.

This work below, *An excursion in Cornwall in 1857*, was at least partly compiled when he was still a student, and was subsequently published in the Annales des Mines, Vol. XIV pp. 77 – 276, (1858).

He married Eugenie Alexandrine Beugnot in 1859 and had two sons:

Jean Vincent Léon (1860 – 1937), an engineer of roads and bridges, and
Louis Joseph (1864 – 1900), a marine engineer.

In 1869 he succeeded Rivot as Professor of Assaying at the Ecole des Mines and held that position until 1877, when he left state employ to enter industry, having already published at least six major studies on mining, geology and mineralogy and assaying, including several with a Cornish connection.

He later returned to state service, retiring as Chief Engineer of Mines in 1893.

Described by a contemporary as 'a scholar as distinguished as he was modest', he was awarded the title of Honorary Inspector-General of the Corps of Mines, being regarded, along with Elie de Beaumont (of The Academy of Sciences) as one of the fathers of the geological map of France.

Léon-Vivant Moissenet died on the 2nd of February 1906, at Chaumont (Haute-Marne).

Introduction

Existing descriptions

The mechanical dressing of Cornish tin ores has been described on several occasions, both in England and in France (1).

About 1758, Borlase, Rector of Ludgvan, near Penzance, described the procedures followed in the west of the county; in 1778, Pryce provided several additions to the work of Borlase, and produced, in detail, drawings of stamps and other apparatus that the latter had described.

Later, Dr. Boase published, in the 2nd volume of the *Transactions of the Royal Geological Society of Cornwall*, an account of tin ore dressing in the St. Just area, with special reference to the ores of that district which carried copper associated with the tin.

---

1. Borlase. *Natural History of Cornwall*, p. 177, (1758)
2. Pryce. *Mineralogia Cornubiensis*, p. 215, (1778)
3. Dr. H. Boase. *Trans. R.G.S.C.*, Vol. II, p. 386, (1828)
4. W. J. Henwood. *Trans. R.G.S.C.*, (read October 1828) Vol. IV, p. 145, (1832)
5. De la Bèche. *Report on the Geology of Cornwall*, p. 575, (1839)
6. Dufrénoy and Élie de Beaumont. *Annales des mines*, 2nd s., t. X, p. 33, (1825)
7. Coste and Perdonnet. *Annales des mines,* 2nd s., t. VI, p. 3, (1829)

W. J. Henwood, in the 4th volume of the same publication, described the somewhat different methods currently in use in central Cornwall (the districts of Camborne, Redruth etc.), the information that he gave applying to the year 1828.

In 1839 de la Bèche, in the 'economic' section of his major work on Cornwall and Devon, after having reviewed the relatively crude and simple methods employed by the ancients in former times, dedicated several pages to a comparison of the main points as described by both Pryce and Henwood.

On the same subject, the 'Annales des mines' included the report of Dufrénoy and Élie de Beaumont (1825), and that of Coste and Perdonnet (1829).

From the observations of de la Bèche, it appeared that the methods and procedure of tin ore dressing had not been much improved during the 50-year period that had elapsed since the description of Pryce and that of Henwood.

Progress made

In contrast, during the following 30 years, although the basic principles of operation had stayed the same, the introduction of steam stamps, nowadays generally and widely used, has tended to concentrate work on to large dressing floors. The presence of large quantities of material at one location has led to the invention and introduction of specialised apparatus and the improvement of old techniques, and has, at the same time, reduced both labour costs and metal losses.

If there still remains much to do in this branch of the mineral industry, it is no less true that there are profound differences between recently established large dressing floors and those of 1758, or even 1828.

Principal interest of this study

Interest in the study of Cornish mineral dressing today is, therefore, fully justified by the notable improvements introduced, as the similar nature of the necessary operations should, at least to some extent, give the engineer a type of generally applicable method for the water treatment of diverse ores and materials of varying character.

In fact, there are great difficulties. Ores of a mostly 'weak' character (*less pronounced characteristics*), in which the mineral is finely disseminated, are not well retained during treatment, and the reduction of the ore to a fine powder is necessary from the very start. Further, the demands of metallurgy dictate the production of a very rich marketable concentrate, the sole advantage available being the significant difference in density between the tin oxide and some of the gangue minerals.

In comparing this with the recovery of copper and lead ores, one can see the essential simplification of the process into the multiple sorting of those ores, done as far as possible on material in small pieces. Copper ores need little upgrading to be rendered marketable; as for galena (*lead ore*), its treatment often presents its own characteristic difficulties, on which I will not dwell, but in every case, the treatment of copper or lead fines and/or slimes is performed in Cornwall with identical apparatus to that used for tin.

In addition, nowhere better than on Cornish tin dressing floors can one observe the way in which the English carry out the always very delicate treatment of fine sands and metalliferous slimes.

With reference to these various points, I thought that it would be useful to put together the information collected during two visits to Cornwall.

Dressing floors visited

In 1855 I went through the dressing floors of the famous old Great Wheal Vor mine, recently restarted, and those of Providence Mines (*Carbis Bay*), Great Polgooth and Drakewalls. In 1857 I saw, in addition, Balleswidden, Tincroft, St. Day United, Carvath United, Carclaze, Pentuan and several others, as well as several times visiting the dressing floors of the Par Consols mine, near St. Austell.

The high price of tin at the time of my last trip (1) was the cause of great activity everywhere, and at several places the leavings of former activities could now be worked to advantage (2).

To these favourable circumstances, I can add the kindly welcome I received everywhere from the managers of the mines, and the inexhaustible obligingness of the Captains and agents on the dressing floors, so I may be permitted to mention among the former: Mr. F. Pryor of Redruth and the late Mr. Puckey of St. Austell, and among the Captains: Capt. Blight of Tincroft and Capt. W. Neetle of Par Consols mine.

---

1. During August and September 1857, high quality tin ore was selling for £80 per tonne. A short time afterwards, the price fell back to £60.

2. Since the writing of this report, I have visited many other dressing floors

in 1858, notably those of Dolcoath, Carnbrea, Polberro, Wendron Consols and Levant.

Divisions adopted

I have split this study into the following sections:

1. An outline of Cornwall – types of tin deposits and the nature of associated gangue minerals.
2. (a) A general description of treatment methods and the series of operations as conducted.

   (b) A description of several particular dressing floors and methods of treatment employed.
3. A description and operation of particular pieces of apparatus and equipment.
4. Economic data and considerations.
5. A note on methods for assaying tin ores.

SECTION 1

An outline of Cornwall – types of tin deposits, and the nature of associated gangue minerals.

Worked since ancient times, Cornwall has never ceased to be one of the principal centres of world metal production. It carries a great variety of types of mineral, and, besides metals, furnishes a large quantity of first choice building and construction materials.

Supplies of fuel are its only deficiency, but these can be brought in, at moderate cost, from the great coalfield of south Wales.

Thus, there is a great deal of coastal traffic; copper ores are loaded at Cornish ports and carried to the Swansea smelting plants, while coal comes by return. The main consumption of fuel is on the mines, for steaming large numbers of pumping and winding engines and stamps etc., while tin and lead smelters, foundries and forges also use a significant quantity.

Before giving some figures relating to actual Cornish metal production, it will be useful to review, briefly, the origins of the metal trade and those business transactions, so important nowadays, between the county of Cornwall and Wales (1).

(1) This information is taken from the work of de la Bèche, and that of J. Hawkins, *Transactions of the Penzance Geological Society, Vol. IV*.

Tin was already being worked and smelted on the spot in the time of the Phoenicians, who had made their colony of Gades, on the west coast of Spain, their main facility for this branch of commerce.

Historical information

In the time of the emperor Augustus, Diodorus of Sicily told how the Romans were purchasing tin from the Cornish, delivered to them on the 'island of Iktis' (*supposed to refer to St. Michael's Mount*), transporting it on horseback in a 30-day journey across France, to load it on board ship at the mouth of the river Rhone.

The demand for tin increased in the 6th and 7th centuries, for the casting of (*bronze*) bells, destined for the many cathedrals of this era, and later by the invention of artillery. In the 13th century, the Belgian city of Bruges was the home of the principal market for the metal, and in the 14th, Italian merchants were transporting it to the countries of the Levant (*areas of the Mediterranean east of Italy, as far as the Nile and the Euphrates, including the coastal regions of Syria, Asia Minor and Egypt*).

King John, in the year 1201, then, later, Richard Duke of Cornwall, and King Edward the 1st in 1305, granted charters and privileges to the producers of tin (*Tinners, Stannators*), thereby establishing their original special courts, known to this day as The Stannary Court, where the general affairs of the mines are regulated and any disputes adjudicated on and settled.

For a long time, exploitation was confined to alluvial tin; when these types of deposit became less productive, lodes were worked, and the search for tin led to discoveries of copper ore. In 1600, Carew stated that copper ores were already being shipped to Wales, probably for the sake of economising on the cost of fuel necessary for smelting.

Around 1700, Cornish tin smelters began to replace 'blowing houses', using wood charcoal and turf as fuel, with reverbatory furnaces fired by coal, with the first steam pumping engines being erected on mines at about the same time.

The Wheal Vor (*tin*) mine had one of these, of the Savary or Newcomen type, from 1710 to 1714. Newcomen engines were erected in significant numbers from 1720 to 1778, before being superseded by those of Watt, whose performance has since been perfected, up to the present day.

To summarize, it can be seen that tin has been produced in Cornwall from very ancient times, and then, as today, the treatment was complete, including the metallurgical stage (*of smelting*). Copper ores, doubtless worked a little before the year 1600, were, from that moment on, managed and controlled in Wales, and the industrial use of the coal of that country, in Cornwall, dates back only as far as 1700, due to its introduction at that time in the process of tin smelting, and the exploitation of the power of steam engines.

As for the extraction and processing of silver-bearing lead ores, this began well before that of copper ores, and their exploitation is today one of the important branches of the mining industry of the region, where two plants smelt a large proportion of the Cornish produce in situ.

Without going further with these general remarks, I will explain the actual current production of the main minerals by means of some statistics.

Mineral production in 1856

During the year 1856, Cornwall and Devon furnished:

Item	Tin	Copper	Lead	Silver	Zinc
	Tons	Tons	Tons	Ounces	Tons
Ores	9,350	206,177	13,112	-	3,977
Equivalent metal	6,177	13,534	8,597	325,892	-

The copper ores sold for 31,045,628 francs (*around £M1¼*).

The tin ores sold for 16,596,250 francs (*around £660,000*).

To these must be added:

8,000 – 10,000 tons of iron pyrites.

26,750 tons of hematite iron ore.

500 – 600 tons of arsenic trioxide (as the refined product).

A small quantity of nickel and uranium ores.

The granites of Dartmoor in Devonshire, those around Liskeard, those of Penrhyn and Constantine, near Falmouth, and those of Lamorna, near Penzance, are extensively exploited for larger maritime projects such as slipways and docks etc.

The altered granites in the neighbourhood of St. Austell, and those of Breag, near Helston, give rise to a production of close on 100,000 tons of china clay and china-stone, mostly sent to the potteries of Staffordshire.

Near Camelford, in the great excavations known as the Delabole Quarries, excellent quality slate is extracted.

The serpentines of The Lizard Peninsula are made into very beautiful fireplaces and mantelpieces, as well as other decorative and ornamental objects.

These figures will give the reader some idea of the mass of products coming from Cornwall each year. As to the consumption of coal today, I have no exact figures, though Mr. Henwood's statistics tell us that in 1837, the mines burnt some 56,860 tons. The total consumption nowadays, including smelters, is probably above 100,000 tons per annum.

Ports Following the north coast around the peninsula, the main Cornish ports are Padstow, Newquay, Portreath, Hayle, Penzance, Falmouth, Truro, Pentuan, Charlestown, Par, Fowey, Looe, Morwelham and Calstock. At many points, the broad mouths of the short rivers allow access to wharves and buildings at some distance from the coast, so the river Fal is navigable as far as Truro, and the Tamar as far as Morwelham. At other places, canals have been constructed, such as those at Par and Liskeard.

Railways For some years, a 27½-miles long railway from Penzance to Truro has served the mineral district of Camborne-Redruth, with branch lines from Redruth to Portreath and Devoran.

A main line from Truro to Plymouth, connecting Cornwall at this point with the English network by a junction with the Great Western Railway, is virtually complete save for an extension to Falmouth. It will be open to traffic when the major undertaking of Mr. Brunel, the Saltash Bridge over the Tamar, is finished, most probably during 1859.

Tramways Horse-drawn lines, or tramways, run in several directions, such as that from Par to Newquay, with a yet unfinished central section, the little line from St. Austell to Pentuan, which follows the valley where, from a long time ago to the present day, there have been large, active, alluvial tin streamworks, and the 6-miles long inclined plane from Cheesewring to Moorswater, near Liskeard, which crosses the Caradon mining district. For tin ores, which are of especial interest to us, transport from the mine to the smelter is by rail or by cart.

Tin smelting works The nine tin smelting houses are all located in the area from Penzance to Truro, except that at Charlestown, near St. Austell:

Smelting House	Proprietors
Calenick	Mitchell & Co.
Cavedras	Daubus & Co.
Treluswell	
Charlestown	Enthoven & Co.
Angarrak	Bolitho & Co.
Chyandour	
Trethellan	Williams, Harvey & Co.
Mellanear	
Bissoe Bridge	Bissoe Bridge Co.

The various machines and apparatus needed for underground work, and on the mechanised dressing floors, are manufactured by several foundries spread over various districts. The large Hayle Foundry is first-rate; I will mention, besides, others such as Copper House, near Camborne; Tucking-Mill, in the village of the same name; Perran, on the Truro River; St. Blazey, near St. Austell; that of Mr. Thomas at Charlestown; that of N. Holman & Sons at St. Just, and Roseland Vale, near Liskeard.

Foundries

The sales by auction of machinery and materials from abandoned mines often allow adventurers to equip themselves at very reasonable cost.

Although the rates of pay for manual labour in Cornwall are always fixed fairly low compared to other regions in England, in recent years they have seen a significant increase, like everywhere else, but particularly here due to the large-scale emigration of miners to Australia.

Labour

The workforce on the dressing floors is made up of mechanics/drivers of machinery, foremen, supervisors (*'grass Captains'*) and, above all, the wives and children of miners. Boys are permitted to work underground, though almost all are 15 years of age (1); only a few of this age are retained for harder, more laborious dressing work.

The following figures for monthly pay may be cited:

Mechanics/drivers	£3. 10s.
Manual labourers	£2. 15s.
Women, and girls over 17 years of age	£1 to £1. 15s.
Girls of 14 – 17 years of age	Up to 25s.
Girls of 12 – 14 years of age	Up to 14s.
Girls of 9 – 12 years of age	Up to 10s.
Boys over 14 years of age	£1
Boys of 12 – 14 years of age	Up to 15s.
Most boys below 12 years of age	Up to 10s.

Cornwall is formed from a series of granite upthrusts and transitional strata. On leaving Lands End, the extremity of the peninsula, five large granite massifs and nine smaller ones are met with, more or less connected with the former (2).

Geological outline (2)

(I) Annales des mines, 1857, part 6, Bulletin: *On the mortality and death rate of miners etc.*

(2) See the following works:
- (i) Dr. H. Boase. *Trans. R.G.S.C.* Vol. IV, p. 166.
- (ii) De la Bèche. '*Report*' etc. (op. cit.).
- (iii) W.J. Henwood. '*On the metalliferous deposits of Cornwall and Devon*'.
- (iv) Dufrénoy and Elie de Beaumont. *Annales des mines*, '*Voyage en Angleterre*'.
- (v) Elie de Beaumont. '*Systèmes de montagnes*'.

Granite massifs

Large massifs	Small massifs
St. Just, St. Ives etc.	-
Crowan, Wendron, Penrhyn, Gwennap, etc.	St. Michael's Mount
	Tregoning & Godolphin Hills
	Carn Brea
	Carn Marth
-	Cligga Head
St. Austell, Luxulian, St. Dennis etc.	Castle-an-Dinas, Belovely Beacon
Bodmin Moor	Kit Hill
Dartmoor, Devonshire	Gunnislake

One may add the Isles of Scilly, and the island of Lundy, at the entrance to The Bristol Channel.

Considered as a whole, these massifs form a broken line. If one joins the centre of The Scilly Isles to the centre of Bodmin Moor, and from this point take a line across Dartmoor at its widest point, you have two directional lines representing, respectively, the systems of Finistère (E. 21° 46′ N.), and that of The Netherlands (E. 14° 55′ N.).

Sedimentary rocks

The sedimentary rocks are essentially schists (killas), of which part, at least, is Silurian, as shown as a result of the discovery of Silurian fossils made some years ago by Mr. Peach, on the south Cornish coast between Falmouth and St. Austell.

Devonian layers exist to the east, the schist passing at times into greywacke, with subordinate limestones.

At several places around the granite intrusions, notably on the northwest coast of the St. Just massif, and near St. Austell, are found green amphibole rocks, or 'greenstones'.

The mines can be grouped in districts, as follows:

District	General position
St. Just	1. West. To the west of a line from Hayle to Marazion.
St. Ives	
Gwinear & Crowan	2. Central. To the east of the former, and west of a line from Truro to Cubert.
Marazion	
Helston	
Camborne & Illogan	
Redruth & Gwennap	
St. Agnes & Perranzabuloe	
St. Austell	3. East. East of the former, as far as the River Tamar.
Liskeard, Caradon	
Callington, Calstock	
Tavistock	4. Devonshire.

Metalliferous districts

The central region is the area with biggest production of copper and tin, after which comes the western district, for tin, and Devon, for copper. The Caradon district, where workings are relatively recent, seems destined for a magnificent future.

Tin ore is found:
1. In small strata, veins or lodes.
2. In 'stockworks', or networks of little 'strings'.
3. Disseminated throughout alluvial deposits.
4. In definite major lode structures.

Types of tin deposit

1. Veinlets or 'strings' of tin are found especially in those areas of killas immediately bordering the granite. They also exist at the junction of these rocks and, in a similar manner, in the granite itself. They should be regarded sometimes as lode branches, sometimes as contemporaneous deposits.
2. Stockworks are met with either in the granite or in large masses of elvan. Carclaze, the most remarkable example, is in the granite.
3. The tin is distributed in alluvial material as fine sand and pebbles of greater or lesser size. Where it is found in association with quartz and chlorite, which constituted the original lode gangue, then no sulphide minerals are met with. Actual production from such streamworks has now become insignificant.
4. Several types of lode system have long been recognized in Cornwall. I may comment on some developments in connection with this subject later, with regard to tin lodes, but for now will list verified types of lode:

Lodes

Lode type		General directional limits
Lodes in the elvan	-	Approximately east-west
The oldest tin lodes	-	East 8 to 25° N., except St. Just area, West 35° N.
More recent tin lodes	-	
The oldest copper lodes	-	As above.
More recent copper lodes	-	West, 5 to 35° N.
Cross-courses	-	North, 20° E. to N 20° W.
	-	(lead, iron, barren)
The most recent copper lodes	-	About E. 15° N.
Barren	Fluckans	As cross-courses
cross-courses	Slides	As lodes

This list gives the lodes and faults in chronological order, as far as can be established from the study of faults so far made. Elvans must be treated as exceptions, as they are generally cut by all the others, but in some mines, themselves cut the older tin lodes.

Copper and tin

It would not do to think of these types as absolute definitions, as many lodes carry both tin and copper at the same time, as may be seen from some examples.

1. At Tincroft, I have seen a lode in which all the zone immediately adjacent to the wall carried only tin. Immediately above, although nicely distinct, there was an intimate mixture of tin and chalcopyrite that filled the lode to the roof.

2. At Par Consols, a tin lode where the pyrite was only found disseminated as tiny specks, but deeper, it occurred in considerable masses.

3. The mines of Dolcoath and Carnbrea, after having been very productive for copper, now yield large quantities of tin in depth.

Tin lodes

In a general way, one can say that tin is one of the metals that has more of a relationship with the granite. Tin lodes are met with especially in the neighbourhood of the granite, but extend as well both into this rock and into the killas. At the same time, those tin mines working solely in the killas, though fewer, are the more productive.

Gangue minerals

The main gangue minerals are quartz, chlorite and iron oxide. It is known that, very often, a cross-section of a lode shows here and there a median line, a certain symmetry as to the nature of the infilling, and it has been noted that, depending on the surrounding rock, various gangue minerals occur in the following order:

Granite	**Surrounding rock**	**Crystalline tin oxide**
	Quartz	Crystalline quartz, wolfram
	Quartz	Chlorite, crystalline tin oxide

Killas	Quartz	Crystalline tin oxide
	Chlorite	Crystalline tin oxide
Elvan	Tin oxide	Crystalline tin oxide

In granite, the gangue is generally a pale green felspar, of a confused crystalline nature, showing some nice crystals and groups of needles of tourmaline and quartz. There, the tin is distributed in crystals, rarely larger than a pea, and most often very fine. Sometimes, the lode is very 'quartzy', and there the tin is very 'strong', as it is in the Great Work mine, near Helston. At Balleswidden, where there are no proper lodes to speak of, but a series of small, parallel tin veins, extending into the granite at great length, as in the Carclaze stockwork, the veinlets of tin are almost pure and associated with no more than a little quartz, tourmaline and felspar.

1. In the granite

In the killas, the lode usually carries a very hard gangue of quartzose schist (capel), generally mixed with chlorite, sometimes with tourmaline and rarely with felspar. There, the tin is even more finely disseminated than in lodes in granite, and is always accompanied by a lot of mineral to make dressing difficult, such as iron pyrites, mispickel (*arsenical pyrites*), wolfram and either earthy or 'quartzy' iron oxide.

2. In the killas

I shall not dwell overlong on the minerals long known to be associated with tin, but simply review the characteristics of tin deposits from the point of view of any resulting difficulties in dressing.

Summary, tin and gangues

The following may be mentioned:

1. Alluvial tin in grains more or less separated from the country rock.
2. Tin in small veinlets, always quite 'strong'. In granite either in the form of a lode, as at the mines of Balleswidden and Beam, or as stockworks such as Carclaze. In elvan, at the old Budnick Mine and finally in killas, as at Polberro, near St. Agnes, and at Drakewalls.
3. Fairly granular tin in lodes in granite, with quartz, tourmaline, iron oxide, a little pyrite and some little chlorite.
4. Tin in lodes in killas, with quartzose schist, chlorite, pyrite, mispickel, and in certain localities, wolfram. It is here that the tin is the most finely disseminated.

The dressing floors to be described in later parts of this work deal especially with the latter two types of ores.

Tincroft mine, presently working at depth in the granite, has very hard produce, a quartzo-ferruginous gangue with lots of pyrite, mispickel and very finely disseminated tin.

Par Consols, Polgooth and Wheal Vor are worked deep in killas carrying quartz and chlorite. Polgooth has the most finely distributed tin, and Wheal Vor significant quantities of mispickel.

St. Day United (the former Poldice mine) has a quartz gangue with much mispickel and wolfram, the mine being in killas.

At Drakewalls, the veinlets in the killas carry tin grains of particularly large size, extremely favourable for treatment. However, this advantage is here offset by an abundance of wolfram.

Produce from treated material

Some portions of rich lodes sometimes yield masses of ore of sufficient purity to pass directly for smelting, Polberro Mine, near St. Agnes, being a noteworthy example of this. After treatment, most of the ores handled today on the large dressing floors do not yield more than 2% (*of the initial weight*) of the ore ready for smelting, known as 'black tin'.

SECTION 2(a)
A general statement of treatment methods, and the series of operations conducted.

Work on bulk material

Ragging

Spalling

After leaving the shaft, the raw ores undergo a first crushing by sledgehammer (ragging), though only to break up the large pieces. Then a second stage of breaking (spalling) reduces everything to a size needed by the stamp mill, that is, to about the size of a fist. This spalling is accompanied by sorting, producing at least three designated types of material.

1. Rich ore – 'best' work.

2. Average grade ore – 'common' or 'poor' work.

3. More or less barren material – rejected to waste or to 'halvans'.

The presence of copper ore in a great many tin lodes sometimes demands the sorting of a further type. However, distinguishing between 'tin' and 'copper' ores often takes place on the same site, in such a way that the retained tin ore carries only specks of pyrite that cannot be got rid of by sorting. The various parcels of ores, having been weighed and assayed separately (*to determine tributers' payment*) are taken to the dressing floors.

Siting and configuration of dressing floors

The location of the dressing floors has to be chosen with the greatest care, and among the primary considerations are:

1. The distance from the hoisting shaft.

2. The easy provision of a water supply, particularly for the stamps.

3. A definite slope, of sufficient area to contain the activities.

Conditions to fulfil

The second two are more important than the first one, but unfortunately, are to some extent mutually exclusive, and can only actually be satisfactorily applied when using steam stamps. In fact, it was necessary in the past to first of all provide a sufficient fall of water, which, used mostly for driving the stamps, was afterwards used for dressing. The total difference in level available from the point of its arrival to the bottom of the dressing floors had to be split between the diameter of the stamps water wheel (at the ore hoppers) and the slope to be maintained on the surface of the dressing floors. Even with the best solutions, the falls at one's disposal allow the setting up of floors with no more than 3, 4, 6, or 8 heads (*at a time*), spread out in the valleys. Very rarely does one come across water stamps with 16 or 24 heads.

Even today a certain number of concerns, quite often the owners of large concessions, are willing to hire out such small sets of stamps, either to small mines or to groups of tributers. Under these conditions the cost of transport from the shaft to the dressing floor can be considerable.

With steam engines there is no reason for concern over natural topography or motive power, and the number of heads can be carried as far as 60, 80 or 120. These large sets of stamps, centralising an enormous quantity of material at one point, have allowed the introduction of bigger and larger scale apparatus, working rapidly. In the final dressing operations, despite concentration of materials as a result of their enrichment, (*the amount to be treated means that*) one can still feed square buddles etc., and avoid recourse to, as in the past, the use of hand sieves, the appropriate treatment for very small parcels of produce.

At the same time, the sheer quantity of material, making one aware of the importance of simplifying its movement, has led to dressing floors being laid out in the most favourable arrangement. Things that on small, water-powered floors had either been impossible, or a refinement of little use, have today become indispensable or an obvious improvement. Let us see how, on actual large dressing floors, the stipulations made above are put into practice.

As a rule, operations are centred near the winding and pumping shafts, which provide the ore and water, respectively. The distance from the bulk ore floors to the stamps rarely exceeds one kilometre, and small tramways lead to the rear of the stamps, such that the wagons can be emptied directly into the stamps feed hoppers.

Most often, water comes from the mine, the pumps having raised it to the mouth of the shaft instead of discharging it into the adit. After running across the dressing floors, a large proportion of the water is normally returned via underground channels to a sump, excavated in front of the stamps. A pump, connected by a balance bob to the stamps engine, then raises this water back up to the surface of the dressing floors. Neglecting losses by evaporation and soakaway, one can, thus, almost double the quantity of water available. Despite this, it is often insufficient, and work is sometimes restricted solely for this reason. On some mines, such as Tincroft and Dolcoath, water comes from old adits. Nevertheless, large dressing floors of 48 – 80 heads consume, on average, some 2 – 5 cubic metres (2 – 5 tons) of water per minute.

Considering the available lie of the land, things can be set out as follows:

1. A mean slope of significant width, forming a large inclined plane, with channels and apparatus laid out end to end in the most suitable order, though the sideways movement of material can become quite considerable (as at Wheal Vor and Balleswidden).
2. A narrow valley bottom, with room to use both hillsides.
3. A sort of 'hog's back', or ridged hill, the stamps always occupying the highest point, and some of the apparatus arranged on the sides (as at St. Day United).
4. An elongated hillside with a fairly steep slope in a series of tiers or terraces, on which a layout like No. 1 is arranged in a sort of zig-zag (as at Par Consols).
5. Almost flat ground, extremely unfavourable and requiring considerable transfer of material, either by shovel or wheelbarrow (as at Tincroft).

In every case, material carried by water to be separated by apparatus must have a natural flow, and every effort must be made to reduce the manpower involved in transferring material from one place to another. An elongated sloping hillside is most advantageous. It is obvious how much the average slope and surface area of large dressing floors can vary. In respect of the latter, one can have a ½-hectare (*1¼ acres*) at Tincroft, and 1½ hectares (*3¾ acres*) at Par Consols, without counting the space that tailings, sands and slimes, can occupy along the length of valley floors, when they are not carried away to the sea.

Separation on the floors of 'best' and 'common' work

The stamps can extend on both sides of the engine. Each side of the dressing floor receives from the stamps, sands from a certain type of ore. One portion of the products from 'best work' (*the richest ore*), (*the strip 'heads?'*), is upgraded separately up to final preparation, and so by-passes being mixed with other, poorer material. The rest of it undergoes the series of treatments with the 'common work' (*average grade ore*).

Division of materials from the point of view of treatment

Stamped ore is split into two portions:

1. Sands retained in the strips ('crop').
2. Fine slimes, carried over into pits.

Crop

The treatment of crop sands yields rich sands, poor coarse sands (known as 'roughs'), and some additional slimes.

Roughs

The roughs still carry some tin, usually 'locked' in association with the gangue, though a little rich sand can sometimes be separated, leaving a significant proportion of sand, tin and gangue, insufficiently stamped, to be sent back again for stamping, under the name of 'crazes'.

Besides the crazes, work on the roughs gives still more fresh slimes, and a great mass of sands judged to be barren and discarded.

Slimes

Sands deposited in the first strips retain some slimes, which are only progressively removed, with each series of operations yielding slimes of a somewhat different nature.

The results of slimes treatment are rich and very fine slimes, poor slimes (discarded), and a quite small proportion of sands, also classed as 'roughs'.

The rich products, as sands or slimes, carry only a small amount of gritty gangue, though, along with the tin oxide are concentrated (*other*) high-density metallic minerals that can occur associated with the tin, and whose proportions vary greatly according to the type of deposit. These can include virtually all the wolfram, most of the mispickel (*arsenical pyrites*), and a large proportion of the iron pyrites and copper pyrites. On a large number of mines, these rich sands have the white metallic sheen of mispickel and pyrite and are called by the workers 'tin witts' (1).

---

(1) It is thought that 'witt' could be a corruption of the word 'white'.

Great difficulties were experienced in wanting to push washing operations further, and, on the other hand, of similar products yielding only very impure tin on treatment.

Simple roasting serves to get rid of pyrite and mispickel. The sulphur and arsenic are burnt off, and the iron and copper minerals remain as oxides and sulphates, respectively. The oxides are light and the sulphates are soluble, so that a subsequent washing can remove them quite easily.

Roasting (burning, calcining)

As for wolfram, this is no more affected (*by roasting*) than tin, and it is only after recourse to the use of chemical reagents that, in recent years, wolfram has been able to be removed from Drakewalls ore (*The Oxland Process*).

When chalcopyrite is present in the rich sands in sufficient proportion, after roasting, moistening and suspension in water they yield copper sulphate in solution, and the copper can be precipitated out on to iron (cementation).

The tin concentrate obtained from sands treatment is in grains of noticeable size, and is called 'crop tin'. That obtained from various slimes is extremely fine, and is called, depending on its origin, 'fine' or 'small' tin. These two products are finally mixed by shovel and constitute 'black tin', fit for market. As average limits of admixture, one can take one-quarter to one-seventh, and as extreme limits, one-half to one-twentieth (I)

The proportion of fine tin recovered from various slimes residues (known as 'leavings') varies greatly with the type of tin deposit.

(I) 'Fine' tin in black tin:

Mine	Proportion
St. Day United	One-seventh
Polgooth	One-eighth
Par Consols	One-quarter
Balleswidden	One-quarter to one-third

The grades of 'crop' and 'fine' tin are the same.

Certain operations after roasting yield products, some good, some less so, that are often put to one side, and kept separate until sufficient has been accumulated as one lot for sale.

Below is a diagram summarising:

1. The main divisions of operations.
2. Intermediate products.
3. Definitive products.

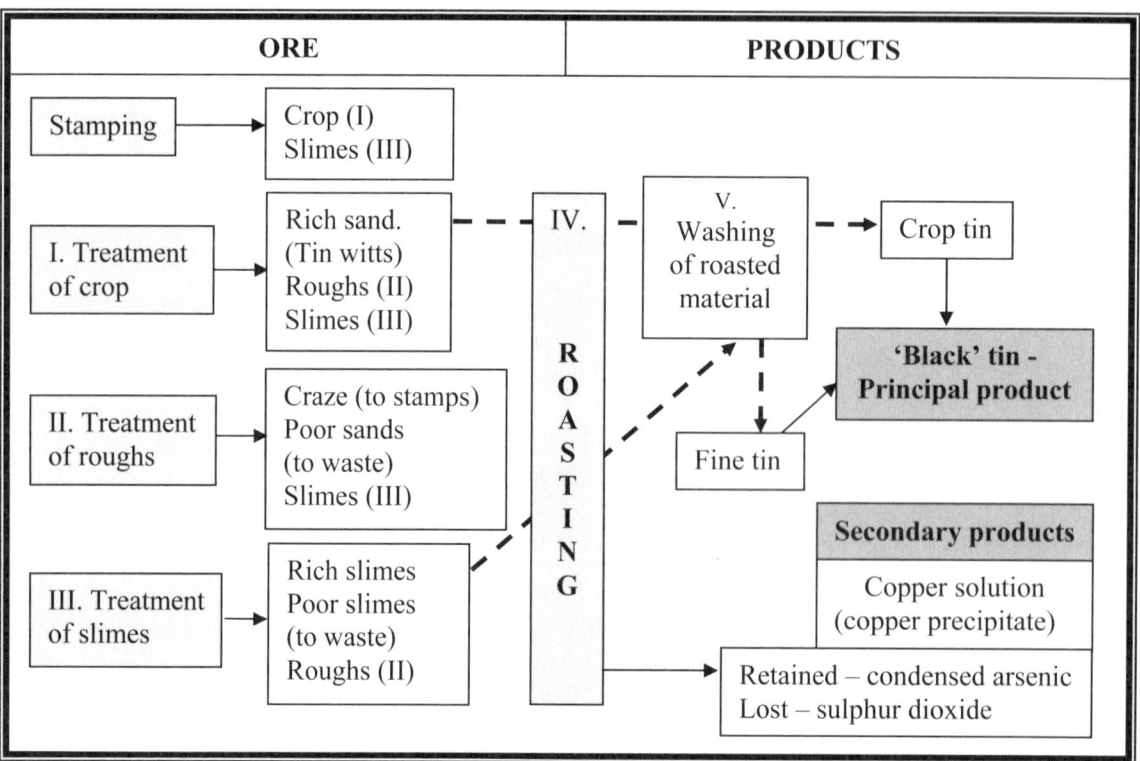

This is a general breakdown, at least concerning operations before roasting. I only know Tincroft to cite as an exception, where the unfavourable location of the dressing floors does not allow treatment of all the roughs.

Apart from alluvial ores, there are only a very few deposits where the total absence of any pyritic minerals does away with the need for roasting, and the washing which follows (I).

(I) The Carclaze stockwork; in the St. Just district, one part of Wheal Bal ores, and near Helston, one part of the ores at Wendron Consols need no calcining.

Bringing the ore to the appropriate condition for roasting is the greatest, yet most delicate, part of the work. Large quantities of material are treated, and the slightest alterations immediately change the expense of manpower, and later on, the yield that one can hope to obtain from a given ore.

Operations before roasting

The intimate structure of the ore, and the nature of sands, always more or less poor, cannot be appraised without long experience and the constant aid of the vanning shovel.

Stamping, the first operation that the ore undergoes on arrival on the dressing floor, definitely demands to be carried out with the greatest skill, as its effect is decisive and extends to all the rest of the treatment. It is a high art to be able to determine judiciously, depending on the ore, what size of sand particles to produce. One has to strive to break the rock sufficiently to free the tin grains from the gangue, while crushing these grains themselves as little as possible. In actual fact, very fine tin is a source of difficulties of every kind, since, on account of its high density, it is found distributed in the sands as well as the slimes. Taken too far, stamping breaks a very high proportion of the gangue as well as the tin, producing a lot of slimes, and here, as everywhere else, the treatment of slime material is still far less effective than that of sands.

Stamping

For any given ore, we are therefore looking to have as little slime as possible, though this is limited by the disadvantages of insufficient stamping (*and liberation*). By reducing the proportion of slimes, that of the 'roughs' is increased, that is, those sands from which the crazes (tin and gangue) have to be separated and sent back to the stamps.

The problem is not that by doing this, the cost of stamping is increased, because, theoretically, the work of pulverisation to an appropriate size would be the same if it were done in one, or two, steps. Every advantage would be gained under this relationship, since the crazes are only ever a small fraction of the roughs, but that the restamped crazes have to go through the whole series of washing operations over again. What is worse, a considerably greater amount of slimes is produced, as the crazing stamps are set out to crush extremely finely, and have to be fed with crazes and ore particles together, so it is necessary to avoid falling back into this disadvantage.

Here, as in almost all methods of mineral separation, lies a question of maximum importance that has to be resolved.

The best comparison to draw is with certain metallurgical treatments, where the products from primary smelting would be metal, matte (*par-

tially smelted ore) and dross to retreat. It is necessary to obtain as much metal as possible straight away, and to produce enough matte so as to have little dross to retreat. However, not having a proportion of matte to retreat every time can offset the advantages that result from its formation. Similarly here, we are looking to obtain as much good sands as possible for the crop treatment, few slimes, and, yet, a not overlarge proportion of roughs.

Character indications regarding treatment

So, to sum up, an ore giving little slimes and little crazes will be easy to treat, and one yielding a lot of slimes and crazes will be difficult to treat, and treat effectively.

The proportion of crazes to produce is too variable a question to consider definite limits (I).

(I) At Par Consols, they stamp about one-third to crazes and ore, at Polgooth, about one-twentieth, and at Balleswidden only one-fortieth.

Treatment of crop ore

The treatment of 'crop' ore involves the major portion of the stamped material, only those slimes carried beyond the primary strips escaping the first series of treatments. Their proportion, so variable from mine to mine, as is that of the 'fine tin' recovered, has, as average limits, ¼ to ⅖ of the total material, so the crop floors have to handle ⅗ to ¾ of the whole.

There, as in succeeding stages, the idea is to work rapidly, by means of various types of 'roughing' apparatus that quickly separate out a large quantity of relatively poor material, and to pay attention to those manipulations to obtain richer products. There is a successive progression by classification in order of density and size. That is to say, the varying use of apparatus where each of these sorting effects predominates. Having regard to the general fineness of the materials, the size fractions only truly apply to the separating out of slimes. Following through the dressing floor, the richest product will be now sand, now slimes.

Apparatus used

The apparatus used in the treatment of crop ore:

1. Strips.
2. 'Square' buddles.
3. Round buddles.
4. Kieves.

Strips

1. All along the stamps runs planking, about one metre wide, on which stamped material runs off to the strips, which, normally, occupy all the ground in front of the stamps, and are laid out on the ground perpendicular to the stamps axle. In other cases they are parallel to it. One half of these strips receive stamped material while the other is dug out by workmen, movable stops feeding the sands alternately to each of the two series. Part of the stamped product is sent to strips of uniform slope

over their entire length of about 33 feet (ten metres), while some are interrupted by one or two drops in height, producing the effect of two or three strips laid end to end.

In these, for example, the first section occupies three or four metres, with double that for the second.

At the lowest end, vertical partitions carry two slots, in each of which a workman puts small cross-pieces, one on top of the other, creating a movable stop that raises the depth of the deposit in the strip. Water and slimes pass constantly over the top, to recombine in a general channel at the foot of the strip, and run from there into large slime pits.

In each single strip the deposit is divided into three parts:

1. The 'head' of the strip (very small), where the sand is already quite enriched.
2. A middle section, much less rich.
3. The final two-thirds, the 'tail' of the strip, with large grains, often mixed with slime.

In the case of 3-part strips, a small 'head' is divided off in each section and mixed with the heads from long strips. There will often be four definitive portions in the case of a single long strip, and five for those strips already in two separate sections.

When a strip does its job correctly, in the case of very poor ore the tail can be discarded directly to 'roughs'. Almost everywhere, this is done simply by shovel, into a small, rectangular pit, from where the slimes run away to slime pits, while the sands return to the ongoing operations that the head and the 'middlings' undergo.

2. Before the invention of the round buddle, all the strip sands were passed to the 'tin case' or buddle (nowadays known as the 'square buddle' to distinguish it). This is still the practice on all small floors and on some larger ones.

The square buddle 'tin case'

The buddle is a rectangular box of varying dimensions (*and capacity*), 8¼ to 13¼ feet (2.5 to 4 metres) in length, 2½ to 6 feet (0.75 to 1.8 metres) wide, and 2 to 2½ feet (0.6 to 0.75 metres) in depth. It is sunk below ground level, the small, lower side being flush with the surface, and the floor has a definite slope. Materials are fed in at least two ways.

- Most often, the sands are thrown into a hopper by shovel, and constantly washed out by a stream of water on to a triangular, inclined plane, fitted with (*distributing*) strips arranged in a fan-shape. The spaces between these strips act as channels, where the feed material splits up and forms a (*flowing*) coating, the same width as the buddle. This is then evenly distributed by falling on to a small, narrow, sloping board, 1 foot (or 30 cm.) wide and runs away into the buddle. The large, specially constructed 'square buddles' are arranged in exactly the same way.
- The other arrangement consists of having a large board, 0.4 metres

(16 inches) in size, at the head of the buddle, on which the sands are put directly (the 'jagging board'). An attendant continually makes small channels (parallel to the long axis of the buddle) in the material with the edge of his shovel (*to aid its flow and distribution*). Water from a circular hole flows on to the already loaded board.

Formerly, buddles were all arranged in this way, and were only of relatively small size. This form of buddling has been retained, without any seemingly valid reason, for several small buddles used for the treatment of already quite rich material, before or after calcining, going under the name of buddle or 'tin case'.

In both arrangements, water carrying fine slimes escapes from the lower end of the buddle through holes pierced in the 'tailboard' (the partition that forms its foot). Plugs are placed in these holes as the level of the deposited contents rises, and an underground channel conducts the water flow away. Besides one boy to load the sand feed, a second is needed working in the buddle to level out the deposit and keep the top surface as a regular, inclined plane. Nowadays, this workman is normally above, on a plank placed across the buddle, and provided with a long-handled broom. In past times, a boy stood in the buddle itself and produced the effect with his feet, either bare, or shod with wooden sandals (brogues) if the treated sand was fine. I myself, have seen at Wheal Vor, in the case of very fine material, the broom replaced by a large feather attached to a stick, the workman there being seated in the buddle on a kind of stool.

However this is accomplished, once the buddle is full, the Captain (*Superintendent dresser*) marks out appropriate divisions of grade with a shovel, commonly three in number but varying from two to five. The buddle contents are then shovelled out, and those divided materials to be retreated piled to one side in a heap, until the ongoing treatment has produced sufficient identical (or very similar) material to be re-buddled in one go.

On large tin floors where round buddles have not yet been introduced, sands from the strips are treated in four large 'square buddles', the four at Wheal Vor being a good example. Collecting at the head there is a small quantity of enriched sand, all the rest appropriately judged going to 'true roughs', each buddling yielding more or less of these.

The enriched sands first undergo cleaning in a kieve (of which more later), whose main product is sent to small 'finishing' buddles or 'tin cases'. These produce rich heads, sent again to kieves for final, definitive cleaning, leaving roughs or 'leavings' of average richness.

Summing up, the treatment of sands from the strips by buddles and tin cases alone yields:

1. A small amount of **rich sands** for the kieve.

2. A large amount of appropriately judged 'true' **roughs**.

3. **Roughs as leavings**, of a more or less rich character.

3. The round buddle would not completely replace the square type, but it successfully achieves the aim set out previously of working rapidly and cheaply on a mass of material, and quickly separating off a large quantity of well-impoverished sands. The small heads from the strips, and those from the round buddles, only constitute a very small fraction of the total deposit in the strips, and go to smaller square buddles, where the careful and more expensive manipulations of this type of apparatus can be applied.

The round buddle

The round buddle is a large, circular, masonry pit, whose diameter varies from 14¾ to 20 feet (4½ to 6 metres), and depth at the rim from 2⅓ to 3 feet (0.7 to 0.9 metres). The floor is conical and normally planked over. In the centre is a conical column of wood or cast iron, supporting a bearing on which turns a vertical iron shaft. This shaft carries a sheet metal feed box, whose sides reach a little below the top of the central column. A wooden launder brings feed material, as slurry, into this box, which is fitted at one-third of its height with a false base pierced with holes, allowing the slurry to pass through and run into the apparatus, all around the central column. On the outside of the feed box two sheet metal crosspieces are fitted, into which go two wooden arms, from which two rectangular brooms, each half as long as the radius of the buddle, are hung by cords. As the central shaft rotates, it sweeps the brooms around, (*automatically*) keeping the surface of the deposited materials smooth and conical. These brooms are also steadily raised as the buddle fills up, either by counterweights or by hand. (*It is important to realise here an important distinction. Square buddles needed two men to work each one, whereas a number of round buddles were virtually self-acting, needing far less attention*).

The periphery of the pit has one or two openings, closed up by a barrier of battens or by planks with peg-holes, leading, as with all buddles, to channels for the discharge of (*excess*) water.

When a round buddle is full, the Captain traces two or three divisions and the deposit is divided into annular rings that are marked out.

When the stamped ore is quite rich and when the strips function well, their heads go direct to square buddles. Otherwise, each division of the sand in the strips goes separately to round buddles. In general, dressing floors where the crop sands are treated in round buddles use three of these pieces of equipment for rotating the treatments – see Tincroft and Par Consols.

The definitive treatment products are:

1. **Sands** for the square buddles.
2. A large amount of appropriately judged **roughs**.

4. The rich heads from square buddles are cleaned in kieves, this operation being known as '*tozing*' (or '*tossing*').

Kieves

In all the preceding pieces of apparatus, the feed material is in the form of slurry (*a mixture of solids and water*), and deposition takes place in a weak or slow current of water. In every operation, the water carries off some fine slimes in suspension, but there are some of these particles remaining stuck on to coarser grains, either of rich sands or roughs. By means of the kieve, the intention is:

1. To detach these slimes particles adhering to tin grains by strong agitation.
2. By prolonged knocking (*on the side of the kieve*) to keep the fines in suspension for a long time, such that a deposit is formed based primarily on particle size and not solely on particle density.

Kieves are made of oak, banded by iron, and they are of slightly conical shape. The largest diameter is from 2½ to 3¾ feet, and height from 2ft. 8ins. to 3ft. 8 ins.

Firstly, the kieve is one-third to half filled with clear water, then, while one workman uses a shovel to create a rapid stirring movement, a second adds successive shovelfuls of sands, which is continued until the kieve is nearly full. Then, during the settling of the contents, the side of the kieve is repeatedly struck (this stage being known as 'packing'), prolonged according to the fineness of the material being treated. When the top water has cleared it is emptied by means of a small pail with a handle. The contents are then lifted out by shovel with very great care, and normally divided into three parts, delineated 'Top skimmings', 'Bottom skimmings' and 'Bottom'. This 'bottom', when heads from finishing buddles are being treated, is most often ready for roasting, and is then known as 'tin witts' or 'bottom fit for burning'.

If the ore carries a lot of iron and copper pyrites, these minerals are concentrated in the two upper layers as well as the bottom, and it can be advantageous to make a second 'bottom skimming' already rich (*in tin*) but carrying a lot of pyrite (I).

(I) This pyritic material has to be roasted several times, the product from the first roasting being known as 'ragging'.

When the ore contains much of both mispickel and pyrites, it can be beneficial to give the 'bottom' a repeat first tossing. This produces a secondary layer analogous to the 'bottom skimming' mentioned above, along with tin witts ready for roasting.

Chimming On some mines, the kieve is used a little differently, being inclined at about 45 degrees. Into it is put about 100 litres of water and about 100 Kg. of sands, followed by strong agitation and packing. Water is emptied from the inclined kieve and, finally, the various layers are removed. In this way, the kieve presents less space at the base and more at the surface, the rotational movement is less even and the packing has a more powerful vibrational effect. It is acknowledged that the rich part is deposited more quickly. This procedure is known as 'chimming', and its use, adopted some thirty years ago (*i.e. in the 1820s*) in the Gwennap district, where there is an abundance of mispickel (I), does not appear to be widespread.

(I) Henwood, W.J. Op. cit. pp. 151 and 152.

Summing up, work in the kieve produces:
1. **Top skimmings** – very fine sands, treated as slimes.
2. **Bottom skimmings** – passed separately to small square buddles.
3. **Bottom**. (a) Heads from first or preliminary dressing – to 'finishing' square buddles – 'tin cases'.
   (b) Heads from finishing buddles – **tin witts**, for roasting.

Without going into more detail here, the tables below sum up the operations and the order of use of various apparatus for the treatment of crop sands, intermediate products and definitive products:
1. Where the dressing floor has only square buddles.
2. Where there are also round buddles.

1. Where only square buddles are used:

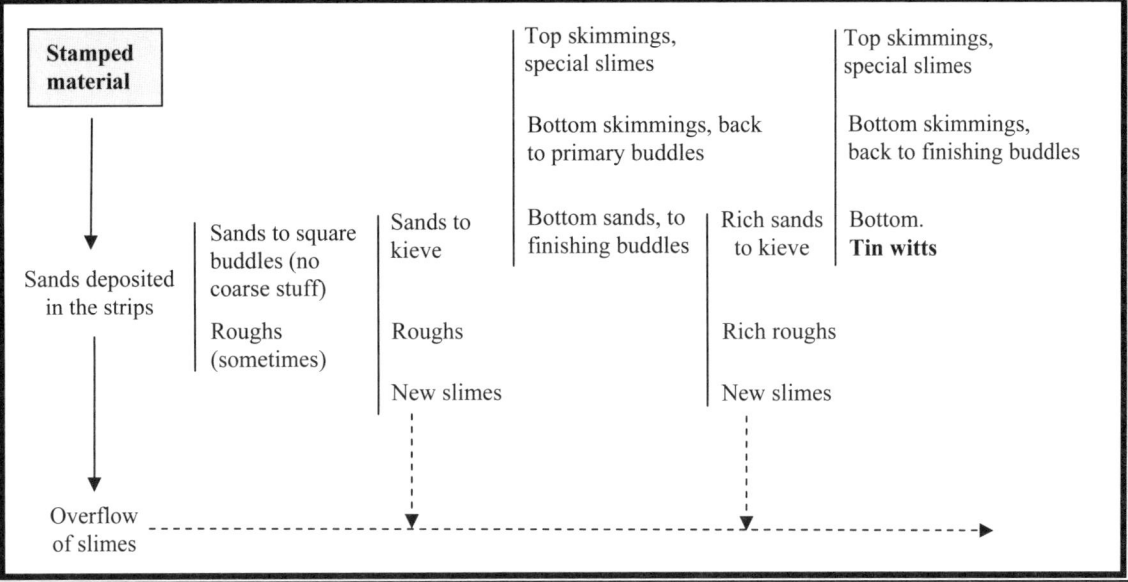

2. **Where there are both round and square buddles in use:**

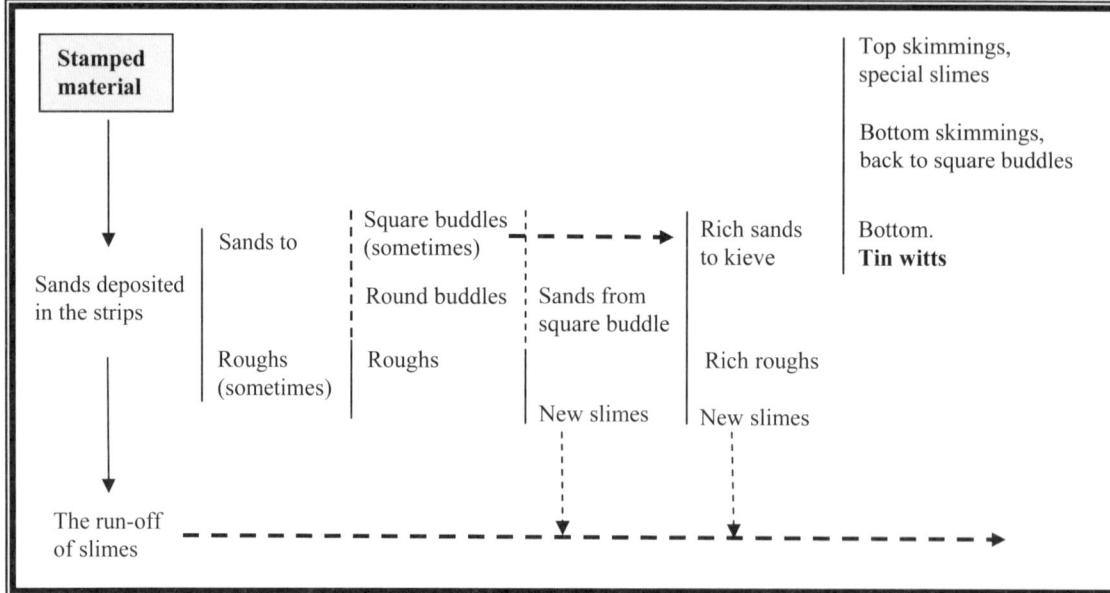

Treatment of roughs

Retreatment of the roughs is carried out on the majority of the mass of material that passes the crop at the heads of the strips; the rich sands, produce from the bottom of the kieve, and the special slimes from top kieve skimmings being the sole exceptions. Effectively, the roughs can be considered as very poor ore, incapable of bearing the cost of intensive manual labour, and so are treated rapidly by means of simple apparatus.

Types of 'roughs'

By their origin, several varieties of roughs can be distinguished:

1. The most important in terms of quantity, those that I will refer to as 'true roughs, appropriately judged' are sometimes at the very end of the strips in the case of low-grade ore, and always the residues of the treatment of crop sands, in large, primary square buddles, or round buddles.

2. Richer roughs, in far smaller proportion, come from treatment in square buddles, either the smaller 'tin cases' or 'finishing' buddles, where they are, naturally, the tailings of these operations.

3. The largest proportion of slimes comes from primary size differentiation, intended to separate out those slightly larger grains that can be entrained and carried over into the slime pits. Those fine sands further taken from slimes are of a very variable quantity and quality, depending on the layout and more or less appropriate operation of any preceding apparatus, and the stage of dressing where slimes are considered and dealt with. They make up the tin case sands and those of poor quality typical of the 'true' roughs.

Summarising, we have to distinguish between:

'True' roughs, originating from

> (a) The very ends of the strips (sometimes).
>
> (b) The residues of round buddles or large square buddles.
>
> (c) The treatment of slimes (sometimes).

Those roughs that are more or less rich, the tailings of the tin cases or 'finishing' buddles.

It is evident that roughs, according to the stage where they enter pieces of apparatus, must carry a large proportion of adhering slimes, and that the first operation applied to them is a cleaning, continued by the action of succeeding washing treatments to which a part of the product of this cleaning has passed.

The 'true' roughs are carried by a flow of water into a long strip or 'drag', following which there is a wooden box or masonry pit, then the large pits to settle out the slimes. Those sands held in the upper part of the strip are enriched in a 'tye', then, if it is worth it, sent to round buddles.   **True roughs**

The tye is a large, wooden channel, at the head of which there is a fairly strong flow of water. The workman slowly adds shovelfuls of material into the water flow itself. The heavy particles settle at the head of the channel, and the action is completed by working the surface of the sands deposit with a shovel or a broom, depending on its fineness. Barren sands and slimes are carried to the tail of the deposit. Its mode of action, very different to that of the square buddle, is, at one and the same time, one of cleaning and of enrichment.   **The tye**

The heads of the tyes are sometimes immediately suitable to go as crazes (*for re-stamping*), if not, they go to a round buddle. There, the centre of the deposit is immediately rich enough for crazes. Round buddles, combined for this treatment can entirely replace tyes (I).

(I) This is about to be done on the dressing floors of Par Consols. (See flow sheet and summary)

The tailings of the tye are put back in motion in the flow of water, and sent to the 'box' and slime pits following, into which all the material not retained in the strip runs freely.

The 'box', being larger and deeper than the strip, allows a rapid slowing down of the flow, favouring the settlement of grains. The freed slimes flow to the surface, and make their way onwards into one or two pits.   **The 'box'**

The roughs in the box do not stay there long enough to congest it. Most often, a workman has the job of continually removing them with a shovel, and transferring them into another channel, where they can once more split into crazes, either at the head, or after washing in a tye.

On several dressing floors, this workman has been advantageously sub-

Discharge valve

stituted by a valve, or 'devil', which controls an opening made in the base of box. It periodically lets out the roughs accumulated in the box into the second channel, and shuts itself again before the slimy water has a chance to reach the bottom.

Summing up, the treatment of the 'true' roughs yields:

1. **Crazes** in variable proportions.
2. A very large quantity of discarded, **barren sands**.
3. **Slimes** in variable proportions.

Roughs of varying richness

The rich roughs, in contrast, do not provide any material to be rejected directly. When they make up the tailings of rich square buddles, the following may be recovered:

1. **Tin witts** ready for roasting.
2. **Crazes**.
3. **Very fine sands** from the square buddle.
4. **Slimes**, for retreatment.

The 'shacking tye'

The first of the above is absent when square buddle tailings of only average richness are treated. The cleaning of rich roughs goes under the name of the 'shacking' process, and is carried out in a unique piece of equipment, in three sections, made of wood (a 'shacking tye').

1. At the head is a hopper to receive the material. It is slightly inclined, and its vertical sides, close up somewhat to narrow the exit.

2. Below this is a box, then a channel for settlement (long pit), and between the two, a wooden plank forming an intermediate level (*for flow distribution*).

In the case of averagely rich roughs, the hopper is loaded from time to time with material, and a current of water carries it into the box, where it is continually stirred by a shovel. The roughs are retained for crazes, and the more or less fine slimes pass into the 'pit'. The head of this pit still carries some small, somewhat gritty material.

If the roughs are rich, they are again shovelled into the same hopper and treated as before, when a certain quantity of tin witts, always very pyritic, will remain behind. The remainder of the material runs out, as previously, and yields the same types of product.

3. The following table summarises the sequence of operations and the series of products. I have distinguished between cases where the dressing floors use only square buddles, and those where both types are used. It is the latter that relates especially to the points made above in respect of 'true' roughs.

Table summarising the treatment of roughs.

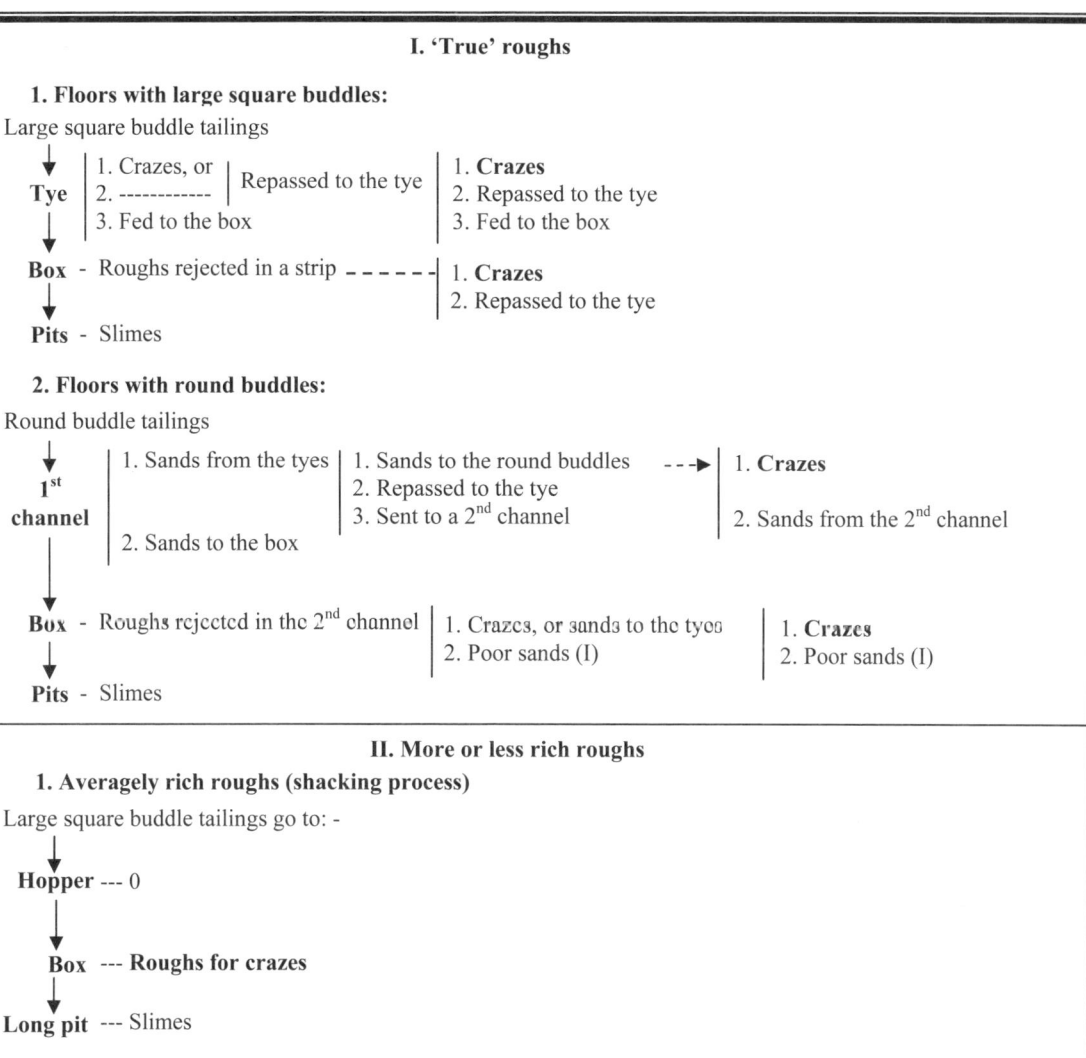

I. 'True' roughs

1. Floors with large square buddles:

Large square buddle tailings

↓
Tye | 1. Crazes, or | Repassed to the tye | 1. **Crazes**
    | 2. ------------ | | 2. Repassed to the tye
↓ | 3. Fed to the box | | 3. Fed to the box

Box - Roughs rejected in a strip ------| 1. **Crazes**
↓ | 2. Repassed to the tye

Pits - Slimes

2. Floors with round buddles:

Round buddle tailings

↓
1st channel | 1. Sands from the tyes | 1. Sands to the round buddles --→ | 1. **Crazes**
                | | 2. Repassed to the tye |
                | | 3. Sent to a 2nd channel | 2. Sands from the 2nd channel
↓ | 2. Sands to the box |

Box - Roughs rejected in the 2nd channel | 1. Crazes, or sands to the tyes | 1. **Crazes**
↓ | 2. Poor sands (I) | 2. Poor sands (I)

Pits - Slimes

II. More or less rich roughs

1. Averagely rich roughs (shacking process)

Large square buddle tailings go to: -

↓
Hopper --- 0

↓
Box --- **Roughs for crazes**

↓
Long pit --- Slimes

2. Rich roughs (special shacking process)

Large square buddle tailings go to: -

↓
Hopper --- **Tin witts** (very pyritic), ready for roasting

↓
Box --- **Roughs for crazes**

↓
Long pit | 1. Fine sands to square buddles (if worth treating)
             | 2. Slimes

(I) These poor sands are normally discarded. They can be worth retreating in a second box in series with pits, a third channel for the roughs from the box, and tyes for the sands from the third channel. This is how this treatment is arranged at Par Consols, where a third channel receives all the residues (leavings), sands and slimes, and carries them to the so-called tributers' floors, below.

The treatment of slimes

4. The treatment of slimes is not a matter of equal importance on all dressing floors, but it presents the same difficulties everywhere. The quantity of slimes varies with the fineness of stamping, and we have seen that it generally constitutes from ¼ to ⅖ of the total material. Slimes are made up of particles of all sizes, from very fine sands to impalpable dust (*particles so fine that they cannot be felt in suspension*).

Slime, looked at in its entirety, is a very dilute and tenuous mixture, and yet the relationship between the average diameter of one of its grains and that of one of its impalpable fines can be far greater than the analogous relationship between a fragment of ore from the stamps and a sand grain of the roughs. There, tin ore, softer than the quartz gangue, is partly reduced to very great fineness, and, consequently, in the treatment of certain slimes, one has to contend with the following difficulties:

Difficulties

1. Variation from general dilution to compacted mud.

2. Very poorly defined size classification.

3. Tin mineral of a general extreme fineness.

Varying sorts of slimes

Given that it is necessary to keep separate, as far as possible, those (*individual*) slimes generated by the various operations described above, one can make distinctions between:

1. Principal slimes, recovered from the large slime pits after having bypassed deposition in the main strips.

2. Slimes from the small slime pits. Work on the crop (*from the strips*) in round and square buddles yields slimy water that most often carries away some 'true' roughs from the first strip. Slimes in this water, and those that are detached from these roughs, are retained in the small pits after the 'boxes'.

3. Small quantities of slimes from the 'shacking' process.

4. Top skimmings from the kieves, which are always quite rich.

5. Secondary slimes, the residues from work on other slimes. These can be mixed in with the principal slimes and treated with them.

All these various types will be reviewed further.

The pieces of apparatus intimately concerned with slimes treatment are:

Apparatus

1. Classifier 'boxes'.

2. Paddle trunks.

3. Square buddles.

4. Frames, or stationary tables.

5. Kieves.

The only remaining pieces of apparatus yet to be described are paddle trunks and frames.

Paddle trunks

The essential purpose of the paddle trunk is to dilute and separate (*compacted*) mud, in order to discard those extremely fine particles that cannot be treated.

In past times, a trunk was built in three sections analogous to those of the 'shacking tye'. The 'strake or streke', where charged material was mixed with a current of water, the 'cover', an intermediate box, and the 'hutch' or catch pit for settlement.

The cover was not meant to recover a product; a workman, armed with a shovel, continually agitated the (*diluted*) mixture to allow it to wash into the hutch. From the year 1825 (I), the operation of trunking began to change, and be conducted by means of mechanical paddles.

(I) Henwood, W. J., Op. cit.

Today, trunks are ranged alongside each other in groups of 24 or 32, and the various covers are merged into one long, transverse channel, running across the head of a series of hutches. A horizontal shaft, about one metre above the channel and supported at its ends by journals, is fitted with as many arms as there are hutches, and each arm is provided with a wooden paddle that dips several inches into the mud in the channel.

The strakes are replaced by one, two or three boxes, where the slimes are stirred by shovel, and from where roughs are taken out, when appropriate.

Water entering these boxes carries slimes into the transverse channel, where the paddles stir it, and with each alternate movement received from the drive shaft, each of them passes a certain amount into the corresponding hutch.

The shaft itself is turned either by a linkage from the stamps, or by water wheel, or by a boy on horseback moving in a circle at right angles to the paddles, moving a counterweighted arm.

Various types of slime frames

The (*tin*) frame, or 'rack' is the English stationary table, those used in Cornwall being of various sizes and constructions, but having in common the (*vertical pivoting*) rotation of the table on its long axis for the discharge of washed material.

This apparatus consists essentially of a rectangular table, constructed of planks held tightly together by a framework forming a raised edge or rim. The short sides of the table are fixed at different heights, in such a way as to give the table an appropriate slope.

Beneath, are two or three compartments, intended to receive the products from washing, and whose relative length corresponds to the desired divisions of the washed products. At their foot is a channel, catching water and slimes leaving the table during its operation via a slot, several centimetres wide, between the planks and the lower edge. Each cycle of operation normally has three periods:

- Feeding of material and the catching and retaining of the rich parts.
- Washing (*cleaning*) of the retained products by a flow of clear

water over the table surface.

- Rotation of the table on the pivots until vertical, washing off of the retained material into the compartments below, and the return of the table to its position as an inclined plane.

A wish to improve (more or less effectively) the various parts of the operation has led to the introduction of numerous modifications. Certainly, one has in view the saving on manual labour and the reduction of tin losses, the second being somewhat subordinate to the first.

Without going into a detailed description of these frames, it is nevertheless necessary to have an idea of the main types in use in order to understand the part that they play on various dressing floors.

The old 'hand frame', the only one mentioned in the studies of 1828 and 1829 (I), receives material by shovel on to a board fixed above the head of the table, serving the same purpose as the jagging board of the tin cases, that is to say, the feed is there divided into channels, and carried on to the table by a flow of water.

(I) Henwood, W. J., and Coste and Perdonnet, Op. cit.

Between this fixed board and the moving table proper, continuity of flow is achieved, here, as on all such frames, by a small board in the form of a flap, that drops down from the upper board of the frame during normal operation, and is lifted back up at the time of discharge, on an axis at right angles to that of the table. This flap is connected to the fixed board, either by two bands of leather, nailed at the ends, or by two small pivots, engaging in two eyes.

When the girl has passed the feed on to the table, spreading it out proportionally on the small board, flattening out the lumps of mud at the head of the table, and evening out the material with a sort of rake that she passes alternately from side to side and up and down, she allows on clear water to clean the deposit. Then, she lifts a catch and pushes the table aside, where it assumes a vertical position, a second catch keeping it there if necessary. With the aid of a water feed, or bullock's horn fitted with a handle, she draws clean water from a cistern, which, thrown on to the table, washes the (*cleaned*) retained material into the two rectangular boxes placed below. To operate the hand frame, the girl is continually occupied during the first and third period, besides having to load the feed by shovel on to the jagging board.

Her labour has been greatly lessened by the use of machine frames (I), where the feed material arrives (*already*) in suspension in water from a launder, to fall on to a triangular headboard fitted with batten partitions (*as at the head of a square buddle*).

(I) As at Wheal Vor, as an example.

The essential difference between the hand and machine frame is analogous to that which exists between the tin case and the large square buddle, that is, in the mode of arrival of feed material. It is evident that here, even more so than with the square buddle, it is of the greatest importance to first of all thin the material down (*with water*).

Thanks to this stipulation, machine frames have been able to be placed in parallel rows, often to lay them out in two lines with the heads touching, and the frames in opposing inclination. The arrangement has an appreciable slope, at right angles to the inclination of the frames. Two channels run the whole way down the line, one to deliver the slimes slurry and the other for clean water.

A single girl can then manage two, four or six frames at the same time, depending on the nature of the material, though she still has to perform manually the washing-off of the frames by water. Small collection boxes are replaced by planking in the form of channels, taking all the products of heads, middles and tails to separate pits at the end of the line of frames, so these pits can be emptied without interrupting the work of the frames.

This task has itself been done away with in those frames called 'self-washing'. A channel, made from two planks nailed at right angles (*i.e. a V-shaped box*) is supported on two pivots in a horizontal position above the table. It is (*gradually*) filled with water during the two first operating periods, and the table, as it rotates, trips a catch, tipping the box so that its contents flow over the table to wash off the deposit. After being emptied, the box is returned to its initial position by counterweight.

'Self-acting frames' (I) work themselves, and need only supervision in case something goes wrong with the mechanism. Here, the 'second period' (*the extra washing of the table contents*) has been done away with, and the rotational movement of the table is achieved by making use of the flow of the slimes feed itself as it crosses the table. To do this, the lower table pivot point, instead of being in the centre of the frame, is moved towards the side that dips down as the table turns. Underneath, near the bottom corner of this long side, a box of suitable capacity is nailed, which receives, during the normal treatment, a surplus portion of the feed flow, and when it is full enough, its weight tips the table. This empties the box at the same time, and when it is empty the weight of the table swings it back into its original position, due to the offset axis of the pivots.

(I) As at Carnbrea, as an example.

Other self-acting frames (as at St. Day United and Tincroft - Capt. Teague's frames), instead of leaving the execution of the various movements to the action of water, quite irregular and variable with the state of maintenance of the apparatus, have given it over to a mechanism operated by a small water wheel that controls a whole bank of frames, operating and rotating them at regular intervals, all at the same time, one boy being sufficient to supervise about fifteen such frames.

(*N.B. these pre-date Vincent's automatic 'rack frames', introduced three years later.*)

I. Principal, or main slimes

1. The principal slimes bring together (*and display*) all the conditions of difficult treatment. The large slime pits receiving them are masonry basins sunk below ground level, and if the slope of the ground allows it, one side is free on the outside and has openings for the removal of the deposited material. When the slimes have settled, and the 'top water' is almost clear, it can be run off to the sump for the supplementary stamps water pump, or first sent conveniently to second pits for further clarification. The solids are left to dry out slightly, because varying dryness and humidity cause unequal contraction of the mass of material and reduces the ease with which these earthy particles can be removed. If the pit has a clear face, the slimes can be recovered by a current of water, if not, then they are shovelled out into a 'box' where they are washed with water, leaving behind most of the roughs mentioned previously.

The well-diluted slimes run from the box to be deposited in a first row of 'paddle trunks', where they are split into two portions. The tails pass to a second row of paddle trunks, where they are split again. The second tailings are either directly discarded (I), or sent to another section of the dressing floors.

(I) At Par Consols, the tails from the second paddle trunks are run away to the sea. At Wheal Vor, they are treated away from the main site, along with all the secondary slimes that run from there. (*i.e. at 'The Flow'*)

The heads of both rows of trunks are not of equal richness, and undergo separate but analogous treatment.

A first washing by frame yields two divisions of different character, which each receive the same treatment, but separately. Each goes to 'doubling frames', that is to say, those that work on the products from the first frames. The heads from the doubling frames are ready for the kieve, the 'bottom' of which goes to roasting, while the two upper portions (skimmings) are returned to frames. Tailings go to a third series, known as 'redoubling frames'.

The table indicates the general scheme of treatment. Any variations are commensurate with the potentially very varied nature of the material, and so there is no space to go into them further.

It can be seen from the table opposite that the first product made ready for roasting is that which has passed the 'box', the first paddle trunks, two treatments on frames, and the kieve, where it constitutes the 'bottom'. **Table summarising the treatment of 'principal' slimes**

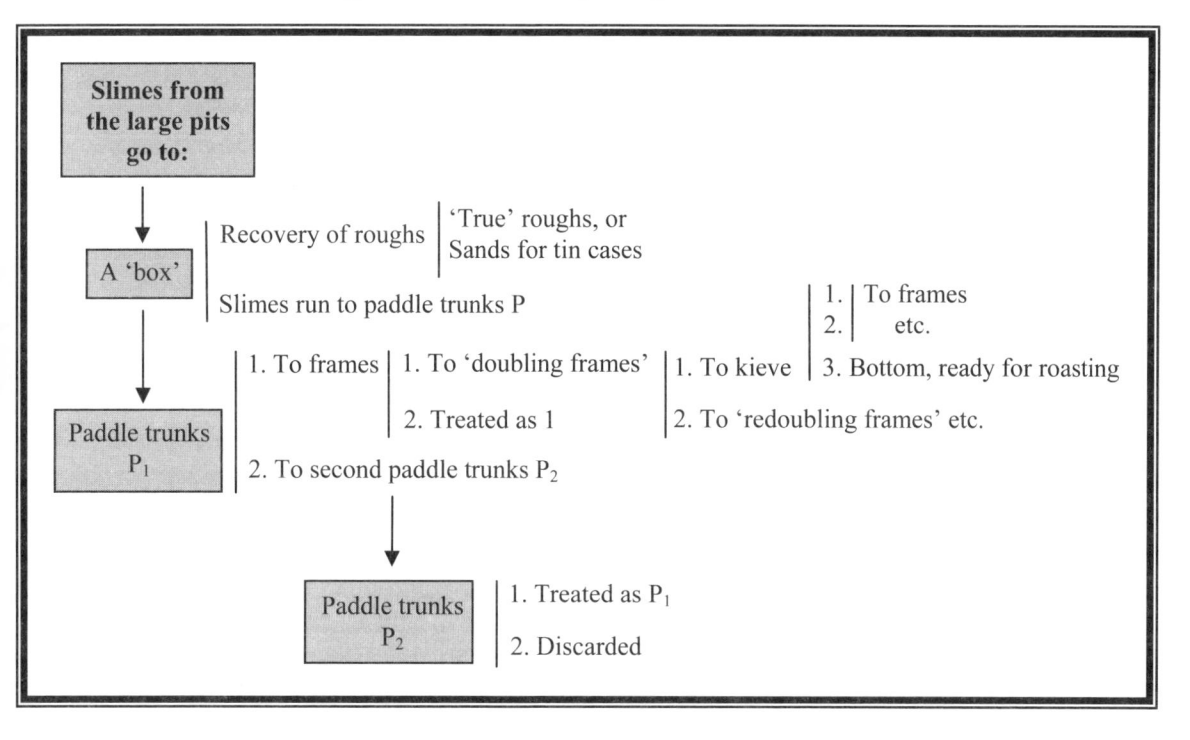

```
Slimes from
the large pits
go to:
         │
         ▼                    │ 'True' roughs, or
    ┌─────────┐  Recovery of roughs │ Sands for tin cases
    │ A 'box' │
    └─────────┘                                                    │ 1. │ To frames
         │        Slimes run to paddle trunks P                    │ 2. │   etc.
         ▼        │ 1. To frames │ 1. To 'doubling frames' │ 1. To kieve │ 3. Bottom, ready for roasting
    ┌─────────┐   │              │ 2. Treated as 1          │ 2. To 'redoubling frames' etc.
    │ Paddle  │   │ 2. To second paddle trunks P₂
    │ trunks  │
    │   P₁    │
    └─────────┘
                         │
                         ▼
                    ┌─────────┐ │ 1. Treated as P₁
                    │ Paddle  │ │
                    │ trunks  │ │ 2. Discarded
                    │   P₂    │
                    └─────────┘
```

On the other hand, if, instead of considering the heads, we look at the inferior products, treatment on frames will have to be repeated to come to the use of the kieve. I judge that the top and bottom skimmings from the kieve, treated on frames, will yield heads either ready for roasting or needing a second tossing, depending on the nature of the slimes.

However, the definitive products are:
- **Rich slimes** for roasting.
   1. Mainly from the bottom of the kieve.
   2. From frame heads.
- **Secondary slimes**, from all of the slimy water that runs over the frames, and sometimes from the tailings of the second paddle trunks.
- **Very fine, poor slimes** that are discarded, the tailings from the second paddle trunks.

II. Slimes from small pits

2. Slimes from the small pits are far easier to treat. Firstly, they contain no roughs, as a result of already having passed through a 'box'. Moreover, neither do they carry those ultrafine slimes that that would give the material some 'plasticity', but approximate more to the very fine sands content of ordinary slimes. On some dressing floors there are, following the box, two successive pits. The first retains the coarsest slimes, and the second is somewhat elongated, where the heads are regarded

as coarse slimes, and the rest as fine such, being divided again into two sections that receive identical but separate treatment.

At the slime pits, a classification by size is sought for. I will refer again to the tests that there is reason to attempt in this regard.

The coarsest material goes to frames, either directly or after having been passed through a tin case. The frame heads are either ready for roasting or for the kieve, where the 'bottom' is roasted.

The fine material undergoes treatment analogous to that of the frame products coming from the heads of paddle trunks, inasmuch as they go to frames and the kieve etc.

III. Slimes from the shacking process

3. The slimes from the 'shacking process' are quite similar to those above, as they also come from the cleaning of roughs, the long pit where they settle classifying them quite as well as those somewhat larger, and the head of this channel can constitute a fine sand for the tin case yielding sands for the kieve, and that, a bottom product for roasting. The tailings (or even the whole of the channel) is treated successively by frames and the kieve. The less rich by frame, and the rich and coarser by kieve, giving, respectively, a head and a bottom product ready for roasting.

IV. Top skimmings

4. The principal 'top skimmings' are produced by the kieves, which treat the heads from the 'finishing' tin cases. These are very fine sands, well classified by size, already rich, and needing only to be treated by frame. Each treatment by frame yields a head product for roasting. Last of all, the head can be copper ore fit for sale, as certain top skimmings can carry an abundance of this, as at Par Consols.

Sometimes, the tails from the first frames still contain some large grains, of both tin and gangue, which are extracted from the slimes by shacking and sent to the stamps.

As for the upper layers in the kieves, where one of the enriched slimes of species 1, 2, or 3 are treated, we have seen that the top and bottom skimmings were having to go back to frames, but in order to enrich these materials, it is often necessary to repeat the use of the kieve, because it is less efficient in dealing with fairly fine sands than it is with tin case sands. Rich slimes, such as come from the heads of frames, are finer and finer, and the end of their treatment yields that very fine tin specially referred to as 'small tin'.

V. Secondary slimes

5. The secondary slimes, or tailings from preceding washing processes, are saved in more large pits where the site locality allows it, or where there is an advantage in doing so. They pass to a single range of paddle trunks, whose heads undergo the same treatment as the principal slimes, and whose tails definitively go to waste.

Summing up, treatments before roasting have given the following **definitive** products and localised variants:

Treatment	Source or origin	Products	Destination
Crop	Bottom of kieve	Tin witts	Roasting furnace
Slimes	Bottom of kieves	Fine sand and	
Slimes	Heads of frames	rich slimes	
Slimes	Tails of paddle trunks	Poor slimes	Discarded to waste
Roughs	Tails of strips or tyes	Poor sand	

As a result of the siting of the dressing floor, it is more or less easy to dispose of the always considerable mass of tailings from the treatments. In the case, happily rare, where, as at Tincroft, the slope of the ground does not allow material to run naturally off the floors, it has to be transported to the waste burrows by wagons, which can be a source of considerable expense.

Thus, a large mine that produces 300 tons of black tin, will have to discard, supposing a retention of two parts per hundred by weight, about 15,000 tons, or about 10,500 cubic yards of sand and slimes.

Most often these materials accumulate in the bottom of a valley, where they occupy an extensive space, as they do at Polgooth mine. When the valley comes out at the coast, the flow of water carries a large part of this away.

Sometimes, the ancients, whose workings were quite large, left behind in their tailings sufficient tin for them to be worth reworking when the price of the metal had risen, as was done in 1855 at Wheal Vor. In 1857, in the Pentuan valley, a little above the stream works at present in operation, tributers are retreating the residues from former workings.

At Par Consols, the elevation and pronounced slope of the hillside allows everything to be sent down to the sea via a wooden channel on a long structure that comes to an end on the sands of the seashore adjacent to the lead smelting works.

Roasting, calcining

At this point I briefly re-introduce the process of roasting, the principle of which has been mentioned previously, and to which I will refer in detail on describing the types of furnaces in use.

Apart from the rich sands and slimes from stream works, and several mines having no need to roast their ore, other, almost pure, ores need no more than a single roasting. On the majority of dressing floors, the rich products have to be roasted at least twice, and only the very best kieve 'bottoms' pass to the furnace only once.

Operations after roasting

The washing treatment of the roasted ore is especially known as 'dressing', and the site where it is carried out by the roasting furnaces bears the name 'burning house' or 'dressing house'.

The operations carried out on the raw ore are of a general character that

Large variations in individual operational procedure

has allowed me to describe them together in their entirety. In contrast, there is nothing more variable than the treatment applied to roasted material, for two main reasons:

1. The more or less pyritic nature of the concentrate.
2. On any given floor, the great number and variety of products, coming separately from all the operations previously described, and the fact that they are kept separate until the end of their preparation.

The interest that could be had in entering into the details of 'dressing' is somewhat lessened by the consideration that, on the one hand, the principle of the work has not changed, and on the other hand, that even for very pyritic ores, the expense of manpower does not exceed $\frac{1}{10}$ of that before roasting, in spite of the very careful manipulations applied. To try and follow to the end all the various materials that leave the calcining furnace would be to fall into a useless confusion.

Nature of roasted material

The impurities that they contain are principally very fine iron oxide, and grainy gangue, almost entirely with crazes, that is, adhering to the particles of tin. Besides these, there are copper sulphate, ferrous sulphate and iron arsenate, and varying amounts of undecomposed sulphides. Finally, despite the care taken with the roasting, there are agglomerations or partially fused 'frits', where the heat has acted too rapidly.

After cooling, the roasted ore is slightly dampened and left for some time to the action of the air. A part, at least, of the sulphides becomes sulphates, and all the copper is made soluble (I).

(I) However, in the St. Just district, the sand and slime tailings from the washings after roasting are frequently sold for copper.

At Tincroft, the red-hot material falls out of the furnace into water. The iron oxide acquires a browny-black tint and is only washed out with more difficulty. This is evidently a less than advantageous procedure.

Sieving

After treatment begins with sieving, to separate the agglomerates, which are sent to the stamps, like all tailings from the dressing house. The ore goes into a kieve, and, if it is sufficiently coppery, the water is retained after digestion and sent to the cementation tanks. For the copper precipitation old scrap iron from the dressing floor is used, notably stamps grates taken out of service. In order to reduce the consumption of iron, almost everywhere care must be taken to close the tank with a wooden lid (*to exclude oxygen*). The copper precipitate obtained was worth, in 1857, about £50 per ton, or, in other words, gave on assay 50% metallic copper, when the operation was well conducted, that is.

Copper precipitation

Apparatus in the 'dressing house'

The types of apparatus in common or current use in the dressing house are kieves, square buddles (tin cases), tyes, frames and either 'copper bottom' (*mesh*) or 'hair' sieves, these sieves being used in several ways.

1. We shall see them used for passing roasted mineral.
2. They serve as a jig (*with hand manipulation*). The operator puts in two or three shovelfuls of material and half submerges it in a kieve full of water. He jerks it up and down, superimposing a circular movement at the same time. The light portions, which are always those of crazes, come to the top of the deposit, where they are recovered by scraping off. The sieve is repeatedly recharged and used until the weight becomes too considerable. This operation is called 'jigging', and for it 'copper bottom' sieves are used.
3. The operation of 'dilluing' is performed in a 'hair sieve' of very fine texture. An assistant loads about 15 Kg. (30 – 35 lbs.) of material, and the operator plunges the sieve entirely under water, moving and working it as described above. When the light portions have been brought into suspension, he inclines the sieve under water so that they are decanted off from the side of the sieve into the kieve. The deposit in the kieve is recovered and passed to square buddles and again to the kieve, but never gives more than inferior quality tin (I).

Sieves

(I) Before the introduction of large, steam-powered dressing floors, hand sieving was much used for the washing of the raw ore. Dilluing was particularly used to wash the final division made in square buddles.

Tyes are used in the same way as they are for the treatment of roughs, though they can be replaced by square buddles having a strong current of water. The ore is progressively shovelled into the water flow, carrying away at once the large grains of crazes and fine iron oxide. The following are several examples of treatment:

1. **Rich ore, roasted once** (tin witts, 'burnt clean'). A first cleaning is done in a kieve, followed by enrichment by square buddle and a repeat treatment by kieve, when the bottom product is 'crop tin'. The first kieve yields:
   - Top skimmings, sent to frames.
   - Bottom skimmings, retreated, if good enough, either by kieve or square buddle.
   - Bottom product, which goes directly to a square buddle.

Examples of treatments

In the case of very rich tin witts in the square buddle, the head from the first washing is fit for the second kieve. Ordinarily, heads are retreated up to three times, successively.

The middle divisions from various washings by square buddle are treated by the same apparatus until they are rich enough for the second kieve. In this case, the kieve bottom product can still carry a small amount of crazes, removed by jigging in a sieve.

The square buddle tails carry much iron oxide, crazes and, even here, a few coarse grains of tin. If sufficient, the tin is removed before the tailings are sent back to the stamps. In this case, the tails are either passed to a tye, where the head is clean tin, or the same result is achieved by dilluing in a 'hair sieve'.

The top skimmings from various kieves go to frames, where the tails are crazes, and the heads, roasted again if necessary, go to the kieve. There, are produced:

1. Top skimmings, retreated on frames.
2. Bottom skimmings, to tin cases
3. 'True' bottoms (final product), or for retreatment on tin cases.

Treatment on tin cases yields material for the kieves and the bottoms from these is the 'fine tin', of first or second quality depending on whether the kieve feed was best heads or enriched kieve skimmings retreated on tin cases.

The tails from these buddling operations carry no obvious coarse tin grains, being crazes sent directly back to the stamps.

The treatment that I am going to indicate for the top skimmings is a little like that applied to rich, roasted slimes.

2. A pyritic product needing several roastings.

Material roasted once is known as 'rag-burnt', and, after sieving and treatment in the kieve, gives:

1. **Top skimmings**, for frames.
2. **Bottom skimmings** for re-buddling.
3. **Bottom**, for a second roasting.

The bottom skimmings, on buddling, give:

1. **Heads**, for a second roasting.
2. **Middlings**, retreated by buddling.
3. Tails, **crazes** for the stamps.

From here, the treatment is as for type 1. (rich ore, roasted once – see above).

I will set out summarised treatments by mentioning that produced in the dressing house, besides sandy concentrates ('crop'), fines ('fine') and very fine ('small'), whose admixture constitutes, as I have indicated, 'black tin for sale', also roasted crazes of all sizes. The ferruginous water from the buddles and the final operations on frames, are the sole materials that pass with the primary tailings before roasting to the lower part of the dressing floors, where there is a secondary, 'tailings floor'.

Section 2(b)

A description of several individual dressing floors and their treatment methods.

The general, and somewhat theoretical reflections set out above will allow the understanding of the practical and detailed methods followed on some dressing floors taken as examples. At the same time, this, to-

Part of the dressing floors at Great Wheal Vor, 1855

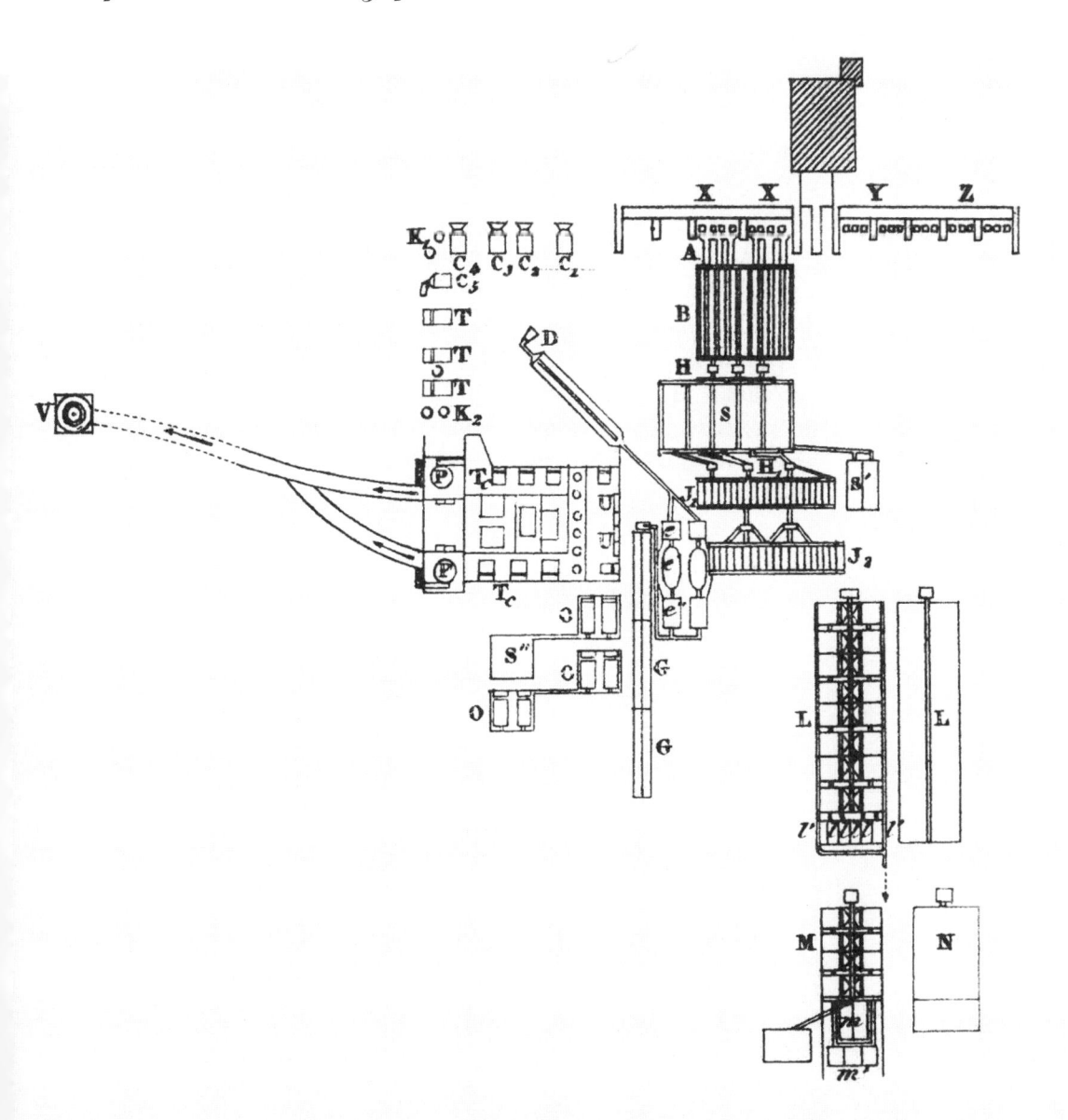

gether with the sketches representing all or part of these dressing floors, will give an idea of the numbers and layout of the various pieces of apparatus. Here again, I will confine myself to a simple partial description for Wheal Vor, Tincroft, St. Day United and Drakewalls, and a complete one for Par Consols, deferring numerical particulars to the continuation of this study.

Wheal Vor in 1855.

The very ancient mine of Wheal Vor, abandoned at one time because of an excessive influx of water, was restarted in 1853, and its tin production climbed rapidly to a high figure. By 1856 this had risen to 425 tons, and in 1855 it was already reaching 313 tons at a time corresponding to the layout of the sketch of the dressing floors given.

On this layout I have left to one side the treatment of both 'best' work and crazes, and it represents that of 'common' work (*which made up the bulk of the ore treated*), the roughs, slimes and the calcining house. An examination of the first two of these (i.e. 'common' work and roughs) will serve as an example of the method of treatment followed, prior to the introduction of round buddles and discharge control valves on the 'boxes'.

1. Treatment of the crop of the common work

The sands from the stamps settle out in two successive rows of strips, **A** and **B**. Strips **A** have two divisions, a and a', while strips **B** have three, b, b' and b". The final division, b", carrying a lot of slimes, is passed to the boxes **H**. Here, the fines rejoin the main slimes in the large pits **S**, and the coarse sands retained in the boxes are washed in the large square buddles, **C**.

The first four divisions of the main strips go directly to the large square buddles, **C**, the products in each of which are divided individually as shown in the table below.

The length of the product divisions varies according to the nature of the sands:

Large square buddles	Number of divisions	Designation of divisions
C_1	2	c_1, c_1'
C_2	4	c_2, c_2', c_2'', c_2'''
C_3	4	c_3, c_3', c_3'', c_3'''
C_4	5	$c_4, c_4', c_4'', c_4''', c_4''''$

The large square buddles receive the following mixed feeds:

Buddle array	C_1	C_2	C_3	C_4
Feed received	Middlings b'	Heads b	Heads a	Heads c_3
	Middlings c_2"	Tailings a'	Heads c_2	
	Middlings c_3'''	Heads c_1	Middlings c_4'	
	Middlings c_4'''	Middlings c_2'		
		Middlings c_3'		
		Middlings c_4"		

The definitive products are all the tails c_1', c_2''', c_3''' and c_4'''', which go to roughs, and the heads c_4, which are cleaned in the kieve K_1. There, they give:

k_1 Top skimmings, fed to frames.
k_1'   Bottom skimmings, retreated separately in square buddle C_5.
k_1"   Bottom, sands already rich enough for tin case T.

The three tin cases T give, as definitive products:

t   Heads, rich sands for the kieve K_2.
t'   Crazes, very pyritic, sent to the stamps.

Kieves K_2 give:

k_2 Top skimmings, fed to frames.
k_2'   Bottom skimmings, passed to buddles C_5 alone or with k_1'
k_2"   Bottom, rich sands for roasting.

2. Treatment of roughs:

The roughs go to the double tye D, laid out to serve as a shacking tye where these buddle tailings give:

d   Heads, good for crazes.
d'   Middlings, re-passed to the tye.
d"   Tailings, carried by a current of water, via a box, into the series of three masonry pits:
e   Small square pit, where coarse sands are retained.
e'   Oval basin, fine sands that go to hand frames.
e"   Rectangular basin, very fine slimes that go to machine frames.

The coarse sands e, recovered by shovel, are made to move down the three long masonry channels **G**, each of which is split into four levels by stops or partitions. The heads of each recover a small quantity of crazes, the rest of the deposit being eventually flushed out of the dressing floors (*to 'The Flow'*).

3. Treatment of principal slimes.

Exactly the same method as described previously is applied.

The slimes pass freely into five pits **S**. Top water from there runs into pits **S'**, where it can clear before being recycled by the stamps pump.

The favourable slope of the ground allows the washing out of the solids from pits **S** by a current of water, without manual assistance. They cross to the boxes **H**, and arrive at **J₁**, the first row of twenty-four paddle trunks. The tailings j' from these trunks pass to the second row of twenty-four **J₂**, where the tailings run to the lower floors (*'The Flow'*). The heads j₁ and j₂ are separately upgraded on the two groups **L** of sixteen machine frames each. There are in addition eight 'doubling frames' **M** and eight 'redoubling frames' **N**, making in all a total forty-eight machine frames.

The burning house contains two rotary calciners **P** (Brunton type), seven tin cases, a big square buddle and a large number of kieves. Off to the side are six hand frames.

At the bottom of the valley, a (*secondary*) floor of considerable size (*'The Flow'*) treats the tailings of former workings. It comprises:

For the old tailings:
- A large strip, in front of which the materials are brought into suspension in water. The head of the settled strip contents goes to water stamps, and the tailings to two round buddles. The stamped crazes yield sand and slimes, which undergo normal appropriate treatment, during the course of which the products of the two round buddles are introduced. After running beyond the strip, the very fine slimes go directly to forty-one machine frames.

For the actual slimes from the top floors:
- There is a first series of sixty machine frames, whose products have to be upgraded on a further twenty-four frames, such that these lower floors have no less than one hundred and twenty five frames for the treatment of all the slimes received there, those from the old tailings and those that are generated by the stamps.

Tincroft in 1857.

The Tincroft dressing floor was entirely modified a few years ago. The almost non-existent slope there compels the forsaking of any secondary treatment of the roughs, and the slimes pass directly from pits to frames

Part of the dressing floors at Tincroft, 1857

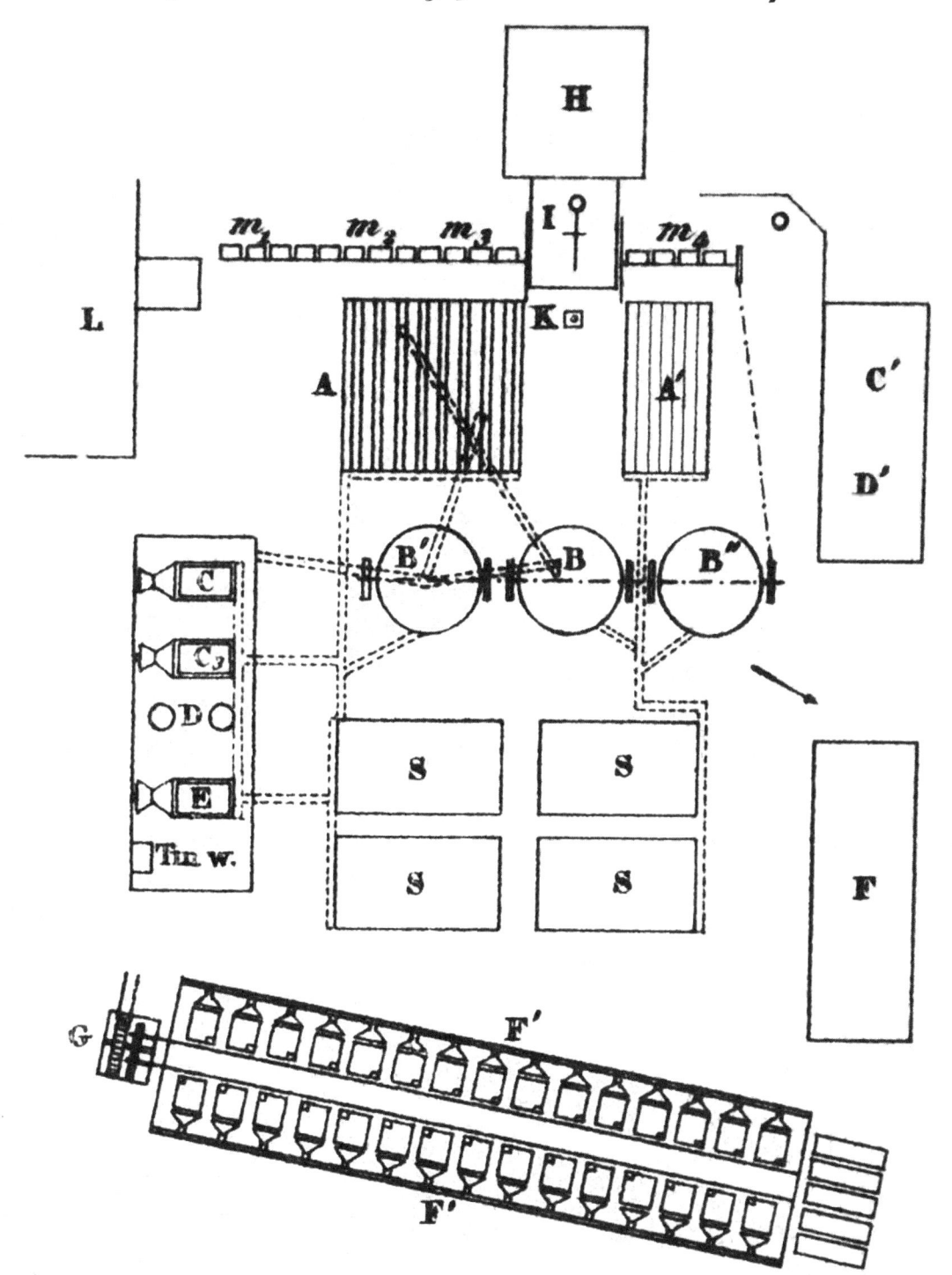

without any intermediate separation by paddle trunks.

Being fairly simple, the layout allows the easy understanding of the use of round buddles in the treatment of crop material.

In 1856, Tincroft produced 151 tons of black tin; in 1857, at the time of my visit, 14 tons of black tin per month were being sold.

Above is a sketch of the relevant part of the floors showing the treatment of 'common work' ore, along with a table describing and summarising the treatment of the crop product. I have described in detail the treatment by large square buddle of the kieve bottom skimmings, and one can rightfully judge the importance that the Captains put on keeping separate those materials that can present some difficulties.

It can also be appreciated that by indicating that sands are *re-passed* to a piece of apparatus, that that implies a series of operations whose detail is not included in a summarized explanation.

Summary of operations and treatment of the crop product from 'common work' ore:

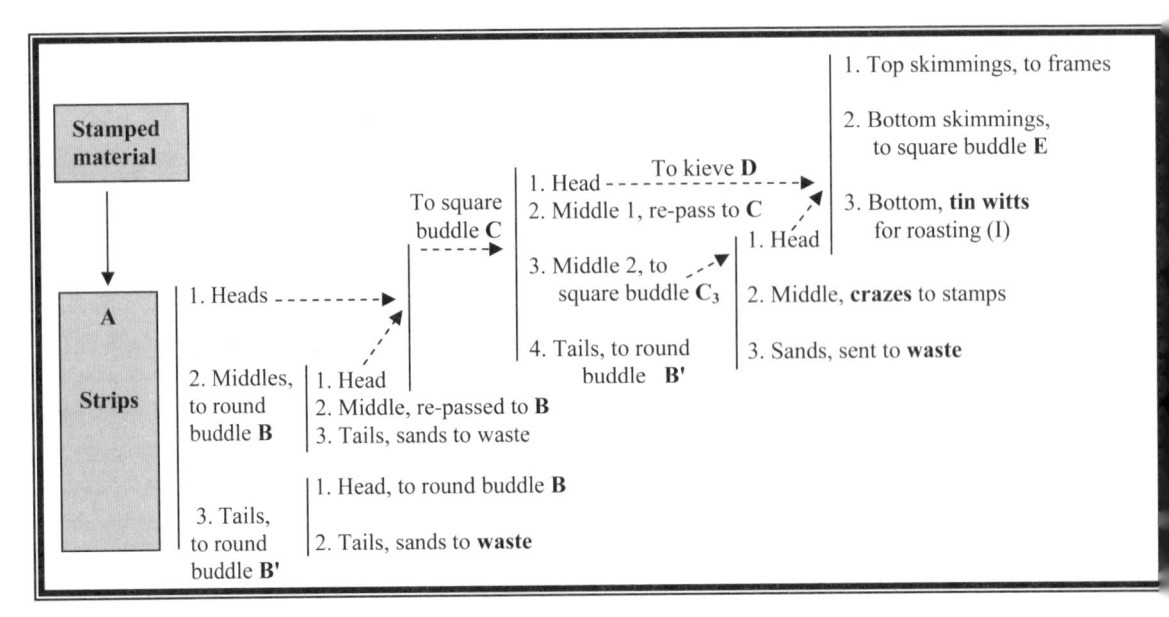

```
Stamped material
    │
    ▼
    A          1. Heads ────────────▶ To square buddle C
  Strips                                  1. Head ──────── To kieve D
                                                              1. Top skimmings, to frames
                                                              2. Bottom skimmings, to square buddle E
                                          2. Middle 1, re-pass to C
                                                              1. Head
                                                              2. Middle, crazes to stamps
                                                              3. Sands, sent to waste
                                                              3. Bottom, tin witts for roasting (I)
                                          3. Middle 2, to square buddle C₃
                                          4. Tails, to round buddle B'
               2. Middles,  1. Head
               to round     2. Middle, re-passed to B
               buddle B     3. Tails, sands to waste

               3. Tails,    1. Head, to round buddle B
               to round     2. Tails, sands to waste
               buddle B'
```

Summary of products:

D_3	Tin witts, rich sands for roasting
D_1	Very fine sands, to frames
$C_{3.2}$	Crazes, sent to stamps
B_3 B_2' $C_{3.3}$ $E_{3.3}$	Poor sand (roughs), sent to waste

(I) Sometimes, sands D_3 (kieve bottoms) are not rich enough, and are re-treated by kieve, yielding:

1. A little top skimmings, which goes to the square buddle **E**, with D_2.
2. A very little middle product, treated separately on the square buddle **E**.
3. Rich bottoms, now fit for roasting.

Summary of various apparatus and how it is used at Tincroft:

Apparatus	Feed material received
Round buddle **B**	A_2 $B_1{}'$ B_2
Round buddle **B'**	A_3 and C_4
Square buddle **C**	A_1 B_1 C_2
Square buddle **C₃**	C_3 (re-passed material)
Kieves **D**	C_1 $C_{3.1}$ $E_{1.1}$
Square buddle **E**	Fed separately for successive re-treatment:
1	D_2 E_2 $E_{1.3}$ and $E_{3.1}$
2	E_1 and $E_{1.2}$
3	E_3 $E_{1.4}$ $E_{3.2}$

St. Day United in 1857. (The former Poldice Mine)

The dressing floors of St. Day United are conducted on exactly the same principles as those of Tincroft, with all the developments that a favourable ground site allows, the small hill, over which they extend, being a slight hog's back. A small, completely separate floor treats the sands generated by the sixteen heads of stamps on the right hand side of the battery – these are not shown on the sketch.

In 1856, St. Day United produced 140 tons of black tin; in 1857, production had risen to up to 16 tons per month.

The third round buddle, **B"**, works specially, on the middlings of the two ahead of it, its products going to the two neighbouring large square buddles **C"**.

The roughs, provided by the tailings of all three round buddles along with those of some square buddles, are carried by slightly turbid water away from the apparatus to the valve **G**, where very fine sands are separated off. These run continually to the two small pits **H**, while any coarse sands that periodically cross the valve go to settle as crazes in the long channels **K**. In this way, the separation of the roughs is greatly simplified, replacing the whole system of boxes and pits at Wheal Vor.

The principal slimes, from the pits **S**, pass from paddle trunks **R**, to six self-acting frames F_s. Their products are upgraded on six ordinary frames F_0, in conjunction with energetic tossing in kieves.

Part of the dressing floors of St. Day United, 1857

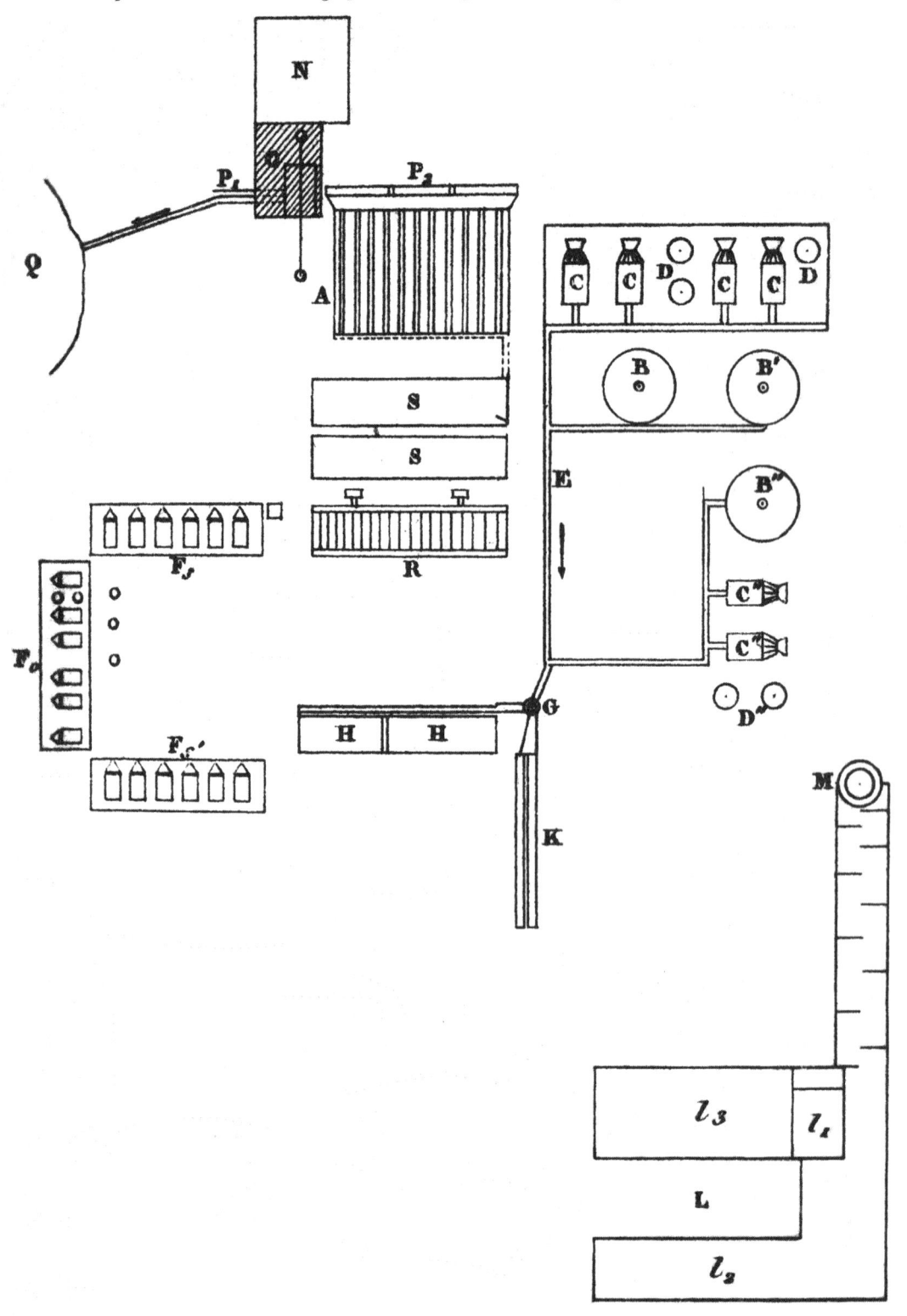

Six further self-acting frames F_s', handle the slimes from the small pits **H**. It can be seen that before roasting, this section of the floors needs no more than eighteen frames in total. Fine slimes are not plentiful at St. Day United, the gangue being particularly quartzose.

The ore carries a great deal of mispickel and wolfram. The former of these impurities needs careful calcination and yields considerable arsenic trioxide, retained in the partitioned chambers (*of the flues*) leading to the chimney. The presence of the latter notably lowers the value of the tin.

Par Consols in 1857.

Par Consols mine is, at this moment, the most prolific tin producer among those of the 'eastern' district (I). In 1856 it produced 316 tons, and in 1857 was selling 27 tons of black tin per month.

(I) In 1856, production was exceeded by only two mines, both in the 'western' district. Dolcoath, 417 tons and Great Wheal Vor, 425 tons.

In the adjoining tables I have set out the methods of treatment of the raw ore. As to procedures after roasting, refer to the remarks previously set out at the end of Section 1 under 'examples of treatment'.

I had no obligation to keep to theoretical divisions, based on the nature of the materials, which can easily be deduced from the rest (*of the information*). The detail in the table is far from covering all the operations practised on the dressing floor, and should be considered as providing no more than a general indication, though, I believe, sufficient to follow the expedient variations applied to the sands and slimes to be treated.

Several methods are not described right to the end, though it is possible to deduce these from the relevant preceding information.

Concurrently, within the table, is a complete list of the numbers of individual pieces of apparatus employed, and shown on the drawing of the dressing floors.

Par Consols can be considered as an example of a large dressing floor that is favourably sited and, in general, well laid out.

Stage	Apparatus	Material treated	Numbers	Designation
Stamping	Heads employed for each task	Best work	12	a
		Common work	36	b
		Crazes (old type 'flosh' stamps)	20	c
		Copper ore	8	d

Crop		Best work	6	**A**
	Strips	Common work	2	**A'**
		Crazes	2	**A"**
	Round buddles		3	**R R' R"**
	Square buddles	Best work	2	**B**
		Common work	2	**B'**
		Secondary products from **B'**	2	**B"**

Roughs	Long strip	Receiving roughs	1	**E**
	Tyes	Heads from **E**, and due to be replaced by 2 round buddles, also to treat **G₁**	3	
	Box	Roughs go to tributers	1	**F**

Slimes	Top skimmings	Best work	1 frame	**D**
		Common work, heads of frames, **M**	3 frames	**β**
	Slimes from small pits	Small pits, for slimes from roughs and 'best work'	2	**G**
		Large square buddles, treating heads from **G₁**	2	**H**
		Frames, treating products from **H**	1	**μ**
		Frames, for slimes **G₂** and **G₃**	2	**I**

		Large slime pits	2	**K**
		Roughs box	1	**α**
		Paddle trunks	32	**L**
		Box	1	**α'**
	Main slimes	Frames, treating **L₁** after **α'**	4	**M**
		Paddle trunks	32	**N**
		Frames, working **N₁**	12	**O**
		Frames, for secondary upgrading	1	**O₁**
		Frames, for secondary upgrading	2	**O₂**

The letters of designation, as used on the drawing of the floors, are given in the tables, and frequently thereafter in the subsequent text.

Below the dotted line is the 'tributer's floor', where all tailings arrive into a long channel or drag, δ. They first undergo a primary sizing classification in two boxes and pits, **S** (analogous to roughs treatment at

Wheal Vor). There are, besides, two tyes, **Tδ**, a second strip, **δ'**, and two further tyes, **Tδ'**. In addition there are four frames, **T**, for the slimes from pits **S**, two more slime pits, **P**, thirty-two paddle trunks, **Q**, and a small floor, **R** with twelve frames accompanying kieves.
In the 'burning house' there are:

- 3 rotary calciners (Brunton type).
- 4 square buddles and 8 attendant kieves.
- 1 'tin case' / tye
- 1 large frame.
- A black tin store. (continued on page 63)

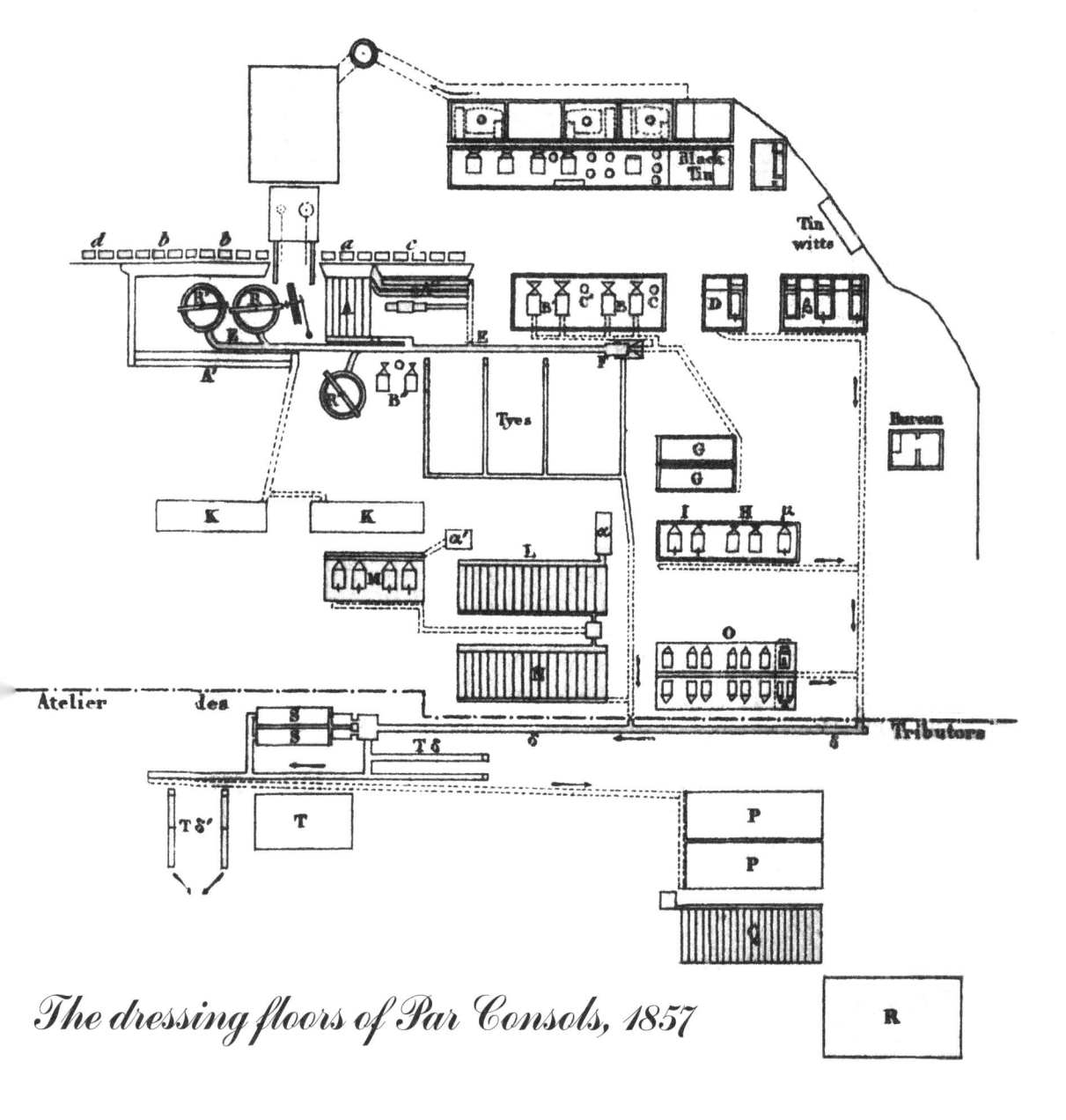

The dressing floors of Par Consols, 1857

I. Par Consols - treatment sands from stamped 'best work'

Strips A

Receive stamps sands

1. Heads, go to square buddies **B** - - →
2. Middles – go with heads **A₁'** of 'common work' strips to round buddle **R**
3. Tails, after cleaning, go with middles **A₂'** of common work to round buddle **R'**
4. To transverse strip
   - Heads go with product 3
   - Tails go to long strip **E**

1. Heads to kieve **C** - - →
2. Re-pass to buddles
3. Re-pass to buddles
4. Cleaning ('shacking') - - →
5. Tails go to long strip **E**, unless the ore is very poor

1. Top skims go to large frame **D** - - - →
2. Bottom skims, re-passed to the buddle
3. **Bottom**, ready for single roasting

1. **Hopper product**, ready for roasting
2. Box. **Crazes** for the stamps, normally rich. If not, then to round buddle **R''** with heads of tyes
3. Head of long pit, goes to square buddle
4. Tails of long pit, go to frames

1. **Head**. Ready for single (or double) roasting
2. Re-passed to the frame - - →
3. To 'shacking'

1. **Crazes** for stamping
2. Slimes, treated as **D₂**

1. Head, to Kieves
2. Re-passed to buddle
3. Tails, to long strip **E**

Products 1 and 2 re-passed to the frame till good enough for kieves. - - - →
3. Discard, to 'Tributers' floors'.

1. **Head**, ready for roasting
2. Re-passed to frame

1. **Head**, ready for roasting
2. Re-passed to frame

Top, re-passed to frame
Bottom, ready for roasting

1. **Copper ore**
2. Discard to **waste**

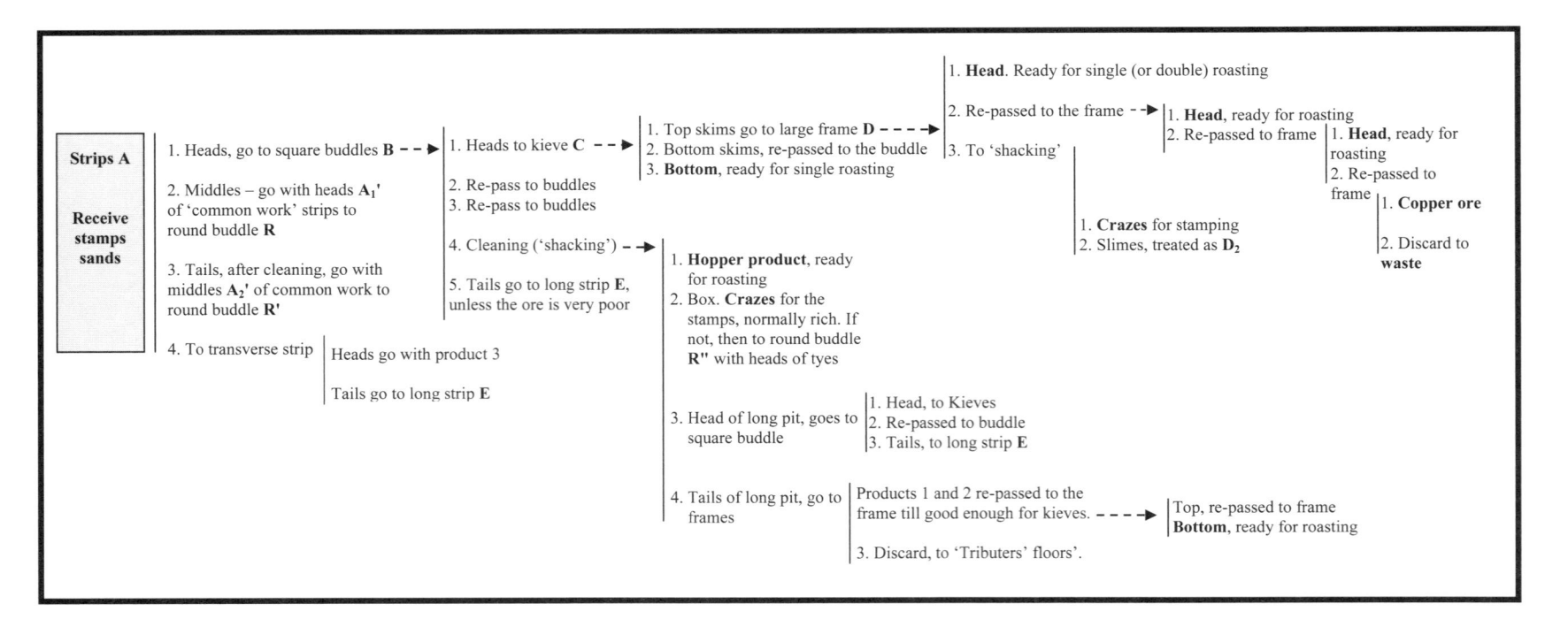

II. Par Consols - treatment of the sands from stamped 'common work'

Strips A'

Receive stamps sands

1. Heads, go with A₂ to round buddle R - - - →
   - 1. Heads to square buddle B' - - - →
     - 1. Top skims, to the large frame β - - - - - →
       - 1. Re-passed (as above for 'best work' **D₂**)
       - 2. as necessary until ready for **roasting**
       - 3. Tails, discarded to tributers' floors
     - 2. Bottom skims, re-passed to square buddle
     - 3. **Bottom**, ready for one roasting (or two)
       - 1. Heads, to kieve C'
         - 1. Heads, ready for roasting
         - 2. To kieve, as β heads
         - 3. Discarded to lower Tributers' floors
       - 2. Re-passed to square buddle
       - 3. Tails, to cleaning ('shacking')
         - 1. Box, averagely rich **roughs**
           - 1. Re-passed to the frame
           - 2.
           - 3. **Bottom**, for roasting
         - 2. Long pit, goes to large frame β - - - →
           - 1. Head, to kieves
           - 2. Re-passed to frame
           - 3. Discarded, to tributers' floors

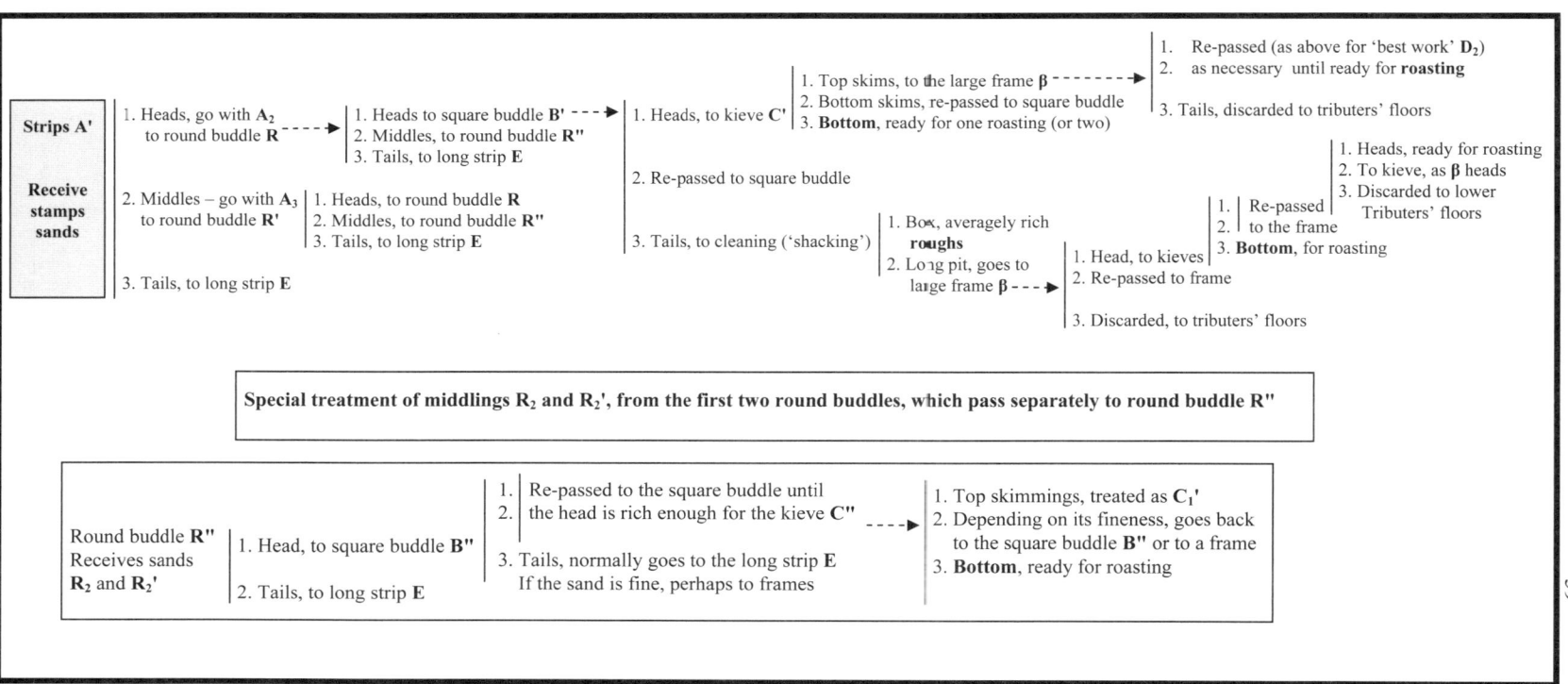

2. Middles – go with A₃ to round buddle R'
   - 1. Heads, to round buddle R"
   - 2. Middles, to round buddle R"
   - 3. Tails, to long strip E

3. Tails, to long strip E

Special treatment of middlings R₂ and R₂', from the first two round buddles, which pass separately to round buddle R"

Round buddle R"
Receives sands **R₂ and R₂'**

1. Head, to square buddle **B"**
   - 1. Re-passed to the square buddle until the head is rich enough for the kieve **C₁'** - - - →
     - 1. Top skimmings, treated as **C₁'**
     - 2. Depending on its fineness, goes back to the square buddle **B"** or to a frame
     - 3. **Bottom**, ready for roasting
   - 2.
   - 3. Tails, normally goes to the long strip **E** If the sand is fine, perhaps to frames

2. Tails, to long strip **E**

III. Par Consols - treatment of sands and slimes rejected by operations I and II (excepting those that pass to the 'tributers' floors')

§ 1. Sands from heads of strips and round and square buddles, collected in the long strip E.

Long strip **E**
- 1. Heads whose nature varies with the materials fed, and which have to be kept separate. The method and operations used can present these variations.
  - 1. Head, goes to round buddle **R"**
    - 1. Head, gives poor crazes
    - 2. Tails. to tributers' floors
    - Note: These tyes are about to be replaced by two further round buddles.
  - 2. Middles, re-passed to the tye — Normally, these are sent to tyes
  - 3. Tails. to tributers' floors.
- 2. Tails carried to the box **F**, where the sands are recovered and sent to the tributers' floors.

§ 2. Slimes from the cleaning of sands settled in the long strip E, and slimes from the four square buddles B and B' (two of each).

Small slime pits **G**
- 1. Heads, go to square buddle **H**
  - 1.
  - 2. Re-passed to the buddle until the heads are rich enough and free of sands to go to frame **μ**
  - 3. Tails, to tributers' floors, along with all those from first and second washings in the buddle
- 2. Middles, to frames **I**
  - 1. Top skimmings, go to the large frame **O₁**
  - 2. **Bottom**, ready for roasting
  - 1. **Heads**, ready for roasting
  - 2. Re-passed to the frame
  - 3. To the tributers' floors
- 3. Tails, treatment analogous to **G₂**

Large slime pits **K**, receiving slimes from stamped material overflowing from the strips
- After decantation of surplus water, the solids are recovered, re-pulped with water and stirred by shovel in box **α**
  - 1. Fine sands, shovelled out for 'shacking'
  - 2. The majority of material is in suspension and runs into the first row of paddle trunks **L**
    - 1. Average size sands, treated in square buddles etc. as **G₁** (Operation III)
    - 2. Finer sands, going directly to frames and treated as **G₂** (Operation III)

IV. Par Consols - treatment of 'principal slimes'

- 1. Heads, put into suspension in box **α'**
  - 1. Coarse sands from the box, treated with sands from the long strip **E**
    - 1. Goes to large frame **μ** - -▶
      - 1. Heads, to kieve
      - 2. Re-passed to the frame
      - 3.
      - 1. Re-passed to the frame **μ**
      - 2.
      - 3. **Bottom**, ready for roasting
    - 2. Re-passed to the frame
    - 3. Goes to second trunks **N**
  - 2. Slimes in suspension go to frames **M**
- 2. Tails, sent to the second row of paddle trunks **N**
  - 1. Heads, go to frames **O**
    - 1. Treatment analogous to that of **M₁** and **M₂**
    - 2.
  - 2. Tails, sent to waste (on the beach)

V. Par Consols - the 'Tributers' Floors', treating tailings, sands and slimes from the main floors.

(Excepting the tailings from the secondary Paddle Trunks, which are discharged to the beach)

No. 1 Long strip (drag) δ, receiving all the material	1. Settled heads, going to tyes 2. Tails, retained in the box, and the sands are sent to	**Long drag δ** 1. Heads, taken for **crazes** 2. Tails, sent back to	1. Heads, sent back to long drag δ 2. Tails (coarse sands), discarded to the sea as waste
		The sands from this long drag go to tyes	1. Top skimmings, re-passed to frame 2. Bottom skimmings 3. Bottom — — — → Treated on a square buddle etc., as G_1, (Op. III)
No. 2 Small slime pits **S**, receiving very fine sands that escape settlement in the long drag	Very fine sands go to frames **T**	1. Heads, to a kieve 2. Re-passed to the frames	
No. 3 Large slime pits **P**, receiving fine slimes escaping Nos. 1 and 2	Very fine slimes, going to Paddle Trunks **Q**	1. Heads, go to frames **R** for treatment analogous to that of L_1 and N_1 2. Tailings, discarded to the beach as very fine slimes waste	

VI. Par Consols - treatment of the sands obtained from the stamping of 'crazes'

Strip A"

Receiving the crazes stamped by the 20-head battery of 'flashers' **c**

1. Heads, go to square buddies
2. Middles, go to round buddle **R** etc.
3. Tailings, go to cleaning ('shacking')
   1. Box, goes to round buddle **R'** etc.
   2. Head of the long pit goes to frames
      1. Re-passed until the head is rich enough for the kieve, the rest treated as products from kieve **C'** (Op. **II**)
      2.
      3. Tailings, going to long strip **E**
      1. Heads, go to kieves
      2. Re-passed to the frame
         1. Re-passed to the frame
         2.
         3. **Bottom**, ready for roasting
         1. Heads, go to kieves
         2. Re-passed to the frame
         3. **Bottom**, ready for roasting
         2. Tails, go to tributers' floors

Summarising, the principal pieces of apparatus are:
Three round buddles, twelve square buddles, forty-three frames, of which six are large and three arrays of thirty-two paddle trunks each.

Drakewalls in 1855

At Drakewalls, the tin ore is found under very anomalous circumstances, as much by the size of the tin grains as the abundance of wolfram. The gangue is principally composed of killas and quartz, and carries large amounts of both iron pyrites and mispickel (*iron/arsenic sulphide*).

After hoisting, and a preliminary sorting at the shaft mouth, breakage by hammer is followed by a second sorting, which removes the greater part of the wolfram. The ore is then transported, not to (*normal*) stamps, but to rolls crushers (*like those commonly used on the softer copper and lead ores*), and after crushing, it is upgraded by tyes, sieves and jigs, operations that closely resemble those for the treatment of those ores, particularly copper. A very small portion of the roughs produced passes to a small set of stamps, when the sands product undergoes the normal treatment for tin ores. For all of its interest, an account of this method would be out of place here.

It is at Drakewalls that the Oxland Process, for the separation of wolfram from tin, has been applied, by the chemical attack of 'soda ash' or sodium carbonate. This is the sole point that I shall lay stress on.

The Oxland Process for separation of wolfram

The tin witts need to be roasted as at other floors. In 1855, for a monthly production of 25 tons of black tin, no less than 14-15 tons per month of arsenic trioxide were recovered in the calciner chambers. The roasted ore is then washed as normal, though barely 3 tons of black tin ready for sale are obtained by the various operations on the floors. The rest is tin concentrate carrying, on average, about 5% of wolfram, which it is a question of removing for purification.

This treatment is carried out in a reverbatory furnace with an elliptical bed, 10½ feet in length and fitted with cast-iron plates. 9 cwts. of damp sand is charged, then, when this is dried out, ¾ of a cwt., or 84 lbs. of carbonate of soda in powder form. The roasting is continued for six hours, rabbling and turning over the bed every half-hour. The fire grate consumes 4 cwts. in 24 hours, so that 1 cwt. is required for each operation. The heat is directed such that the soda attacks the wolfram completely, and a temperature is maintained such that the tin is unaffected, as far as possible.

After leaving the furnace, the material is in the form of more or less agglomerated blackish powder. Some white grains of excess soda can be seen, but no flakes of wolfram.

Originally, the tungstate of soda was dissolved out by lixiviation, and crystallised by evaporating the solution in sheet metal vats.

It was hoped to find a market for this product by recovering the wolfram, either in a metallic state for use in alloys, or oxidised or combined for paint and the colouring of glass.

These attempts not having come to fruition, it was dispensed with in 1855 for a preliminary washing (I).

(I) In 1858, the tungstate of soda and wolfram were acquired by German chemists, whose aim was to use them in the fabrication of a new type of steel.

After chemical attack by the carbonate of soda, the agglomerated matter was sent directly to the stamps, where, despite the light weight of the heads, it was necessary to add 330-440 lbs. of quartz per ton of material to prevent thickening to a paste. The settled solids in the strips were subsequently enriched by washing, analogous to that which follows conventional calcination.

The grainiest material, being little agglomerated during the process, could be washed without a preliminary stamping, and about two tons of black tin recovered.

In order to treat 2,315 lbs. of material, reducing to 1 ton (2,240 lbs.) of purified black tin, the calcining furnace uses:

Item	Weight	Cost
Carbonate of soda at 12s. per cwt.	176½ lbs	18s. 11d.
Coal at 16s. per ton	254 lbs.	2s.
Labour at 3s. per day	1.2 days	3s. 7d.
Total		**£1 4s. 6d.**
Stamping and washing, at most		£1
Approximate total cost per ton of black tin		**£2 4s. 6d.**

To this cost, the potential tin loss, as much by chemical attack as in the following washing, must be added, on which I have no information, but which cannot be negligible.

Here, in comparison to the average value of black tin over a year, is the approximate price realised per ton at Drakewalls with that at St. Day United, another mine whose ore carries wolfram:

The reduction in black tin price realised, by the presence of wolfram

Year	Average value of 1 ton of black tin	Price Drakewalls	Price St. Day United
1853	£68	£77	-
1854	£64	£78	-
1855	£68	£77	£55
1856	£71	-	£58

This shows just how much the presence of wolfram depreciates the value of the tin mineral. When it is present in significant quantity, the price of a ton of black tin can fall to £40 or even less. Thus, the importance of an economic process for its removal is evident.

Section 3

Description and function of various pieces of apparatus.

§ I. Stamps.

Stamps are installed on the upper part of the dressing floors. The batteries form a horizontal line, with the engine occupying a place near the centre. On both sides of the engine, and sideways on to the dressing, are the great cam barrels rotated by the action of the engine.

General layout

Behind the stamp batteries, and from six to nine feet above them, stands the tramway bringing the ore, which is fed directly from wagons into ore hoppers with an inclined base, there being one hopper to supply ore for each mortar box of stamps. Material falls (*from the hopper*) by its own weight and by the vibration of the machine, aided in its movement by water near the end of its travel. It enters the box through an opening made in the rear face, is subjected to the action of the stamp heads, and leaves, as a highly liquefied, free-flowing mud or slurry, through front openings (sometimes also on the sides of the box), either fitted with a screen grating or not, as the case may be.

The water, charged with sands, runs away down an inclined plane running all the way along the front of the boxes, and is directed into the settling strips.

The engine houses comprise two adjoining buildings. The lower one, to the rear, contains the steam boilers, and the other, at a higher level, the engine itself.

Every stamps engine that I have seen has had a vertical cylinder and balance beam, the admission and exhaust of steam etc. being governed by valves.

Normally, the engine house has part of the balance beam projecting outside, and very strong foundations, extended in front of it to support the bearings for the drive shaft (*connecting to the stamps axle*), have slots and spaces necessary for the cranks and flywheels.

The cam barrel is constructed in several connected sections, supported separately by a strong and robust wooden framework, and adding or removing sections is easily accomplished. Each section of this barrel relates to a set of four boxes or 'covers', each of which contains either three or four heads and lifting 'stems'. Nowadays, stamps in sets of four are generally preferred.

At this point I shall not enter into a detailed analysis of the construction

Stamps engines of steam stamps engines. It will be enough to indicate the more important dimensions of some, and the conditions under which they work, so that one can assess:

- The motive power necessary for stamping on various dressing floors.
- The corresponding consumption of fuel (*coal*), which accounts for a significant fraction of the total cost of tin preparation.

The adjoining tables contain numerical information for twelve sets of stamps, relating at the time of compilation to the engines and the apparatus they drove. I have compiled this information from several sources:

'*The Cornish Engine Reporter*'. W. Browne. (Nos. 1, 2 and 3).

'*The Engine Reporter*'. Th. Lean. (Nos. 4 and 5).

Statements that I have had occasion to make. (Nos. 6, 7 and 8).

Combes, '*Annales des mines*', 3rd series, Vol. 5, 1834. (Nos. 9, 10, 11 and 12).

	Mine	H.p.	Cylinder & stroke	Hds.	Active	Average drop height	Total weight (head + stem)
1	Tincroft	77	36", 9 ft. d. acting	64	48	10"	840 lbs
2	Great Polgooth	Brazier's 73	35", 10 ft. d. acting	120	-	10"	364 lbs
3	Great Polgooth	Gover 34	24", 7 ft. d. acting	60	-	10"	400 lbs
4	Carnbrea	-	32", 9 ft. s. acting	96	-	9"	650 lbs
5	Dolcoath	Old stamps	26", 9 ft. d. acting	64	-	10"	650 lbs.
6	Gt. Whl. Vor	-	36", 10 ft. d. acting	80/120?	-	10"	380 lbs
7	Balleswidden	-	36", 10 ft. d. acting	96	68	10"	672 lbs
8	Par Consols	-	2-cylinder compound	76	68 for tin	10"	644 lbs.
9	Gt. Whl. Vor	Old stamps	24", 6½ ft. d. acting	34	-	10½"	372 lbs
10	Gt. Whl. Vor	South stamps	27", 5 ft. d. acting	48	-	10"	390 lbs
11	Gt. Whl. Vor	Bratt's stamps	16", 5 ft. d. acting	24	-	10½"	394 lbs
12	Balleswidden	-	24", 5 ft. d. acting	32	-	10½"	391 lbs.

	Mine	H.p.	No. of drops per rotation	Revs. Per minute	Flywheel diameter	Crank radius	Source & date
1	Tincroft	77	5	10	22'	-	Browne Jul. 1837 (a)
2	Great Polgooth	Brazier's 73	-	-	25'	-	" (b)
3	Great Polgooth	Gover 34	4	-	15'	-	" (c)
4	Carnbrea	-	5	8.5	20'	4'	Lean Jun. 1857 (d)
5	Dolcoath	Old stamps	5	9.4	25'	4'	" (e)
6	Gt. Whl. Vor	-	5	9	-	-	Jul. 1855
7	Balleswidden	-	5	9	-	-	Sep. 1857
8	Par Consols	-	5	10	-	-	"
9	Gt. Whl. Vor	Old stamps	5	9.65	12'	3'	Combes Jun. 1833
10	Gt. Whl. Vor	South stamps	4	9.12	15'	2½'	"
11	Gt. Whl. Vor	Bratt's stamps	4	10.48	14½'	2½'	"
12	Balleswidden	-	5	-	13'	2½'	"

(a) Works a 17" diameter plunger, 7' stroke, taking water 4 fathoms. Draws 40 wagons per day up an inclined plane to a height of 15'. Has 3 boilers, weight 35 tons. Engineer, J. West. Built by Perran Foundry Co., 1835.

(b) Raises 30 wagons per day of 2,800 lbs. each, up an inclined plane to a height of 21'. Has 2 boilers, weight 20 tons. Engineer, W. West. Built by Hodge's Foundry (St. Blazey?), 1848.

(c) 8 cwts. of coal per day allocated for working the round buddles. 2 boilers, weight 10 tons. Engineer, Webb. Built by Hodge's Foundry, 1844.

(d) Works a 16" diameter plunger, 4¾' stroke, taking water 6¼ fathoms. Raises a part of the ore to be stamped to a 12' height. Works 45 paddle trunks, with 1/9 of the total coal consumption being allocated for this work. Some heads are inactive.

(e) Works a 10⅞" diameter plunger, 8' stroke, taking water 6 fathoms. Draws the ore to be stamped up a height of 15'. Works 50 paddle trunks and 5 round buddles, with 1/7 of the coal being allocated for this. Feed water is cold.

The majority of these engines are 'double-acting', though some single-acting engines are employed to good effect, that at Carnbrea (No. 4) being an example. It is obvious that uniformity of speed of rotation is not a necessary working condition, and the flywheels employed here are sufficient for the job in hand.

Types of engines

At Par Consols, the engine is a double expansion compound type, based on the Woolf pattern. The two cylinders are entirely separate, almost constituting two machines, each with a balance beam and crank arm. The cranks themselves are keyed to be offset by 90°, avoiding a 'dead point' (*in the rotation*).

The engineer James Sims also builds 2-cylinder compound engines (Sims combined engines). The layout adopted consists of positioning the larger cylinder, where the expansive power of the steam is used, following, and on the same axis as the smaller, both pistons being fixed on the same piston rod, and the intervening space between the two in permanent connection with the condenser. Steam comes from the boiler to the head of the smaller cylinder, acts on the small piston, and, having done its work, passes to the lower face of the large piston. During the first stage of movement, the large cylinder is in communication with the condenser. The relationship between the two piston diameters is, at most, 2:1, that is to say, the volume of the larger cylinder does not exceed four times that of the smaller.

This system has been successfully applied to a certain number of pumping engines, and to both horizontal and vertical rotary engines. One of the latter, having pistons of 24″ / 48″ diameter, respectively, drives a stamp battery of 64 heads.

Power

From the tables above, it can be seen that it would be useless to look for a relationship between the power of any one engine and the number of heads that it drives. That mainly favours those somewhat larger mines that have been furnished from the start with quite powerful pumping engines, compared to the presumed increase in production by adding new sets of stamps. Besides, the weight of the stamp stems is very variable, so their number alone would be no indicator of the work that the engine has to do.

Nevertheless, it can be concluded that with a cylinder of 36″ diameter and a stroke of 9 or 10 feet, up to 120 heads of reasonable weight will be able to be driven, and there is enough power to meet the needs of treatment on a considerable scale.

Comparing No. 6 with Nos. 9, 10 and 11, it can be seen that at Wheal Vor, in 1855, there was one 36″ engine, 10 ft. stroke, driving 80 heads (this number would subsequently have to be increased to 120), whereas, in 1835, three engines were in use for 106 heads.

A single powerful engine allows a considerable amount of work of the same nature to be concentrated all at the same place, and I have already commented on the advantage of having one large floor instead of several small ones, but it is only a genuine advantage if the work to be done is proportional to the power of the engine.

When, following unfulfilled expectations, a powerful engine is only driving a certain number of stamps, the work is far too little, and the expansive power of the steam could well be pushed to its upper limit.

But, it will always be necessary to slightly close the regulator, to restrict the passage of steam, which will be the cause of a permanent significant loss of useful effect (engine 'duty').

Most of the engines brought on to the scene are very strong and durable, since that is necessary in order to drive the stamps. However, there is reason to see that they often have additional, very important supplementary work to perform. Besides the pump set up in front of the engine house to recycle the used dressing water, they frequently operate the round buddles, the paddle trunks, and draw wagons up the inclined tramway to the stamps.

Speed

Since any machine has been built to work between certain speed limits, it is in the overall interest, from the point of view of useful work, that they do not exceed these.

Here, the operation of stamping itself, and the never varying layout of the mortar boxes, grate screens and strips, exert a fair regularity on proceedings.

Each stamp head strikes 40 or 50 times per minute. In other words, with 5 cams, the cam barrel turns 9 or 10 times during the same period. It is possible to reach 60 or even 70 blows per minute, but this forcing of the work becomes more difficult and disadvantageous.

Force in h.p.

Taking one stroke of the piston at 10 feet, and 10 r.p.m., the speed of the piston will be 200 ft. per minute or 3.33 ft. per second (*20 ft. = 1 complete stroke of the engine*).

Here is the practical rule that Browne uses to calculate the force in h.p. of a rotary engine. He states:

If the pressure per square inch acting on the piston = 10 p.s.i., then the speed of the piston = 250 feet per minute.

Now, taking as an example the Tincroft engine (No. 1):

Diameter of the piston = 36"

Surface area = 1,017.94 sq. inches.

1,017.94 x 10 x 250 = 2,544,858 lbs. lifted at 1 ft. per minute.

Dividing this number by 33,000 (I), 77 h.p. is obtained.

(I) The English h.p. is equal to 33,000 lbs. lifted at 1 ft, per minute, or 550 lbs. lifted at 1 ft. per second.

Engine 'duty'

The 'duty', or useful work performed by steam engines, is calculated nowadays in millions of pounds weight raised 1 foot for each 1 cwt. (112 lbs.) of coal consumed. Some years ago, it was calculated according to the work done per 'bushel' of coal burnt. Welsh coal weighs 94 lbs. per bushel (*the bushel being actually a volume*), so that it can be seen that the old figures need to be raised proportionally by about $1\frac{1}{5}$, or $^{112}/_{94}$ for comparison with today's actual numbers.

As a working example, let us compare the calculations of engine duty for Nos. 1 and 8 in the table above. That is, the stamps engines at Tincroft and Par Consols, respectively, considering only the weight of the stamps lifted and neglecting any accessory work.

* (Author's note: After carefully working through Moissenet's figures with a reliable calculator, I have come across a few slight differences in the actual results, and one or two typographical errors, such that, in the end, I decided to quote *my* results in place of those in the original manuscript - A.J.C.).

Tincroft

48 heads, with a total new weight (*head, stem and lifter or tappet etc.*) of 840 lbs. each. The stamp heads are replaced when reduced by wear to one-third of their original size. At Tincroft, the actual new heads themselves weigh 560 lbs, the stem and tappet 280 lbs.

Therefore, $280 + \frac{2}{3} \times 560 = 654$ lbs. for the average weight of a half-worn stamp.

At 50 blows per minute, and a height of drop of 10",

$48 \times 654 \times 50 \times {}^{10}\!/_{12} = 1,308,000$ lbs. raised 1' in 1 minute.

With a coal consumption of 2 tons, or 40 cwts. per 24 hours, 1 cwt. is burnt every 36 minutes.

$1,308,000 \times 36 = 47,088,000$, or **47.1 millions 'duty'**.

The corresponding h.p. is $1,308,000 \div 33,000 = $ **39.6 h.p.**

Par Consols

76 heads, with a total new weight of 644 lbs.

Here, $224 + \frac{2}{3} \times 420 = 504$ lbs. for the average weight of a half-worn stamp.

400 bushels (or 335 cwts.) is burnt per week, so 1 cwt. is burnt every 30.1 minutes.

So, $76 \times 504 \times 50 \times {}^{10}\!/_{12} \times 30.1 = 48,039,600$ or **48 millions 'duty'**.

The corresponding h.p. is $1,596,000 \div 33,000 = $ **48.4 h.p**.

When the diverse additional secondary work done by these engines is taken into consideration, one can arrive at a somewhat higher figure for the actual engine duty, but it is obvious that, even with careful reckoning, the evaluation of the majority of the work done is 'tainted' with inexactitude.

The following respective stamps engine duties can be found:

Mine	**January 1857**	**February**	**June**
No. 4 - Carnbrea	57.7	65.5	63.8
No. 5 - Dolcoath	45.6	-	-

For January 1858, for four engines, Browne gives an average duty of 45.7 millions.

I submit that, taking 45.5 millions as an average duty would, on the whole, be rather under than over the true figure.

It is interesting to compare the performance of these engines with that of those employed for pumping. Mr. Lean, who reports on about twenty pumps, gives an average duty for the first six months of 1857 as 54.166. Mr. Browne gives 58.2 as the average for ten engines during January 1858. I think that one may take the average as 56.

Coal consumptiom per h.p. per hour

It is easy to reduce these numbers to those for coal consumption per h.p. per hour, that we are used to taking into account.

If:
- x = the coal consumption, in pounds weight, per h.p. per hour.
- N = the number of millions of pounds weight lifted at 1' per minute.
- m = the number of minutes taken to burn a cwt. of coal.
- D = the engine duty, expressed in millions of pounds weight.
- C = the number of effective h.p.

Then, we have:

$$N \times m = D, \text{ and,}$$
$$N \div 33{,}000 = C.$$

Or, $x = \dfrac{112 \times 60}{m \times C} = \dfrac{112 \times 60 \times 33{,}000}{D} = \dfrac{221{,}760{,}000}{D}$

From this formula, we obtain:

Engines	Duty	Coal consumption Per h.p. per hour
Stamps	45.5M	4.87 lbs.
Pumps	56M	3.96 lbs.

From which we can infer that the useful work of stamps engines at this time is 81% of that of pumping engines.

Progress made in stamping engines

In 1825, Dufrénoy and Élie de Beaumont announced that, a few years before, steam engines were applied to stamp mills in Cornwall, rather than water-power (*by water wheel*). They cited the mines of Wheal Vor, Great Hewas, Dolcoath, Poldice and Polgooth. In the preceding table, Nos. 9, 10 and 11 are those engines at Wheal Vor, very probably for the first time.

If we look at the duty for June 1833, we have, per cwt. of coal:

	No. 9	No. 10	No. 11	No. 12
Duty	28.56	27.60	13.36	25.39

Giving an average of 27.2M for the three highest duties. During the same period, 59 pumping engines had given an average duty of 54.96M. Comparing the relative figures for 1833 and 1858, we therefore have:

Type of engine	Duties 1833	1858
Stamps	27.2	45.5
Pumping	54.96	56.09

In other words, while the performance of pumping engines had stayed almost the same (I), that of stamps engines had increased by 67% or ⅔.

This progress has been attributed to several causes:
- The various improvements made to the engines, notably the lengthening of the cylinder, allowing the expansive power of the steam, the relationship between the stroke of the piston and its diameter having risen from between 2.2 and 2.5 to one of 3.3 or 3.4.
- The improved construction and installation of stamp batteries, particularly in respect of the guides for the stems.

(I) Pumping engines had received a great number of improvements in regard to their construction, but the majority of engines in service today are somewhat old, which tends to lower their average duty.

Materials to be stamped are:
1. Ore that has been broken by spalling to about the size of a fist (about three inches).
2. Insufficiently stamped sands, returned under the name of 'crazes' from various parts of the dressing floors.

Stamps with discharge screen grates can be used for both types of these feeds, though nevertheless, on most mines, the crazes are still passed to the older type of stamp, without screens, and with an overflow discharge weir of variable height in an opening in the front of the mortar box. These stamps go under the name of 'floshers' or 'flashers'. In both systems, feed material arrives under the heads via an opening made in the rear of the mortar box.

Stamps with screen grates — I will refer only to the first type. The layout and placing of the screen grates varies on different floors, the following being some examples:

Mine	Screen layout
Tincroft **St. Day United** **Wheal Vor** ('best' work)	4 screens, 2 in front and 1 at each side of the 4-head mortar box

Wheal Vor ('common' work) **Balleswidden**	A single screen on each side of the mortar box

	Par Consols	3 screens, 1 large one in front and 2 others on the sides of the mortar box

Stamps in sets of 5 heads **Polgooth**	2 screens, 1 large one in front and one other to one side

With stamps in sets of four heads, and four screens, the two middle heads have a drop of 8″ or 9″, and the outer two 9″ or 10″, one inch more. The ore arriving in the middle is directed to each side by two inclined planes, and the more violent blow of the outer heads discharges the muddy sands, throwing them against the screen grates.

In boxes of three heads, it is supposed that there is but a single plane, sloping towards the screen side, and the heights of drop of the heads, inwards from the screen, are 10″, 9″ and 8″, respectively.

At Par Consols, where the front screen occupies almost the whole length of the box, the four heads all have the same drop height of 10″.

I shall now describe in detail a 4-screen stamp, the type generally used for ores to be crushed fine.

Detailed description of 4-screen stamps

The drawings below do not represent any particular stamps apparatus, but result from summaries I made of the stamps at Wheal Vor in 1855 and at Tincroft in 1857.

A 'set' is made up of four boxes of four heads each, separated from each other by a gap of 16 inches. Each box is constructed from strong oak planks, 3½ inches thick for the long sides and 4½ inches for the shorter. The width of the working space is 14 inches, the total length 3 feet 6 inches and the depth, from the base, is 3 feet 3 inches. The top is covered over by a plank, cut out in such a way as to allow the stamp stems ('lifters') to pass through.

Stamps box, 'coffer' or 'cover'

The two short sides are assembled slotted into two pieces of wood, 7 inches square and 8 feet long, which rest directly on the foundations. Iron braces, fitted on the exterior of the two long sides, cross over these bedplates and are bolted down underneath.

The interior of the boxes is fitted with ½-inch thick cast iron plates to a height of 2 feet 6 inches from the base. The wood is grooved and the plates are held in place by small, obtuse-headed countersunk bolts, the nuts being on the outside.

The aperture allowing access for the feed ore and water (I) is 15 inches wide, with its bottom on a level with the floor of the box.

(I) At Wheal Vor the boxes of the 'common work' stamps, with only two lateral screen grates, have two vertical slots in the rear face, feeding clean water directly close to the screens, in addition to that which enters in the middle with the ore.

The openings in the front face and sides are 8 inches wide by 7 inches high. The gap between the two rear openings (*for the additional water*) is 8 inches. All of these openings stop 2 inches above the base, though at St. Day United this is reduced to 1 to 1½ inches.

Inclined plane and hopper

The ore comes down an inclined plane of planks, with raised edges. The slope is determined by graphical construction, in as much as an isosceles triangle is drawn, whose base is 14 and whose sides are 12. One of the sides is held vertically against the face of the box, and the other gives the line of inclination of the slope, whose base is thus set at 18½°. This inclined plane is 4 feet long, and between the partitions it is 15 inches from the rear opening in the box and 2 feet above it.

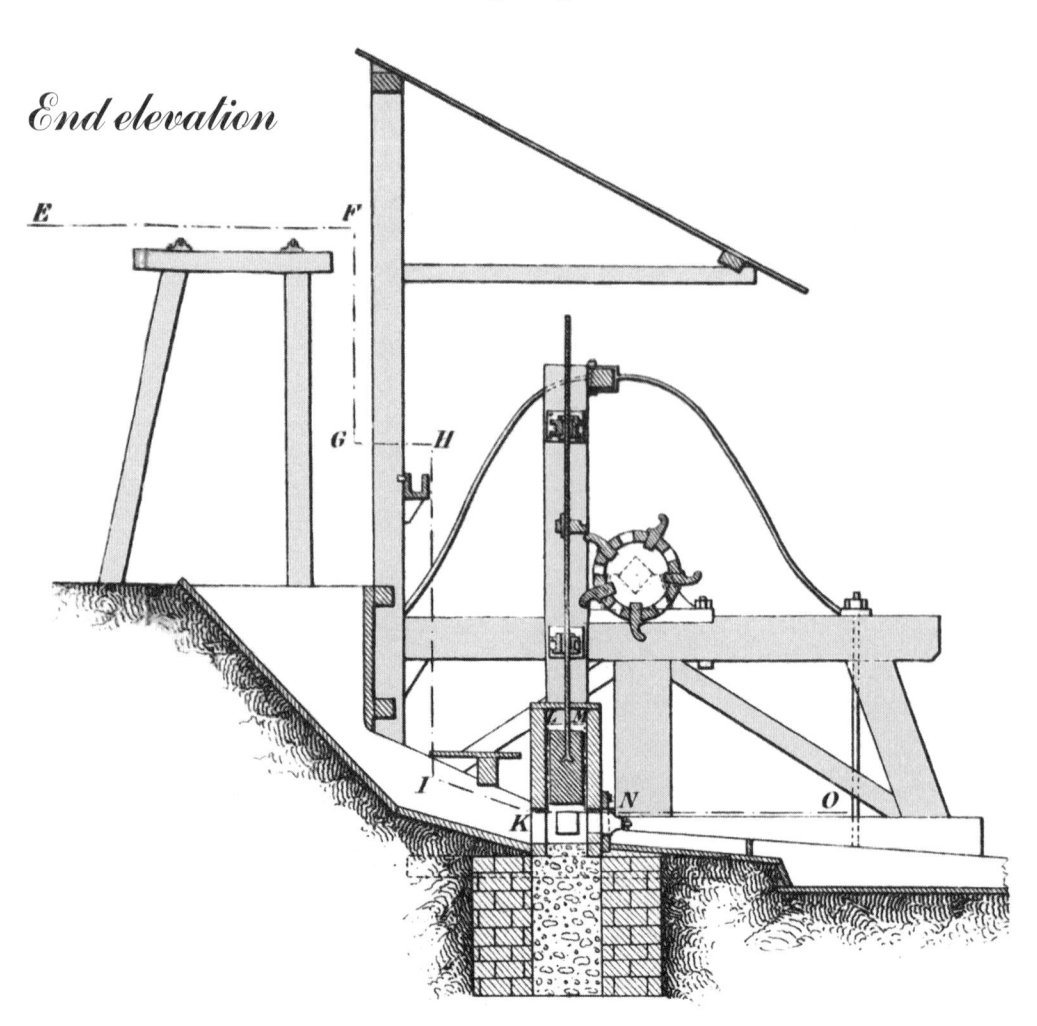

End elevation

The discharge hopper for the ore wagons is 5 feet wide, and 5 feet in vertical depth to the head of the inclined plane. Its floor slopes at 45°.

Screen grates, plates and framework

The screen grates are of sheet iron or copper, 9 inches wide by 8 inches high overall, with a corresponding perforated area of 7 inches by 6 inches, and are held in the centre of a metal plate and framework. This plate is sometimes made of wrought iron, but more commonly of cast iron, 1-inch thick, 14 inches wide and 18 inches high, with a central rectangular opening for the screen, and incorporating the means of attaching it to the coffer box.

The sides of the plate are pierced with six holes. The upper two serve to bolt it to the face of the box, the middle ones take two bolts whose heads are countersunk into the wood, the bolts protruding about 5 inches beyond the plate, with ends pierced to take a cotter pin. The two lower holes are below the level of the 'discharge plank' (*the board on which the stamped discharge runs away to the strips*), and are only used for turning the plate around when its opening has been worn away through contact with acid water and sand. At the end of six or seven months (at Tincroft), the base of this rectangle is completely deformed, when the plate is then turned around and lasts a further equal period of time.

Screen plates

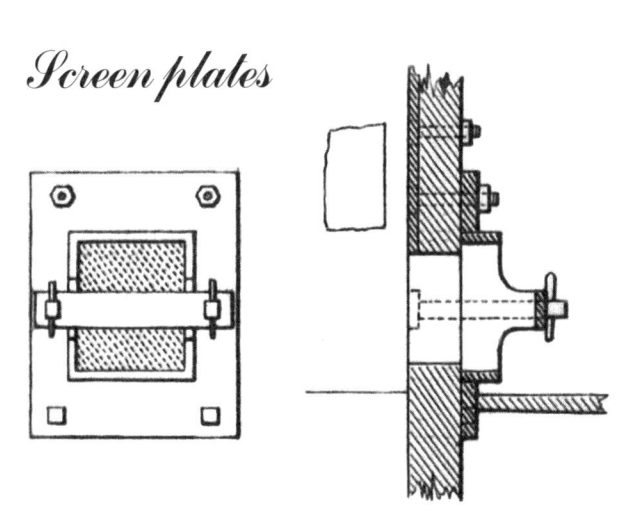

When the screen is in place, an iron framework is placed over it, ½-inch thick and 2 inches high, with two extending lugs that project about 5 inches in front of the screen. An iron strip, pierced with two holes fits over these lugs and locates on the two protruding middle bolts mentioned above, being held firmly in place with two cotter pins. The operation of replacing the screen is thus easy and quickly done.

In front of the run of coffer boxes, all along the set of 16 stamps, there is a 3½-foot wide plank with a slope of 1 in 12 (i.e. 3½ inches), enough to prevent any settlement of material discharged from the stamps on the plank itself. It acts as a transfer point, and below it run the strips.

Stamps. Heads and lifters

The stamps themselves are in one piece. The head is of cast iron, the lifter is of flat iron, and penetrates well into the head. The end of this bar of iron has been split into four, and separated into a sort of claw. When the stamps are run, the iron head envelops these protrusions, such that there is no fear of it pulling out.

At Tincroft, a new head is 23 inches high, 12 inches deep parallel to the short side of the box and 7 inches across, parallel to the front of the box. The lifter is 10 feet 9 inches long, and 4 inches by 2 in cross-section.

In the St. Just district, two-piece stamps, joined only by an iron wedge are also used. The cast iron head has a 7-inch tapered hole, and the lifter widens out at the end.

Guides There are two guides (*in which the 'lifter' or stem travels*). The first is located at 16 inches above the top of the coffer box (or 4 feet 9 inches above the base), the second 5 feet 6 inches higher.

Each of these is made up of a fixed part, bolted permanently to wooden mountings forming extensions of the short sides of the coffer box, and a movable part, connected to the first by three bolts, fitted with nuts at each end. These two close-fitting pieces make four spaces for the iron bearings and the lifters.

The bearings are hollowed out, three-sided prisms, 7½″ high and ⅛ of an inch thick, with raised external edges at both ends. They fit into each other within the fixed part of the guide. The stamp and lifter is put in place, and, lastly, the moving piece of the guide is adjusted appropriately, with a projection fitting between the two faces of the bearing, making it form the fourth surface for the smooth sliding of the lifter. The advantage of these bearings is obvious. The main part of the guides has an almost indefinite life, while the bearings are replaced as needed.

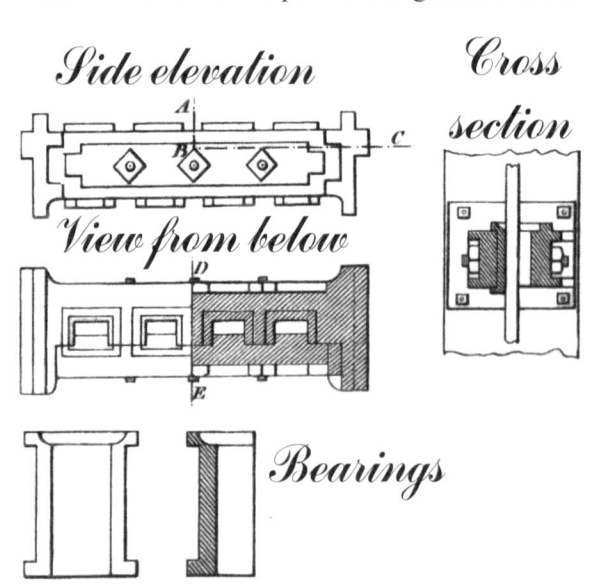

Side elevation

View from below

Cross section

Bearings

By an ingenious arrangement, the upper edge of the bearings at the Wheal Vor stamps have been made in the form of a bowl, to accept lubricant grease.

After what has been stated above, the work to be done in replacing a stamp is freely conceded. The engine must be stopped. At several stamps, a block and tackle, on a horizontal girder above the stamps, is moved straight to the stamp to be lifted out.

Plan and section EFGHIKLMNO

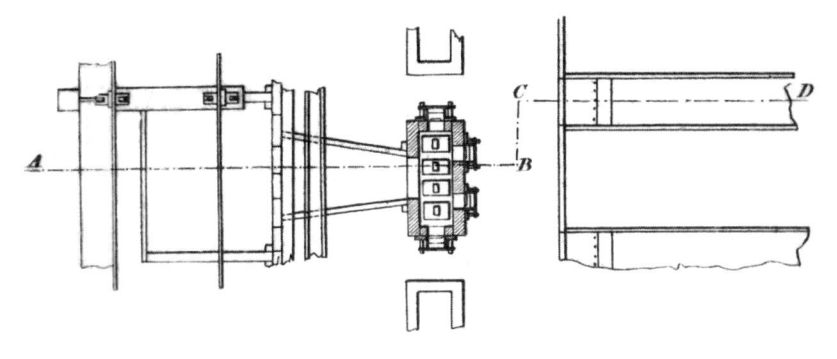

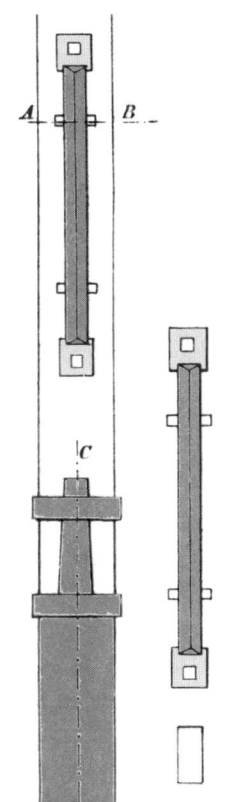

The tappets or 'tongues'

The tappets or so-called 'tongues' are cast iron, in the form of a hammer head. They are also often made of wrought iron, with steel-faced contact surfaces.

In order to fix a tappet on to the lifter of a new stamp so as to have, for example, a drop height of 9 inches, a stick or rod is stood in the coffer box.

With a ruler representing the tappet, and kept horizontal, the movement of the cam is followed, which eventually passes out of contact with it. This point is then marked on the rod. The length between this point and the lower end of the rod is reduced by 9 inches, and marked on the lifter from the point where it leaves the head. This gives the level to set for lower face of the tappet (I).

(I) It has recently been proposed that the tongues be made to project on both sides of the lifter, with the cams doubled, or like the prongs of a fork. The point of contact is then always in the centre of the lifter, and the contention is that this arrangement reduces much of the friction in the guides, and entirely allowing the easy shifting of the tappet to the right position when the stamp head wears.

Axle and cams

The cams are, in Cornwall as almost everywhere, five for each stamp. They are cast iron, 5 inches wide and 11 inches long in total, projecting 6 inches out from the axle.

The axle is also cast iron and hollow. The external diameter is 27 inches and the thickness of the metal 3½ inches. Each cam fits through a 5 by 3-inch wide slot, its 5-inch tail protruding beyond, into the hollow axle.

On one side of the cam there is a 1-inch deep notch of the same length as the thickness of the axle and it is fixed in place by driving in an iron wedge on the opposite side. The section of the casting is 4 by 3 inches, and between each cam slot an oval hole is pierced in the axle designed to lighten its weight (*without reducing its inherent strength*).

The twenty cams, in four series, are arranged in such a way that they can be looked at as fixed in four equidistant helical arcs around the axle circumference.

The axle is set up so that between the lifters and the nearest point there is about 7 to 8 inches. There is about 2 inches left between the end of the tappet and the axle, and a little less between the cam and the lifter.

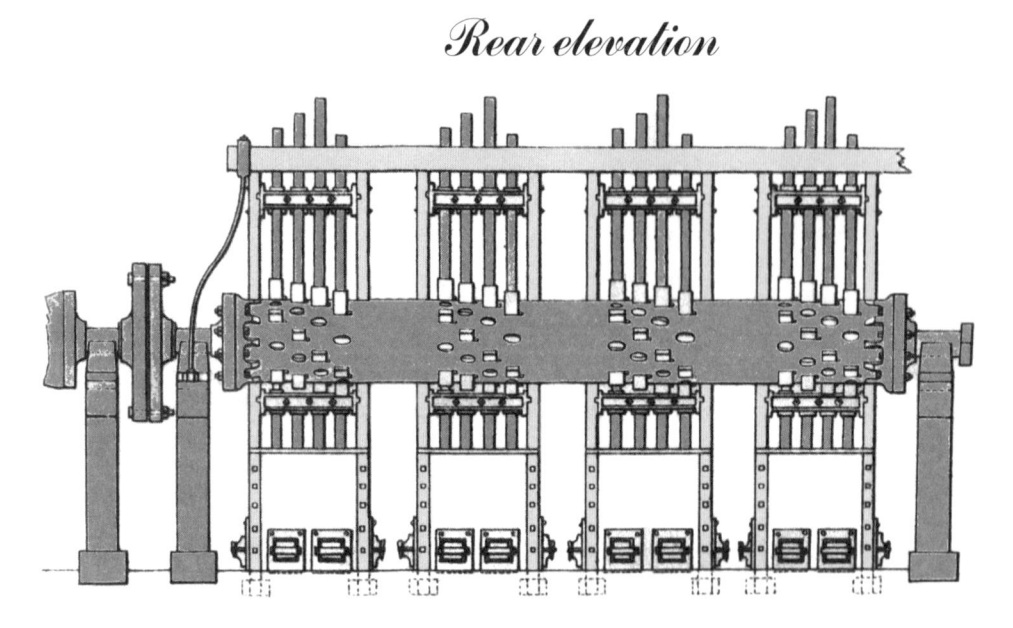

Rear elevation

Let us suppose a lift of 9 inches is needed. The tappet at rest is 4½ inches above the centre line of the axle and the cam takes it through an angle of about 28° per lift. For a lift of 10 inches, the corresponding numbers are 3½ inches and 32°.

Let us consider a mean arc of 30°. Between two cams in the same series, the angle is 72°. Taking the 20 cams of the four series it is 72 ÷ 4 or 18°. It can be seen that for any set of four stamps there will be only two in action at any one time, and similarly, that to the moment that one of the two drops from the cam, the axle turns through 2 x 18° – 30° = 6°, picking up only one more stamp, which does not take more than one-tenth of a second (I).

(I) From this, neglecting friction, the theoretical effort imposed on start-up of the engine can be calculated.

E.g. No. 4, Carnbrea: 96 heads weighing about 60,000 lbs. Length of crank

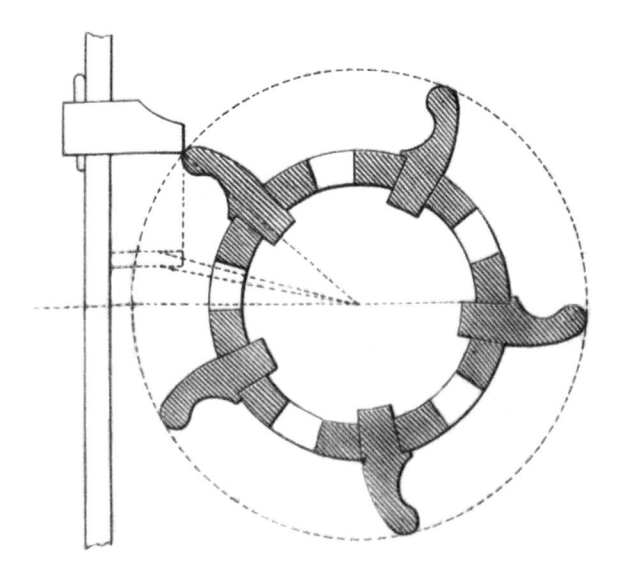

48 inches. Mean radius of contact of the cams 13½ inches + 3½ inches = 17 inches. Half of the stamps in action.

The coefficient of reduction = $^{17}/_{48}$ x ½ = 17.7%, supposing that the engine came to rest at 90° to the 'dead point'.

Force exerted on the piston, 10,620 lbs. or, with a diameter of 32 inches, about 13 lbs. per square inch – showing that the engine will be easily set in motion.

The axle is about 20 feet long. At its ends are bolted strong journals (*the parts of the axle that rest on bearings*) 9 inches in diameter, extended by a square head. The coupling together of various sets is done by means of double iron flanges fixed to the square heads of adjoining journals, and connected by two large bolts.

The connection of the actual engine to the stamps is more complicated. The head of the engine crank ends in a plate with a raised edge in which turns a ratchet wheel, mounted on to the square head of the first axle journal. A spring catch, fixed at a point on the edge of the crank plate bears on the ratchet wheel, and the cam barrel cannot be made to rotate except in the proper direction. This arrangement prevents the ensuing breakage, should the engine driver mistakenly start the engine up in the wrong direction. It also applies in the case where the engine has been stopped almost at the 'dead point', stopping it moving backwards in coming to rest. Finally, the supplementary stamps water pump can still be run even when the stamps are stopped.

Depending on the nature of the ground on which the stamps are sited, the foundations are laid out in various ways. In general, it is enough to excavate a pit three or four feet deep, and the length of a set of stamps. It is made sufficiently wide to accommodate the construction of two full length, 18-inch wide walls. The coffer boxes are simply laid on top of

Stamps foundations, coffer bases and walls

these walls at the desired height, and the space between the two walls is completely filled in with fragments of very hard quartzose schist. Stamping is started, feeding the stamps with killas, and after four to five hours of work, the floor is quite hard and compacted enough to begin the stamping of tin ore.

When old stamps are dismantled, at the bottom of the boxes, a layer of pulverised and agglomerated tin ore, twelve to eighteen inches thick, is found, which has accumulated over a long time with the action of the stamps and the compaction of the filling of the excavation.

If no lateral walls are constructed, two long wooden beams, 9 inches across the base, are placed on the floor of an excavation about 18 inches deep. Their axial spacing is at least four feet, and they extend right under the whole set of four boxes, leaving them solidly seated, and the transverse feet of each of these are simply nailed to the beams (see below). The 'beating in' of the floor is then conducted in the same way as in the walled pit.

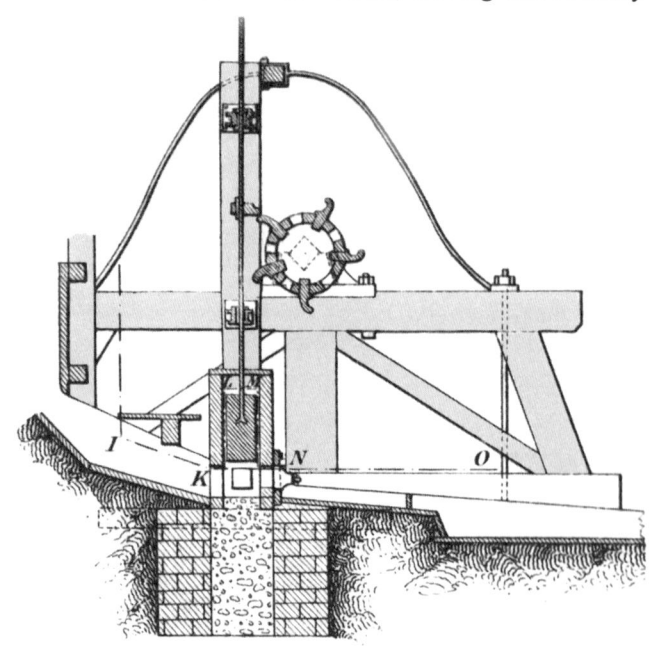

In the St. Just district (except for Balleswidden Mine), only the old-type 'flash' stamps are used, even for the stamping of tin ore. In this case, the foundations consist of granite blocks four feet thick, three feet wide and four feet six inches long. A seven-inch thick block of cast iron, having the interior dimensions of the box is then laid on top, and the box held in place by staples that fix the two transverse feet on to the granite.

Beams

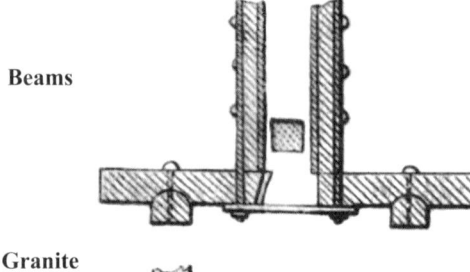

Granite and iron

In the mines in the west of Cornwall, iron lifters are now generally used. In the east of the county, wooden lifters of 'Norway Baulk' are still used on many floors – Polgooth, Carvath United, Par Consols etc.

The arrangement at Par Consols is shown below, which is very suitable and as equally applicable as iron lifters in most mining areas.

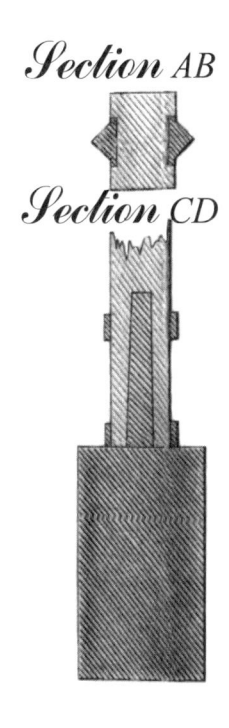

Section AB

Section CD

A new stamp 'shoe' or head is 19 inches high and 11 inches by 7 (in cross-section). Its iron 'tail' is one foot long, and 2¼ inches square near the head, tapering to 2 inches at the end. The wooden lifter is 11 feet long and 7 inches by 5. A lateral hole is made for the tail of the head, a piece of wood inserted and two retaining bands of iron put in place.

As for the guides, these are four iron 'prisms', nailed in pairs on either side of the lifter, which is slotted to receive their ends, leaving a sort of knife-edge at an angle of 60° sticking out. Some small pieces of softwood are held transversely (*in the stamps framework*) at both levels, and can be adjusted by bolts until the knife-edges just make grooves in them (*as they slide*).

Wooden lifters at Par Consols

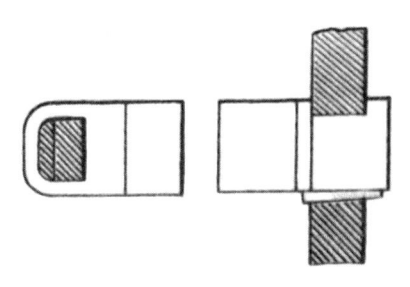

The tappet has a tail that passes through a slot in the wooden lifter and is held in place by a key wedge. When the stamp head has been worn a few inches, the tappet is raised by slotting the lifter and putting in battens below.

Stamps with screen grates can be easily altered for use as 'flashers' or 'floshers'. The screen and its mounting are taken out and a wooden channel put in place, whose base is nailed on the lower edge of the front opening, raising this by about one inch, that is, at three inches above the base of the box. This depth is raised again so that the overflow level for the sands is about twelve inches from the base. The working head of the stamp is always under water, since its own level is not more than ten inches (depending on the height of drop set).

With each blow, a certain quantity of muddy and sandy fluid is thrown up and overflows into the channel. Often, this flow is made more even by fitting a small, movable flap in the upper part of the opening, on a leather hinge.

'Flash' stamps for crazes engines

Stamping

Floshers for ore stamps

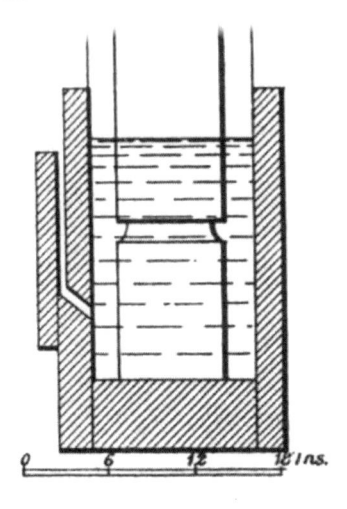

The 'flasher' stamps of the St. Just area have, as stated, a cast iron sole plate. The product openings start at 2 inches above this base and the discharge has to run down across a 3-feet inclined plane with a 9-inch drop. Some vertical sliding ports control the flow of material (I).

(I) Notwithstanding the fineness of the tin in the mines of this district, I do not hesitate to consider the use of these 'flashers' with a cast iron base as, in every way, disadvantageous for direct stamping of the ore.

Influence of the chosen arrangement

Let us first of all examine the influence that operation of the various arrangements discussed can have on the final result. Firstly, the stamping of ore.

In all stamping operations, one has in view the object of removing, as quickly as possible after the preceding stamping blow, that material already reduced sufficiently fine. The size is (*largely*) controlled by the screen, and it is the water that carries the material through. With each blow of the stamp, the pulverised material and slimes are splashed up against the screens, and are, effectively, sieved. It is understood that there would be an advantage in increasing the screen area as much as possible, to the base of the box, but, a certain depth of water must always be retained in the coffer box during stamping, and, the greater the screen area for any given hole size, proportionately more water is consumed. Normally, the quantity of water available is rather limited, and one is led, then, to the following conclusions:

Boxes (stamps coffers)

- For fairly coarse stamping, two side screens are sufficient. The holes are (*relatively*) large, the sand is easily discharged, and the appropriate water level can be maintained in the box.
- For most fine stamping, the arrangement already described, of four screens, becomes necessary. The total screen surface area is doubled, but the very fineness of the holes in the screen necessitates this.

At Par Consols, the front screen is 23½ inches by 7 inches, that is, equivalent in area to three ordinary screens. There also, the grain of the tin is very fine.

Boxes for three-head sets of stamps, with two screens (one on one of the sides), are hardly made any more. At Polgooth the stamping is very fine, but the heads are relatively light, and for three of them, the surface area of two screens can cope with the discharge. This arrangement presupposes a sideways movement of the material in the box, and the tappets have to be readjusted every week, in order to keep the drop heights close to the desired 10″, 9″ and 8″, respectively. Here, new stamp heads, as in those set-ups with two or four screens, have an enhanced effect on the discharge. That is, those placed near the side screens.

Stamp weight

The total weight of each stamp (*head, lifter etc.*) is a matter of judgement, certain very hard ores necessitating heavy stamps.

As already indicated, the choice of screen is of the utmost importance, since all the rest of the treatment depends on this.

Screens

Screens are calibrated No. 1 to No. 36. The screen gauge is a conical iron rod, 6 inches long and ¼-inch diameter at the base.

It is divided into 36 equal parts, No. 1 corresponding to the base diameter itself (¼″). The rod is inserted into the holes in the screen, and a reading taken of the division where it stops. The numbers most frequently used for tin ores are those from 30 to 36, that is, those less than 0.001 metres in diameter (= *1mm. or ¹⁄₂₅ of an inch or 1,000 microns, in modern parlance*).

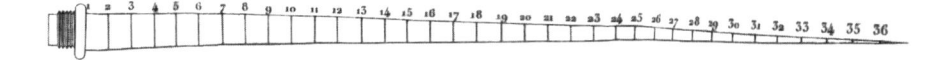

I can quote the following screens used:

    Wheal Vor Nos. 34 and 35
    Polgooth Nos. 34, 35 and 36
    Tincroft No. 36

Because of the way the screens are fabricated, (*by punched holes*) (I), the holes themselves are 'elongated' (*on the side opposite to that punched*) into cones, projecting from one side of the sheet metal. In use, this side is the one turned to face the interior of the coffer box, to avoid (*as far as possible*) blockage of the holes by offering the easy escape of the materials passing through.

(I) Fabrication of screens. Most screens are made from sheet iron, of the quality of sheets for tin-plate. They are normally 8″ by 9″ or 7½″ and cost 6s. per dozen. These screens are fabricated in several special workshops, notably that of Mr. Launder, at Redruth. The tools are an upright wooden anvil covered with a thick sheet of lead, a hammer, and an assortment of old (*large*) steel needles, sharpened to fine points.

The workman places two sheets of metal on top of the lead, held there by two hooks. He then makes holes in oblique lines to the edge of the sheet, so placed that three holes form an isosceles triangle. The spacing of the holes, and therefore the number of holes per square inch, is not subject to any rule, but judged from the proposed final hole size. The two sheets are pierced in about an hour's work, and re-passed for those holes that need enlarging.

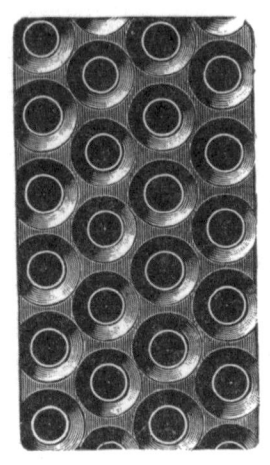

Copper screens, still little widespread in their adoption, will certainly come into general use. They used to be regarded as necessary in those mines where the water used for stamping was very acidic. Today, their advantage has been recognised, even under ordinary conditions. Thus, at Par Consols, some experiments have been made during the current year, 1858.

A large copper screen weighing 1 kg. (2.205 lbs.), lasts three months, as long as seven iron screens. Three screen sheets cost 6d. and are worth 1.1d. on resale so the actual cost is therefore just under 4.89d., that is, about 30% of that incurred by using iron screens.

At Carnbrea, the 96-head stamp battery is kept with copper screens for 9s. 9d. per month, whereas iron screens would cost at least 17s. 3d. The copper sheets used have to be quite thick, in order that the holes, made with a perforating punch, have a tough projecting section. Thus, at Par Consols, screens of 770g. (1½ lbs.) are reckoned much too weak.

In use, the protruding conical section of the hole gets worn away, and the holes themselves effectively enlarged, though unevenly, depending on the position of the screen on the coffer box. The result is that by the time one of these is replaced, it has been delivering for a long time sands much coarser than the original screen number appears to indicate. Often, it is true, the screens are actually damaged by flying fragments of rock, and it is this factor that makes the use of long screens at Par Consols notably more expensive.

Nevertheless, assuming a complete wearing away (*of the cone section*), without any actual damage, the diameter of the holes in quite fine screens does not exceed 1 millimetre.

When the greatest fineness of screen (*in use*) is reached, there is no longer any possible calibration, and for stamps treating crazes the screens are finer than No. 36.

Stamping of crazes

The stamping of crazes is difficult. Except for those that stem from the 'burning house', they have to be mixed back in with hard ore, such as 'capel' (quartzose schist), which, by its nature, adds to the proportion of fine material, in as much as fragments of this rock grind the sands between themselves.

The type of addition, in an arbitrary proportion to new ore, in which crazes are simply thrown back into the upper part of the ore hopper, does not allow any valid comparison between the work performed by 'flasher' stamps and those with screens. Nevertheless, the yield of the former can be confirmed as poor, as might well be foreseen from the mode of discharge of the material.

With any fixed arrangement, the fineness of the products can still be varied by modifying the flow of water, in as much as an excess of water is hardly to be worried about (*apart from the consumption*) with screen stamps, while with 'floshers' it would have the immediate result of discharging insufficiently pulverised crazes.

The stamping of crazes with extremely fine (and frequently renewed) screens has been successfully achieved at several mines. At Par Consols, the same attempt has come to nothing because of the large surface of the front screens, which cannot withstand the pressure of material and rapidly tear apart. At St. Day United, screens finer than No. 36 are used, and the base of the coffer box lowered by one inch, that is, kept at 2″ - 2½″ below the screen opening.

At the time of my visit to Balleswidden, Capt. Tredinnick was performing parallel experiments with 'flashers' versus fine screens, and without being able to specify numbers, the advantage of screens had, for him, become incontestable.

Consumption v. production for stamps

In order to determine the cost of stamping, we have to look at some relative figures of consumption and production.

The amount of water used in stamping is generally reckoned to account for one-quarter to one-third of the total water used in dressing. The information I have been able to obtain is only approximate, and is not based on measurement.

Consumption of water

At Par Consols, each box of four stamps receives water via two ¾-inch holes, fed from a channel under a head pressure of 3 – 4 inches.

At Tincroft, there is only one 1¼-inch hole, and the head of water is 3 inches.

Here are some tentative figures that I have deduced from calculations based on various indications:

Floors	Water (gallons per head per minute)	Comments
Polgooth	1½	The differences between the numbers correspond, up to a point, with the relative weights of stamps (see table).
Par Consols	1¾ - 2	
Tincroft	2 - 2¼	

On average, for fine-grained ores, the water consumption per box of four heads will be 7 – 9 gallons per minute.

One can count up, for all steam stamps:

- Three drivers, only one being present at a time. Shifts are of twelve hours duration, as opposed to the normal eight hours for working miners. Each driver is paid £3. 10s. per month.

Personnel

- Three workmen – watching the stamps, replacing screens, and directing changes of flow to the strips. These are, on the whole, former miners, no longer fit for underground work. At Par Consols there are only two. Shifts are twelve hours long in every case, only one man being present at a time. The monthly pay is £2. 15s.

I will mention here, as a reminder, with regard to the general maintenance and repairs for the entire floor:

Position	Monthly pay
1 carpenter	£3. 15s.
1 boy assistant	£1
1 blacksmith	£3. 15s.

Coal

Coal comes from Wales, and, in general, is not top quality. Mr. Browne estimates that, depending on which coal is bought in Cornwall, the 'duty' or performance of an engine can vary from 8 – 10%.

The coal consumed at Par Consols, for boilers and calciners, has been analysed:

Volatile matter	16.6%	Calorific value - 92,
Cinders (burnt residue)	3%	agglomerated coke,
Fixed carbon	80.4%	lightly 'puffed up'
	100%	

It can be stated that, taken from ports such as Swansea, Cardiff and Newport, coal costs 7 shillings per ton. Shipping to Par is 5s. 6d., which, with the cost of unloading, brings the price up to 12 – 13 shillings. At Tincroft, situated some 12 miles from the port of Hayle, the cost is 13 – 14 shillings. Depending on the distance from the port of arrival to the mine, cartage can account for a further 2 – 3 shillings, or even as much as nearly 5 shillings per ton, so that, delivered on the mine, one ton of coal costs 12 – 16 shillings per ton (*effectively double the cost of the raw material*).

Large mines often import cargoes of 100 – 150 tons at a time.

I have already stated the coal consumption corresponding to a stamps engine duty of 45.5 Million. As a practical rule, I believe that it will be pretty close to the truth to take the coal necessary to lift a stamp of a given weight, per 24 hours, as 10 – 12% of its own weight, or, per month, 3 – 3.6 times its weight. Put another way, a 660 lbs. stamp will require 1 ton of coal per month.

Tallow grease and oil, etc.

The engine uses, for maintenance purposes, quantities of oil and hemp that are far from negligible, for example, oil, valued at 5d. per gallon, and hemp at 5d. per lb. The stamp battery uses tallow grease for the bearings and guides, at £3 - £3. 4s. per cwt. In many mines in the west of the county, this has been advantageously replaced by a sort of 'soft soap', of resin and soda, known as 'anti-friction grease', costing only 12s. per cwt., thus making a considerable saving.

Stamp heads

Stamp heads are 'white cast iron', which has to be both hard and tough, a good stamp head lasting five to six months. On average, after four months' usage, two-thirds of the head is worn away, and it has become too light in weight to be worth keeping. The foundry normally delivers heads with wrought iron tails either one or two feet long, when the lifters are soldered on the mine.

During the summer of 1857, foundry prices were as follows:

                Cast iron alone   8s. per cwt.
Heads with short wrought iron tails   9s. per cwt.
Heads with long wrought iron tails   10s. per cwt.

When an iron stamp is at the end of its useful life, the foundry can repair it for:

                Labour   2s. 6d.
      Additional cast iron   8s. per cwt.
Wrought iron (if necessary)   17s. per cwt.

Old, used materials can be re-sold to the foundry at:

      Cast iron alone   2s. 6d. per cwt.
Used heads with tails   3s. 3d. per cwt.
         Wrought iron   6s. 3d. per cwt.

An iron lifter can normally last through the life of three heads, i.e. about a year.

Norway pine, for wooden lifters, costs 11d. per cubic foot.

Foundry iron costs:

Accessory pieces

    Guides   13s. per cwt.
    Tappets   12s. per cwt.
    Cams
    Screen plates   } 11s. per cwt.
    Interior lining plates

Screens

The working life of sheet iron screen plates varies greatly with the acidity of the water. Under ordinary conditions, a screen lasts, on average, for 15 days. Screens of size 8″ by 9″ cost 6s. per dozen.

Production

It is accepted how much the quantity of material stamped in a given time by a single stamp, on various floors, must vary with the nature of the ore, that is, with the relative hardness of the gangue, the fineness of the tin (which demands a proportional number of screens), and also with the weight of the stamp under consideration.

Difficulty of general evaluation

In seeking to establish a relationship between the number of stamps in a battery and the annual production of the mine, to the causes in variation listed above have to be added those that depend on the greater or lesser activities underground and during dressing. These include:

Causes of variation

- Work slowed down by lack of water.
- The nature of the ore being mined and treated.
- The losses of tin according to the dressing methods and the effi-

ciency of their operation.

- The number of stamps taken into account. Into this come 'flashers', in variable numbers and proportion depending on the type of ore and the 'know-how' of the Captain-dresser.

Here are some examples:

Floor	Total heads	Tons stamped in 1857	
		Total	Per head
Carnbrea	96	20,000	208
Par Consols	68	17,000	265
Balleswidden	63	12,000	176
Tincroft	48	9,000	187
Levant (I)	64	8,000	125
Polberro (II)(1854)	72	30,200	420

(I) 'Flash' stamps.
(II) Very soft ore, coarse tin, screen stamps, 84 heads with 12 idle.

Over 48 hours, a single stamp considered in isolation passes less than 1 ton of material.

With an ore of average hardness, fine grain, and giving 2% (*recoverable*) black tin on (*vanning*) assay, the annual production could be:

With 64 heads of 660 lbs. each, 200 – 250 tons of black tin.

With 96 – 120 heads, a yield of, 350 – 500 tons of black tin.

Small stamps of 375 lbs. weight, in boxes of three heads, obviously do less work.

Thus, at Polgooth, there is one battery of 120 heads, and another of 60 heads (or 180 heads in total), and production has never been more than 40 tons per month.

At extreme limits I will cite, on the one hand, Providence Mines, near St. Ives, where the ore has yielded 15% in recent years, and which, with 30 heads of stamps, has been able to produce 20 – 25 tons per month (256 tons in 1856). On the other hand, we have the stockwork of Carclaze, where the ore yields 0.33%, only demands very coarse screens, and with 12 water wheels driving 36 heads, does not produce more than 2 tons of black tin per month (8 tons in 1856).

Here, as an example of well-conducted stamping, is a detailed breakdown of the costs, as far as I believe verifiable, at the floors of Par Consols for a period of one month:

From 10th March to 27th August 1857,

  7,799 tons were stamped, giving **147.122** tons of black tin
 So, for one month, **1,420.45** tons gave **26.749** tons of black tin

This represents a yield of 1.885%, whereas the vanning assay gave 1.827%.

The costs of one month's work are shown in Table 1, below, and in Table 2, the costs per ton of mineral stamped, and per ton of black tin ready for sale.

1. - Cost per month of stamping with 76 heads at Par Consols (I).

Labour	3 drivers @ £3. 10s	£10. 10s.	£16. 0. 0.
	2 'watchers' @ £2. 15s.	£5. 10s	
	1 carpenter (on call)	-	
	1 blacksmith (on call)	-	
Coal and various materials	Coal, 67 tons at 13s. per ton	£43. 11s.	£50. 14s. 6¾d.
	Grease, 159¾ lbs. at 6½d. per lb.	£4. 5s. 7¼d.	
	Oil, 8.16 gallons at 5s. 1½d. per gallon	£2. 2s.	
	Hemp, 40 lbs. at 4¾d. per lb.	15s. 11½d.	
Cast and wrought iron	Stamp heads, 1.363 tons	£15. 18s. 9½d.	£20. 14s. 9½d
	Small screens, 5 doz. at 6s. per doz.	£1. 10s.	
	Large screens, 3 doz. at 18s. per doz.	£2. 14s.	
	Grill plaques, 122 lbs. at 11s. per cwt.	12s.	
Sundry expenses	Wooden lifters, guides, tappets, cams, and iron frames for screens, plus labour for maintenance and repairs		£12. 0. 0.
	Total costs		£99. 9s. 4½d.
	Less deduction, 8 heads on copper ore		- £8. 0s. 7½d.
	Total, for 1 month, 68 heads on tin ore		£91. 8s. 9d.

(I) Besides the 68 heads working on tin ore, the battery has 8 heads for use on copper ore when necessary.

(II) Per year, 224 stamp heads are used, weighing:

   24.536 tons at 9s. per cwt. - £217. 5s. 9¾d.

Re-sale, 8.178 tons at 3s. 2¾d. per cwt. - £26. 0s. 1¼d.
           £191. 5s. 8½d.

II. – Specific costs of stamping at Par Consols.

Per 1 ton of ore		Per 1 ton of black tin produced	
Special labour, 2½ hours at £2. 15s. per month,	2¾d.	5½ days at £2. 15s. per month,	11s. 9¼d.
Coal, 101½ lbs. at 13s. per ton	7¼d.	2.469 tons at 13s. per ton,	£1. 12s. ¼d
Grease,	1¼d.		5s. 3d.
Cast iron and screens, (iron used 2 lbs.),	3½d.		15s. 3d
Sundry costs, minus deduction for 8 copper stamps,	¾d.		
	1s. 3½d.		£3. 7s. 3½d

At Carnbrea, with 84 heads, some 1,914 tons of ore and fine-grained quartzo-ferruginous gangue, showing a tin content of 1.886 (*recoverable*) on assay, are stamped per month on average, yielding 36 tons, 2 cwts. of black tin.

The total expenditure on stamping is:

    Per ton of ore   1s. 3½d.

  Per ton of black tin   £3. 6s.

It can be appreciated that with a fine-grained ore of average hardness and a tin content of about 2%, the cost of stamping will be variable on large floors:

    Per ton of ore   1s. 2½d. to 1s. 5¼d

  Per ton of black tin   £3. 4s. to £3. 12s.

By contrast, at Polberro, where the ore currently exploited comes mainly from material left behind in former workings and old halvans, the tin is in killas that has been rendered more or less soft by alteration, and a lot more ore is stamped. In 1854, 30,201 tons stamped yielded 234 tons, 14 cwts. of black tin, the yield being 0.78%. The total operating costs, including depreciation, were higher, then standing at £1,950.

    Stamping, per ton of ore   1s. 3½d.

    Per ton of black tin   £8. 5s. 7¼d.

The advantages stemming from the coarse grain of the tin and the relative softness of the gangue are here countered by impurities in the feed water. The extremely acid water rapidly corrodes the boilers, making for increased 'down time', and greatly adds to coal consumption.

Comparison with water stamps It is easy to estimate the saving that can be made by the use of water-powered stamps. Assuming that the ore in question is analogous to that at Par Consols:

A stamp battery of 16, 660-lb. heads would hardly need less than 25 h.p., or a quite considerable water head of at least 13 feet, delivering over 110 gallons per minute. The stamping capacity would be up to 350 tons per month, and the costs would work out at:

	Per month	Per ton of ore
Labour: 2 'watchers', with duties of operation	£6. 0s. 0d.	4d.
Cast and wrought iron: stamp heads, screens etc.	£5. 0s. 9½d.	3½d.
Sundries: maintenance, grease etc.	£2. 19s. 2½d.	2d.
Totals	£14. 0s. 0d.	9½d

Despite the saving on drivers etc., the labour cost is increased by about half because of the low production, and the overall saving is hardly one-third of that of steam stamps.

However, it would not be the same for very small floors, where, for example, a water wheel drives 3 or four heads only. In this instance, labour becomes almost negligible because the workman attends to the stamps while at the same time dealing with the products, and the consumption of cast iron and screens, and wear and tear, is reduced, such that the overall cost comes down to about 4¾d. per ton of ore handled.

It only remains to indicate the initial costs of purchase and 'setting up' of stamps.

At Pednandrea Mine, near Redruth, a very nice stamp battery of 48 heads and a 36-inch engine (which could ultimately drive 120 heads) cost £2,500 new, for the engine and stamps. At Par Consols (76 heads), the cost was £2,000.

Cost of engines and stamps

Public sales, by bids at auction, allow mines just starting up to equip themselves cheaply with secondhand materials.

At Carvath United, a battery of 24 lightweight heads, with wooden lifters, cost £200. I have been told of the sale of 16 heads for £90, whose purchase price new would be £180 - £200, this being the average cost of a good new set of 16 stamps.

The cost of 'setting up' varies very much with the nature and topography of the ground. As for the engine house, the normal cost is £100 – 120, though the price increases with distance from suitable sources of granite construction material.

§ II. Strips

The true treatment of tin ore only commences at the moment when the ore leaves the stamps as a sandy slurry and enters the strips. It is very important that this first stage is well laid out, where the work can be done very cheaply, and the cost is no more than that of recovering settled material.

We have seen that the idea is to retain the sands in descending order of richness, and let the fines pass on. Before describing the layouts adopted for strips, I will concentrate on the actual movement of fine, slimy sands, as most of the observations made in this respect will be equally applicable to square and round buddles etc.

Chances for carrying away and deposition of sands

Chief Engineer of Mines Mr. Gras, in his study of alpine torrents (I), has laid down the opportunities of being carried away of material capable of being moved. I will no more than summarize some of his conclusions by recalling the appropriate expressions that he has adopted to define the main phenomena:

1. The 'limiting velocity of entrainment' is that of a thin trickle of water just sufficiently large to move a given grain of material. Naturally, this varies with the shape of the grain as well as its size.

2. A flow of water is said to be 'saturated' with material when the smallest quantity (of extra material) added to that already carried along brings about deposition.

3. The total weight of material that can be carried along by a supposedly 'saturated' flow is a measure of its 'power of entrainment'. This power is proportional to the velocity, density and depth of the liquid. The bed of the flow staying constant, it varies with the volume, density and shape of the material, and increases or decreases according to those materials becoming more or less mobile.

Consequences:

- An already 'saturated' flow of water can wash away its bed. There is erosion, and the fine material mingles with that already carried along. If the velocity falls, those materials the most resistant to further movement are deposited.

- All the more reason, if the flow is not 'saturated', for there to be erosion but no corresponding deposition. The washing away begins with the finest and lightest material.

- If the 'power of entrainment' of a 'saturated' flow is reduced for any reason whatever, there will be deposition and a consequent increase in the bed height. Those materials more difficult to entrain will be deposited first (effectively, the velocity of flow decreases).

(I) '*Annales des mines*', 5th series, Vol XI, 1857.

The nature of stamped material

The slimes and sands discharged by the stamps are a mixture of very different materials. According to their densities we have:

Mineral	Density
Tin grains	6.96

Metallic	Mispickel	6.00 – 6.40
	Iron pyrites	4.85 – 5.05
	Copper pyrites	4.10 – 4.30
	Wolfram	7.15 – 7.55
Gangue	Quartz	2.65 – 2.80
	Chlorite	2.65 – 2.85
	Killas	2.50

Shape

As regards shape, examination by microscope shows that the grains of tin, copper pyrites and gangues are entirely similar to fragments of rock of the same species, as if broken by a hammer, that is, very irregular and very angular. Iron pyrites, on account of its easy cleavage, keeps its crystalline form down to extremely fine particle sizes (I).

Volume

The volume of the various grains is extremely variable. The largest grains come from the gangue, quartz and chlorite. The tin, already finely disseminated on its own account, has been broken most often between fragments of quartz, so that the average size of the tin grains is much smaller than those of the gangue minerals. Iron pyrites, less resistant and very friable, is normally finely pulverised.

(I) See 'examination of the sands at Par Consols'

Deposition in the strips

At the moment when the stamped materials arrive in the strips, with a great excess of water, their velocity is reduced by the very slight slope and wide profile of the strip. The current immediately becomes 'super-saturated', and remains so throughout its flow down the strip. Deposition of material takes place, starting with those particles least easily carried. Several factors prevent good classification, and materials of very different mobility are mixed together at any given point.

1. The 'muddy' state of the sands is one of the most significant, and its role is even more considerable in buddles and on frames etc. than in the strips. Grains of various sizes are all stuck together. The mode of pulverisation (*stamping*) tends to produce these small agglomerations, which are not broken up, either by passage through even a fine screen, or by running across the planks at the head of the strips. Formed by elements of various conditions, they have average properties as to mobility.

   This has the result, for example, in a large, dense grain, on settling, carrying with it accompanying fine particles. Small dense grains and larger, lighter ones are found together further on, co-deposited with their own, respective fines.

2. A second, and above all generally applicable, cause is the collision of particles during their movement. Grains of very different sizes travel together. The fine and light particles, which, if they were apart, would take up a velocity greater than the others, continually collide with large grains in front of them, pushing them further than they would travel without this extra propulsion. The particularly angular shape of the sands leads to the formation of a quantity of small hollows or cavities in the bed of solids, where fine grains lodge as they come into coincidental contact. This effect occurs especially at the moment when a large grain stops, and where the velocity of the fluid in the immediate vicinity is reduced for an instant.

Let us now consider various parts of the strip, head, middle and tail.

At the head, the flow has a particularly high solids content, and, therefore, there is rapid settlement, though somewhat poorly defined. The tin, essentially made up of quite fine grains, falls and settles. The various materials accompanying its settlement cannot be fixed, but there is a high proportion of fine gangue and also some very large grains, those of average size rolling on the surface.

At the middle, although the solids content is reduced, the settlement is still a little confused, but the 'erosion factor' is stronger in this section of the bed, and any fines that stop there are returned into suspension. The middle is, therefore, mainly made up of coarse sand and fine tin.

Towards the tail, the aim is to retain all the fine sand, and the stop battens are kept above the level of the deposit. There is still a considerable solids content, but the erosion is gradually cancelled out as the end of the strip is neared, leaving a higher and higher proportion of slimes retained there, together with coarse sand.

Beyond the strips the material drops into channels of sufficient slope that everything in the water is carried to the slime pits, where the slimes and fine sand are retained.

Layout of strips

The strips are made of planking, and normally, two strips are used for each box of four heads, with each alternately receiving the stamped sands from the box over a period of twelve hours. Here are exact dimensions and the slope of certain strips:

Floors	Length	Width	Depth	Slope	Obs
Par Consols	12 ft.	14 in.	12 in.	1:72	(I)
Gt. Whl. Vor (a)	13 ft.	18 in.	11½ in.	1:78	(II)
Gt. Whl. Vor (b)	26 ft.	-	-	1:78	(III)
Tincroft	30 ft.	15 in.	14 in.	1:48	(IV)

(I)   First strip for 'best work'……   6 strips, 12 heads

(II)	First strips...............	3 strips, 16 heads
(III)	Second strips...............	9 strips, 16 heads
(IV)	Sole strips for 'common work'	14 strips, 28 heads

The layout at Tincroft, also adopted at St Day United, is the simplest. Division of the strips into sections in a series of tiers has the advantage of interrupting the flow, and creating a genuinly enriched head at the start of each tier, to be added to the tail of that preceeding. At Balleswidden, there is a series of as many as three strips, each 12 feet long and 30 inches wide.

At Drakewalls, material from the rolls crushers is sent to 'strip-tyes', with several transverse 'ridges' or rises in the base. In front of each of these, an inclined board is placed crosswise, against which the flowing material strikes almost at right angles. The very rounded (*here particularly*) grains of tin, which have rolled down along the section, are stopped and precipitated at the foot of the board, and the resultant eddy currents carry away only the lighter material.

Proportion of waste

Following what has been said in connection with stamping, and the fact that each head passes about 1 ton of ore per 24 hours, a strip receives from 4 heads just over 6 lbs. per minute of material, along with 8 gallons of water. If the average, uncompressed bulk density of the sand in the strips is taken as 1.3 (dry state), then it can be seen that it arrives with 13 times its own weight, or 18 times its volume, of water.

(* *Here, it must be argued that the metric system of notation, i.e. 2.8 Kg. of solids and 36 litres of water, enables a simpler calculation of % solids content by weight, being 2.8 ÷ 38.8 x 100% = 7.22%*).

Character of good operations

The character of a well-functioning strip, as far as it can be readily identified, is the smoothness of the settled surface. The slightest 'channelling' (*by running water*) produces little gullies where the velocity of the water increases and carries further away some tin either already deposited or still moving. On both sides and in front of these gullies, the flow slows down and lighter material accumulates there. On the whole, no further classification is possible. If the water from the stamps is overdone, its 'power of entrainment' is increased, but in a properly operated strip, this does not occur.

If the strip is poorly set up and the deposit becomes 'channelled', it either has to be made wider, or, always easier, the slope must be decreased.

It may be noticed that the strips described above are quite narrow, and there are several reasons for this preference. It is desirable that each strip corresponds to one stamp coffer box, so that, if those particular stamps should be stopped, work in all the other strips can carry on as normal.

Now, the cubic volume of material to be handled being known, the strip is first made sufficiently long to achieve proper classification. Then, with the depth of the settled solids estimated at 1 foot, for easier recovery by shovelling out, the necessary width is easily calculated.

Further, the action of the vertical walls, even with a weak head of water, is by no means negligible. Their main effect is to guide the fluid flow and keep it following the longitudinal axis of the strip. With a very wide strip, any 'channelling' causes an immediate corresponding build-up of solids, the water easily starts to meander, and instead of working on the obstruction, adds to it. Eighteen inches appears to be a suitable width, there being no need to exceed twenty.

Method of dividing the deposit

Once the strip is full. The Captain, going on his knowledge of the ore being treated, or, if he judges it appropriate, according to an examination by vanning shovel, marks and indicates the chosen divisions to the workman, which he then takes into account for the removal of the settled solids (*as respective products*).

At Tincroft, for example, with an ore yielding 1½% (*black tin, by weight*), the following divisions are drawn in the strips mentioned in the above table:

	Length		
Divisions	**Absolute**	**Relative**	**Nature of the sands**
Head	2' 6"	$1/12$	Sand for the square buddle.
Middle	7' 6"	$3/12$	Sand for the round buddle.
Tail	20'	$8/12$	Sand for the round buddle, except a small part, of fine slimes, sent to the slime pits.
Strip A	30'	$12/12$	

Personnek

The personnel at this stage varies greatly according to the layout and arrangement of the floors, and depends on whether round buddles are used or not. At Tincroft:

> For the 8 strips on 'best work'   1 boy
> For the 16 strips on 'common work'   3 boys

The heads alone are carried by wheelbarrow to the appropriate square buddle.

The middles and tails are thrown straight away into the wooden channels that take them to the round buddles, and which extend above the strips, these latter being, at Tincroft, far enough below the channels for the 'common work' middles and tails that there needs to be an extra boy there to throw these sands up on to a sort of intermediate platform, from where they are lifted and transferred to the channel.

With favourably sloping ground on the dressing floor, and a good arrangement of round buddles, a single boy will be able to look after 8 strips (or a 'set' of 16 stamps), and will shift 10 – 12 tons per day of damp sand. A stamps boy is paid £1 per month, which works out at 8d. per day.

As an example of the classification effect of strips, tabulated below are the results given on analysis by wet method for the sands at Par Consols:

A. First small strips of 'best work', receiving sands at 19% black tin

Head	24% black tin	Sand to square buddle, **B**.
Middle	8% black tin	Sand to round buddle, **R**.
Tail	2% black tin	To 'shacking', the sands go to round buddle **R'**.

A'. Large strips for 'common work', receiving sands at 4.35% black tin

Head	18% black tin	Sand to round buddle, **R**.
Middle	0.8% black tin	Sand to round buddle, **R'**.
Tail	0.85% black tin	To long strip **E**.

These figures have no absolute value in any other context. In order to carry out assays on samples to obtain results good enough to be able to calculate them, such care is needed as would be impossible for me to have. Nevertheless, they are sufficient to show that there is much to be gained from well-constructed strips. Strips A perform perfectly.

§ III. Square buddles, tin cases.

On those dressing floors where round buddles have not yet been introduced, large square buddles are used to treat all the sands from the strips. Those at Great Wheal Vor are of recent construction, and well set up.

The buddle is constructed of 1¼″ thick planking, 11′ long from head to tail, and 10′ 3″ along the base. Its width is 5′ 6″, and the height of the vertical side walls is 2′ at the head and 2′ 6″ at the tail.

The tapering hopper that first receives the feed material is 16″ by 3″ at the top, and 4″ below there is a metal screen (*to break up lumps and even out the feed*) through which the sands have to pass. At the bottom, below this, they run through an opening 3½″ wide and 4″ high, set in the lower wall of the hopper. A widening inclined plane with raised

Large square buddles at Wheal Vor

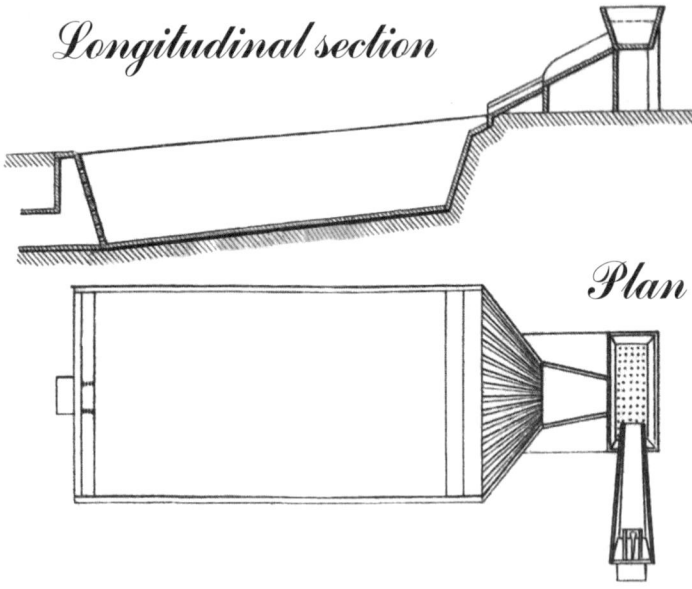

Longitudinal section

Plan

edges takes them on to the feed distribution board, where they arrive as a flow 14″ in width. This inclined board is 18″ in length and is fitted with 14 battens spread out in a fan-shaped arrangement. These battens are 1¼″ high and 7/16″ wide at the head, thickening to 1″ at the point of discharge. Each distribution channel itself widens as it descends, to 3½″ at the lower end.

The separate feed streams then fall 3¼″ lower on to a small, 5″ board, where they recombine to form a single flow that runs into the full width of the buddle. The Figs. above and below show the general scheme of construction and water and feed arrangement.

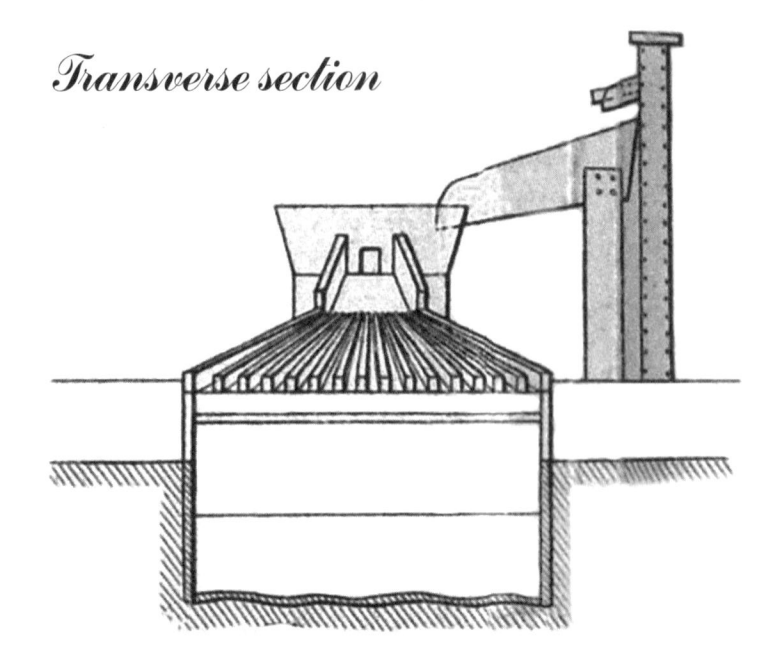

Transverse section

In order for the surplus water to run away from the tail of the buddle, the end board that forms its very foot is pierced with two vertical rows of six holes each, set out so that the difference in height between each is 2″. As deposition of solids proceeds and the bed height rises, these holes are successively blocked off with pegs.

The slope of the buddle floor is 16″ over its entire length, 1⅝″ per foot length, or about 7°. The fan-shaped distributor, and the inclined plane that precedes it, both have a slope of 1 : 2 (or 45°). The 5″ 'splash' board has the same inclination as the base of the buddle, whose head and tail end walls slope outwards at 4 : 1 or 75°.

Sometimes, these large square buddles are made 14 or 15 feet long and 6 feet wide. Except when there are always fairly large batches of sands to fill the apparatus, the deposition of the materials will not exceed similar dimensions to these.

Depending on the nature of the sands, when the operator judges it right to shorten the deposit in the buddle, he keeps closing the end holes right up to the top level, so as to always have a small 'pool' at the tail, where the sands form a sort of slope without reaching the tailboard itself.

Most often, the construction of square buddles is simplified by having a hopper with no grille and a wide mouth leading directly to the battened feed board, i.e. of opposite profile to that described above, when the ore is simply shovelled in.

With various buddles arranged in parallel in the same shed, the water for each comes from the same launder. This is the arrangement adopted for the square buddles at Tincroft, treating the sands both from the heads of the strips and the round buddles. They are 10′ long, 5′ wide, and with a depth, at head and tail, of 20″ and 24″, respectively. Their slope is 1″ per foot, which is enough, considering the fineness of the already rich sands being treated.

At Wheal Vor, 'tin cases' (*or smaller square buddles*) are used to retreat the enriched sands from the larger types, and also the roasted concentrates. They represent the improved version of buddles formerly in use and described by Henwood. In this regard, I thought it interesting enough to provide a drawing (see below).

    Length at the base 8′ 5″
    Width 3′ 6″
    Depth at the head 20″
    Depth at the tail 24″
    Slope 1½″ per foot, 1: 8, 12.5%, about 7½°.

The 'jagging board', on to which the sands are shovelled and divided by little channels, is 15″ wide, with an overall slope of 4½″, nearly 1 : 4. The feed water spreads into a flow above a vertical board and falls from a height of 6″ on to the jagging board. The wooden tailboard, at the foot

Longitudinal section

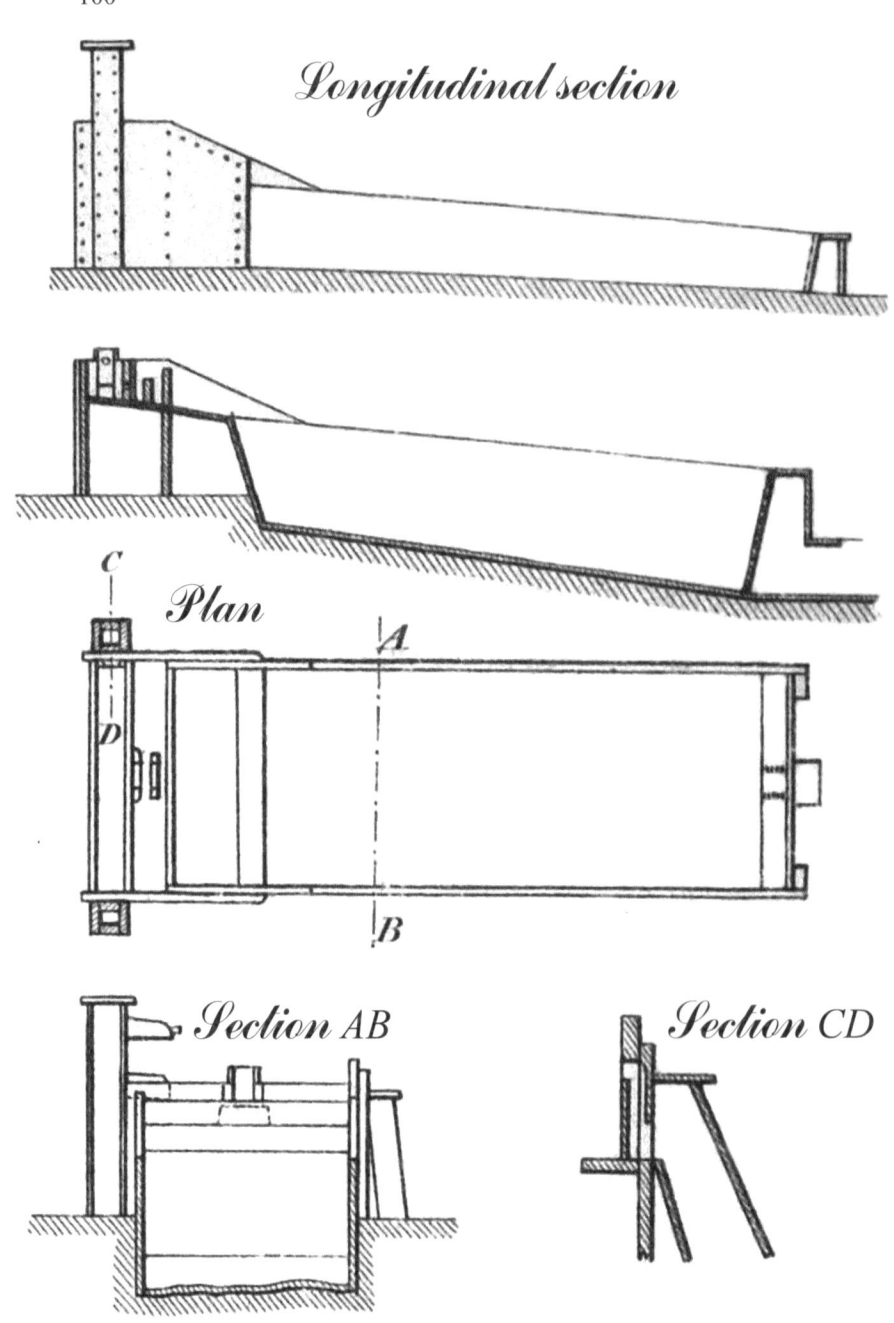

Plan

Section AB   *Section CD*

of the tin case, is pierced with 16 holes in two vertical rows of 8, with a height difference of 1½" between each of these.

Behaviour of material in various apparatus

At the moment when feed material falls into the buddle, as far as possible it has to form a homogeneous fluid slurry, that is to say, it must not contain any large lumps or agglomerates, and there must be no separate rivulets of clean water with no sands content.

Drawbacks of tin cases

The Wheal Vor buddles (*described above*) best fulfil these conditions, the ordinary buddles at Tincroft almost satisfy them, but this is not so with the smaller tin case under consideration here.

Effectively, feed material is only carried from the jagging board into the buddle proper by the eroding action of water in the channels made in the sand, and there is no guarantee that this takes place with any degree of regularity. Also, treatment in this smaller type of buddle is reserved only for rich sands, i.e. those sands made up of material already well classified in terms of size.

The work of the two operators is most meticulous, to avoid any compromising of the results. This will be more easily understood by way of the following explanation.

Depending on the nature of the sands being treated in the buddle, the water flows are as follows:

Proportion of solid to water

Water supplied per minute

	Hole diameter	Volume in gallons	Type of sands treated
No. 1	1½"	7 - 8	Very coarse sands, therefore generally poor.
No. 2	½"	2 2¼	Fine sands, rich or poor.
No. 3	½"	0.89 – 1.1	Very fine sands, rich or poor.

In the case of sands No. 2 (e.g. the large buddles at Tincroft), the quantity of sands fed at the same time is 53 – 56 lbs. In taking a value of 1.5 for the average bulk density of the buddle sand, dry and not compacted, it can be seen that it enters the buddle with only about half its volume, or one-third of its weight of water (*once more, the metric system makes this calculation a lot easier*), or, again, with some 39 times less water than in the strips – in modern parlance, 65 – 70% solids content, (*some 2½ times the value employed for feed to a modern shaking table*).

On the other hand, the relative slopes employed are:

Base slope

For buddles	1 : 7.7	1 : 8	1 : 12	Varying with the
For strips	1 : 48	1 : 71	1 : 78	size of the sands

In other words, some 6 – 9 times steeper in buddles than in strips.

These comparisons indicate the considerable difference between the modes of deposition in these two types of apparatus. Whereas the strip carries a dilute suspension, the buddle is fed with a thick, sandy mixture made to *roll* down an inclined plane. One has thus to take into account the shape and volume as well as the density of the grains, and an examination of the sands deposited at various distances down the buddle confirms this.

Deposition of sands in the buddle

At the head of the buddle is tin of mostly fine size, fine gangue (retained adhering to the tin or otherwise), barely a few grains of average size and *no* very large grains such as are found at the heads of strips.

As middlings, equal proportions of grains of chlorite and quartz (I), both of average size, and a small quantity of entrained tin, not appreciably finer than that in the head.

In the tailings are virtually all the large grains of gangue, that have rolled there most easily, and a high proportion of fines, which are there either by virtue of their adhering to larger particles, or especially as a result of being carried in suspension in the water. Any tin in the gangue is essentially present either as crazes, 'locked' with gangue (*and needing to be re-stamped*), or as extremely fine 'slimes'.

From the preceding observations it may be concluded, firstly:
- That the buddle is nothing more than an apparatus for cleaning.
- That its main aim is enrichment, which will only be as good as any previous size classification of the sands to be treated.
- That it is, therefore, most useful to perform a preliminary 'shacking' of various tailings, judged to be 'slimy', that are required to be treated.
- That the buddle must only be expected to produce, as quickly as possible, the greatest quantity of rich sand for passing on to kieves, and that the kieve will have the job of carrying out the final cleaning.

Secondly:
- That extremely fine material is not suitable for treatment by buddle.
- That proportionally great attention has to be paid to the water and the slope, both elements of 'power of entrainment', in respect of the relative mobility of the particles in the material introduced.

(I) The buddle samples examined for comment are from the dressing floors at Par Consols.

Operators and their jobs

The operators are either two boys or two girls, respectively, a 'feeder' and a 'broomer', the latter taking his or her place on a plank across the buddle, about three feet from the head. He (*or she*) lightly manipulates the material, and by a crosswise movement, gently levels the material deposited at the head, so as to render the surface as smooth as possible. He prevents the formation of 'channelling', at the sides of small deposited lumps or masses of material, and disaggregates these, setting in motion again those sands that tend to come to a stop about the middle of the buddle.

The 'Captain' marks out the respective divisions of the product, and the boys (*or girls*) empty out the buddle accordingly. They pile up to one side those portions to be re-passed, and carry away the rest to appropriate points for further treatment.

It has already been noted that the number of product divisions can vary from two to five, their relative length also depending on the nature of the ore. Experience, aided if necessary by vanning, is here the sole guide.

At Tincroft, a large square buddle works on the heads of both strips and a round buddle, carrying 15 – 18% tin, with a lot of mispickel. There, the following are found

Divisions	Length Absolute	Relative
Head	2' 0"	1/5
1st middle	1' 8"	1/6
2nd middle	1' 8"	1/6
Tail	4' 8"	7/15
	10' 0"	15/15

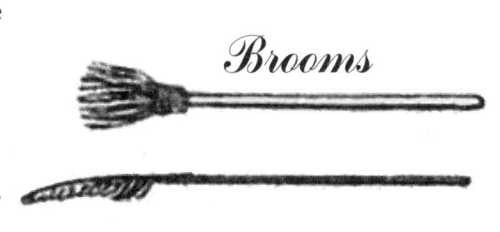

Brooms

It can be observed that the surface of the final deposit in the buddle is not always parallel to the base. In the case of the Tincroft buddle above, the depth of the sands is 20" at the head, and only 15" at the tail, from which it can be concluded that the slope of the buddle is a little too slight, having regard to the richness (low mobility) of the sands treated.

In contrast, when the 3rd division above (the 2nd Middle, finer and less rich than the original material), is re-passed to the same buddle, the depth of bed of the tail is nearly equal to that of the head.

Under these conditions, the Tincroft buddles can handle 400 – 445 gallons (1.9 – 2.0 cubic metres) of feed, and those at Wheal Vor 510 – 556 gallons (2.3 – 2.5 cubic metres). The time taken to fill the buddle varies inversely with the particle size of the sands. At Tincroft it was two hours, so that, during a 9-hour effective working day, two complete buddle operations (*filling and emptying*) could be performed, in other words, some 6 – 7 (dry) tons of material could be treated.

Buddle costs per ton of sand

The two buddle boys, or girls, are each paid 15 shillings per month, or 6d. per day, and the minimum cost of the buddle treatment of 1 ton of material works out at 1¾d. to 2d.

Effectiveness of treatment

As an example of the effectiveness of separation by buddle, below are the results for sands at Par Consols:

Buddle **B** treatment of heads of strips **A**, at 20 – 24% tin

1. **Head** — 42% tin — Sands to kieves
2. **Middle** — Average sample — 10% tin — Sands to be re-passed
3. **Middle**
4. **Tail** — 3% tin — Sands to special 'shacking'

Use of buddles as tyes

We have seen that, at a certain point in the preparation of material after roasting, the square buddle can be used as a tye. A strong flow of clean water is fed directly into the buddle, and the sand is then gradually poured by shovel into the water flow itself. It is only under these exceptional conditions that the buddle is used like the so-called 'German buddle', with which it has often been mistakenly confused. In fact, the tye is, in England, the true equivalent of the German buddle.

§ IV. The round buddle.

The round buddle, invented about fifteen years ago, has brought about a great change for the better in the treatment, not only of tin, but also of the fine sands of lead and copper ores. It is tending to come into general use, and it has been introduced in France, notably at the Pontgibaud lead mines. Nevertheless, in order to be able to count on good performance from this apparatus, it is necessary to impose certain conditions, which I will emphasise later.

Description of the Tincroft round buddle

The Figs. below show one of the three round buddles at Tincroft. It is 18 feet in diameter, the depth of the masonry pit being 2′ 5″ at the periphery. The floor has a slope of 1″ per foot, 1 : 12, 8.33%, or about 4¾°.

Material is fed to the centre head of the buddle by way of a V-shaped wooden launder made from planks nailed at a right angle, receiving a flow of water carrying it into a conical, sheet metal feed box. The slope of the launder is 1¼″ per foot, which can be raised to 1½″. The feed box itself is 18″ in diameter at the top and 20″ high. About 4″ below the top of the cone is a plate pierced with four holes by which it is connected to the rotating drive shaft. The base of the cone extends 3″ below the top of the centre head, leaving between the two an annular opening of about 1½″. The centre head is of wood, covered with a tight-fitting cast iron sheath. Its overall height is 4′, of which 19″ rises from the floor of the buddle. This cast iron sheath is 8″ in diameter at the top and 20″ at the base, with the cone angle being 75°. From each of two arms is suspended a 5-ft. long flap. The diagram shows a self-acting, counter-

Round buddle - elevation

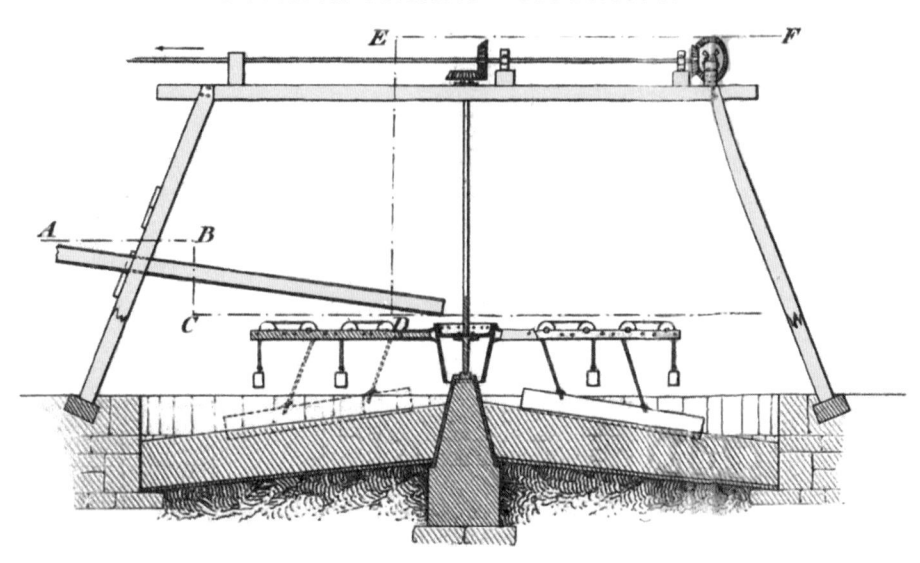

weighted suspension arrangement, though at Tincroft, each arm bears a small crank controlling the cords at the end of the arm, which the 'watcher' has to turn from time to time.

The fluid sands entering the feed box pass through the false base, hit the walls and are directed on to the centre head to run down into the buddle. Surplus water escapes by an underground channel closed off by small battens. As with strips, this can be replaced by a board with holes and plugs, as in square buddles.

Rotation of the arms and feed box is taken from the stamps engine and transmitted to the buddles by line shafting and bevelled pinions, the vertical drive shaft making 5 r.p.m.

Sometimes, both the walls and floor of the buddle are of masonry construction, the diameter varying between 15′ and 20′. Often though, it is

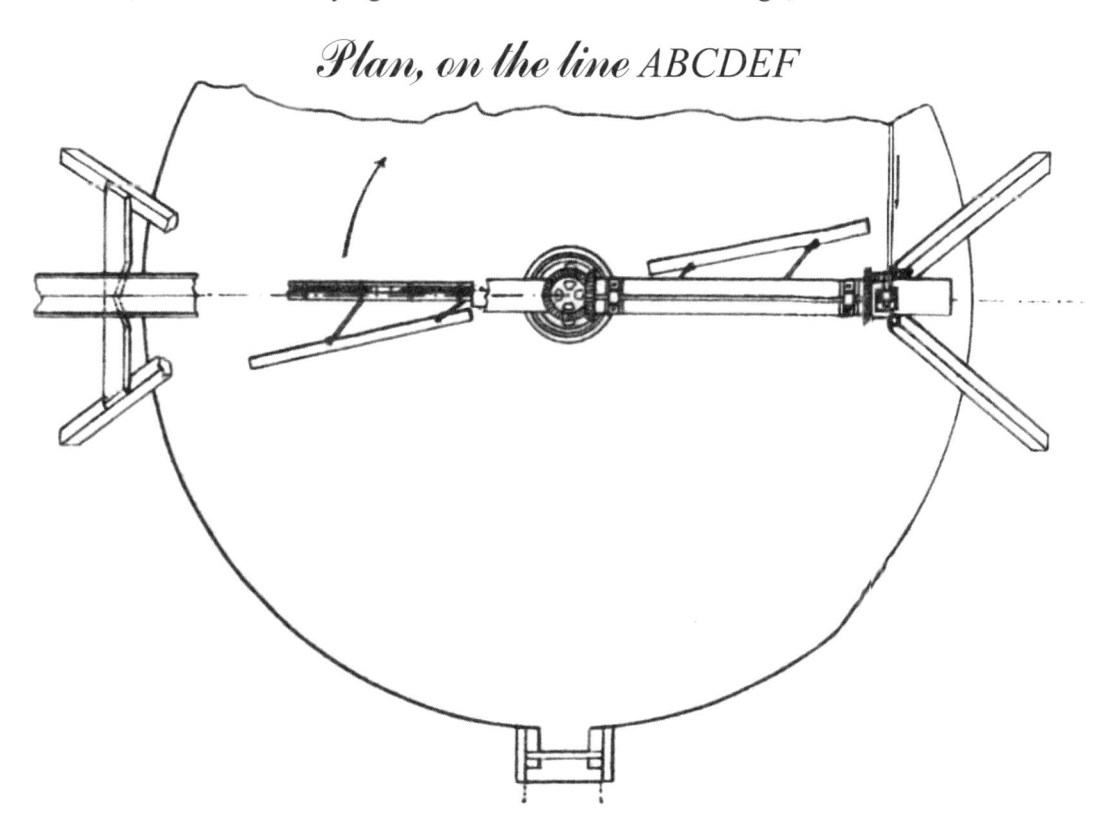

Plan, on the line ABCDEF

enough to fit the floor with planking, only to the centre, with a 5′ radius.

The centre head can be all wood or all cast iron. In the latter case, its base is widened so as to provide a solid 6″ wide border.

Various layout arrangements

As rotating flaps, small wisps of broom are generally used, held between two small planks and clamped by four bolts.

The exit of the surplus water from the tail can be made more regular by having three battened openings, spaced at 120° around the periphery of the pit. At Par Consols, these three openings discharge into a circular channel running right around the pit at 18″ distance from it. When the buddle comes to be emptied, the tailings are discarded directly into this channel, whose slope is sufficient for the water flow to carry them away to the long strip **E** (see diagram of the dressing floors).

Slope of the buddle floor

Depending on the relative fineness of the sands feed, the slope of the round buddle floor is set at:

Floors	Slope	Sands treated
Great Wheal Vor	1¼″ per ft. (10.4%)	Coarse, as previously
Tincroft	1″ per ft. (8.33%)	Fine
Carvath United	½″ per ft. (4.17%)	Very fine

The slope set is much the same as that of square buddles that would be used to treat the same material, save being slightly less for the round buddles.

I have not been able to obtain any specific information on the quantity of water used, but it would not be far out to regard it as being proportionally equal to that used in square buddles, that is, per minute to treat:

Tincroft, fine sand   Dry weight 54 lbs.   44 lbs. water (55% solids by wt.)
Wheal Vor, coarse sand   Dry weight 75 lbs.   57 – 66 lbs. water (53 – 57% solids)

Characteristics of good performance

A simple glance is enough to judge if the quantity of water being used is suitable, as the surface of the deposit being laid down is perfectly conical and smooth. With too little water (*too thick a feed*), there is a build-up of material at the head, ending towards the middle of the pit in muddy streaks. With too much water (*too dilute a feed*), material is carried too rapidly to the periphery.

As with all totally mechanised apparatus, the same rules apply to the round buddle. There, there is no careful eye of the 'watcher' to be counted on to put right any irregularities, so, great care should be taken to steer clear of them in the first place. That is to say, the necessary conditions for good operation should be known, recognised, and strictly adhered to.

After having carefully regulated the water flow, even more so here than with the square buddle, care must be taken to see that the box always receives a well-homogenised fluid feed. This can be simply and more or less efficiently done by feeding the launder from a wooden hopper, where the sands from the strips are always thrown in to excess, in relation to the water that they receive.

If, for want of this precaution, the launder is such that it cannot hold more than a few shovelfuls of sand, it will be enough for the strips 'boy' to interrupt the flow for a moment, so that an influx of clean water does not 'channel' all the tin deposited in the centre of the buddle.

Even perfectly run, the round buddle is not known to be usefully used for already rich sands, at least, not those that are not already very well classified in terms of size. This is a consequence of its form and operation. In effect, the deposited sands diverge from the centre, such that any given small area, for example, the surface of a zone in the middle of the deposit, continually receives a greater quantity of sand and water per minute than an equal area further down, towards the walls of the pit. Because of this, there is a great inequality in the degree of 'packing' of the material, the head being relatively 'hard' and compacted. This can be likened to the compacted section of a tarmaced road, whereas the periphery of the buddle pit represents the newly tarmaced edges.

The head of a square buddle, supposedly treating the same sands, will be softer, because down its whole length it offers the same cross-sectional surface area to the flow of material. Now, the sands of a square buddle, or a round buddle, are always imperfectly de-slimed, and the grains of tin, almost all quite fine, are surrounded by a veritable silt of slimes. So, these small masses of tin and slime will be able to roll *on* the head of a round buddle, whereas they will stop *in* the softer head of a square buddle (I).

The round buddles can only act as a 'roughing' apparatus

Another almost obvious consequence of the mode of feeding to the centre head is that those sands that, despite their fineness can still be treated in a square buddle, can not be treated successfully in a round buddle.

(I) In supposing that a round buddle receives, in a given time, twice the amount of material fed to a square buddle, a calculation indicates about 2′ for the radius of a circle, having the same centre as the round buddle, that can be regarded as the point on the round buddle that handles the same feed rate as that fed to a square buddle.

During the filling of the round buddle, one can only exercise simple observation over the arrival and exit of the water, and there is no specialised manpower available, since it is the job of the 'strips boys' to charge the hopper with sands.

As usual, the 'Captain' marks out the deposit in two or three sections. At Tincroft, for example, the round buddles treat the middles from the strips, and three divisions are made:

	Length, on a radius	**Approximate bed volume**	**Destination**
Centre head	0′ 6″	-	-
1. Head	3′ 6″	$7/24$	To the square buddle
2. Middle	1′ 6″	$3/24$	Re-passed to the round buddle
3. Tail	3′ 6″	$14/24$	Roughs, discarded at this point
	9′ 0″	$24/24$	

The depth of the deposit, as in the square buddle, was 20″ at the head, and 15″ at the tail. The time taken to fill the buddle was:

Tincroft 6 hours to fill with 12 cubic metres, quite fine sands
Great Wheal Vor 4 hours to fill with 14 cubic metres, coarse sands

Only one complete operation (*filling and emptying*) is possible per day.

The size of the workforce needed depends entirely on the layout of the floors, and the distances over which the various products have to be transported. For the rich head of the square buddle, this is never too far and does not involve a lot of material. As for the middle of the adjacent round buddle, performing enrichment, this is most economically carried out by means of wooden launders, across the space between the two pieces of apparatus. Sands are loaded in at the rate at which the round buddle is emptied, a supply of clean water passing above the whole system and providing water for the transfer launder. This is how, at Tincroft, the three round buddles are interconnected (see the diagram of the dressing floors).

In general, the tails make up each time more than half of the total deposit. At Par Consols and at St. Day United, they can be thrown directly into the strip that handles them. At Tincroft, where the lack of slope of the ground does not allow them to be treated, there is no alternative but to use wheelbarrows, taking them by an inclined way as far as the tailings burrow, where wagons come to take them off the floors.

In spite of the considerable extra work, the three round buddles there, handling together about 30 cubic metres, or 38 tons, of material (the dry, uncompacted bulk density being 1.28) need only 5 boys, 2 'shovellers' and 3 'wheelbarrowers', paid £1 per month each.

Cost of round buddle per ton of sand The minimum cost for treating 1 ton of sand by round buddle works out at marginally over 1d. In more topographically favourable conditions, this cost can be reduced to between 0.67d. and 0.86d. per ton. Therefore, we can see that the cost of manual work for the treatment of 1 ton of sands by round buddle is less than half what it is for a large square buddle. Of course, for the round buddle there is always the cost of motive power to add on.

At Wheal Vor, set apart at one side of the floors, a small 6′ x 12″ water wheel, with 30, 6″-deep compartments, and making 20 r.p.m., provides 6 r.p.m. to the round buddle.

Motive power Most often, power is taken from the stamps engine, though it then becomes very difficult to estimate any extra coal consumption resulting from this additional work.

Useful performance Analyses of sands samples at Par Consols have provided the following figures relating to the classifying effect of round buddles:

A. Sands of the same size as fed to large square buddles.

Round buddle **R**, treating | The heads of 'common work' strips **A₁**'
 The seconds from 'common work' strips **A₂** | Sands of 8 – 10% tin

1. Head, 18.5% tin, sands to large square buddle.
2. Middle, 2% tin, sands to round buddle **R"**.
3. Tail, 0.68% tin, roughs.

B. Coarser sands, but very poorly classified as to size.

Round buddle **R'**, treating | Seconds from 'common work' strips **A₂**'
 Cleaned thirds from 'common work' strips **A₃**' | Sands of 0.8 – 2% tin

1. Head, No separate head made, as the ore treated is very poor.
2. Middle, 2.8% tin, sands to round buddle **R"**.
3. Tail, 0.3% tin, roughs.

C. Fine sands, a little like those of 'top skimmings' from kieve C₁, but less well classified.

Round buddle **R"**, treating | Treating *separately* the middles **R₂**
 and **R₂'** (Tables A and B above) | Sands of 2 – 3% tin

1. Head, 11.5% tin, sands to large square buddle.
2. Tail, 1.7% tin, roughs.

Examination of samples of these products leads to the following conclusions:

1. That with sands of quite regular grains, a rich head can be made.
2. For given sands of equal tin content, coarser sands are more easily enriched than finer sands.
3. That a poorly classified sand containing coarse grains will only ever give a poor head product, because fine gangue is also retained.

§ V. Kieves.

The kieve is a piece of apparatus for cleaning already enriched material (*i.e. tin concentrates*) and it is used both for sands from the heads of square buddles and fines from frames. It remains for me only to describe the various possible operating variations, and the beneficial effect.

First of all, the quantity of clean water introduced is one-third to one-half of the kieve volume. Two operators, either young boys or older girls, work together. One of them shovels material into the kieve, while the other maintains a vigorous rotational stirring, this stage being known as 'tossing'. Filling the kieve takes only four or five minutes, though during this time the second operator has to work very hard.

Settling and deposition of material takes place during the second stage, known as 'packing'. A boy repeatedly strikes the side of the kieve with a largish hammer, or often with an upright rod, whose lower end is located in a plank with a hole in it, kept under his feet. When there are several adjacent kieves, and a source of motive power at no great distance, then mechanised means of packing can be set up and arranged, as in the 'burning house' at Great Wheal Vor.

The finer the material being treated, the longer is the settling time, this being 15 – 20 minutes for square buddle sands, but longer than 30 minutes for slimes concentrate from frames.

The clear 'top water' is ladled out by hand with a small pail, and the settled solids are removed by shovel, layer by layer, exercising great care. The operators then carry the various products from the kieves to wherever they need to go for any further treatment. In general, three product divisions are made, though there can be either two or four, their relative importance depending entirely on the nature of the material being treated.

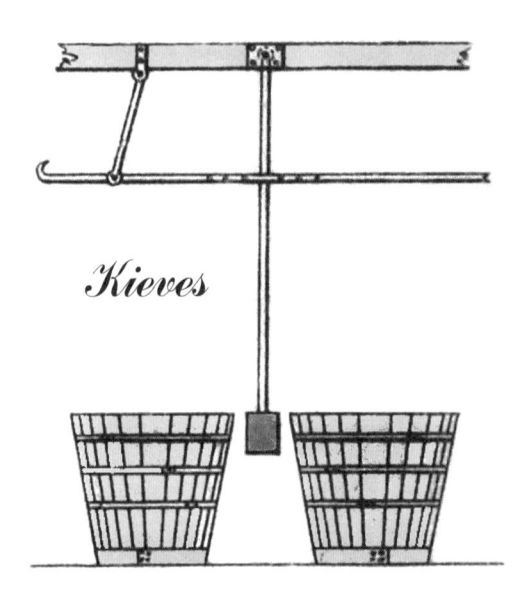

Kieves

At Tincroft, for example, a kieve handling the heads from the square buddles has the following dimensions – upper diameter 40", height 24", height of initial water 14" (or half full).

The overall kieve capacity is 400 litres (90 gallons), handling about 200 litres (650 to 700 lbs.) of sand per operation, giving:

	Layer		
Divisions	Thickness	Volume	Destination
1. Top skimmings	Barely 2"	28 litres (14%)	Goes to frames
2. Bottom skimmings	6"	86 litres (43%)	Goes to square buddle
3. Bottom	6"	86 litres (43%)	'Fit for burning', goes to roasting
Kieve **D**	14"	200 litres	

In 3 of these kieves, and 8 operations overall, about 1,500 litres of sands, produced by the three square buddles on 'common work', can be treated per day.

Treatment cost per ton by kieve

By taking 1.63 as the average dry, uncompacted bulk density of the sand, this is equivalent to 2 - 2½ tons of sands treated per day. The labour needed is:

3 girls, each paid £1 per month, and 1 boy (for 'packing') paid 10s. per month, giving a daily treatment cost of 2s. 4d.

Treatment by kieve of 1 ton of sand therefore works out to be 11¼d. to 1s. 2d., averaging out at 1s. 0½d per ton.

The sands at Par Consols gave the following analyses:

Kieve **C**, treating the heads of square buddles on 'best work', at 40 – 45% tin (I)

Useful effect

1. 'Top skimmings'   11% tin
2. 'Bottom skimmings'   20% tin   (see pages 165 and 166)
3. 'Bottom'   70% tin.

Kieve **C'**, treating the heads of square buddles on 'common work'

1. 'Top skimmings'   7% tin
2. 'Bottom skimmings'   18% tin
3. 'Bottom'   59% tin.

(I) See a previous table for the relative sizes of grains of these 3 divisions – C_1, C_2 and C_3

---

§ VI. Tyes and 'valves'.

The ordinary tye is a long wooden channel, 2 - 2½ ft. wide. According to:

Tyes

- The method of admitting the clean water.
- The quantity, usually three or four times more than in the square buddle, and,
- The way in which the sands are introduced.

The resultant effect is completely different from that particular apparatus. The tye is, at one and the same time, classifier and cleaner.

The least mobile material stays, alone, at the head of the settled solids, while coarse, barren sands and *all* the fines are carried further on. Suffice to say, it is only suitably used for poor material, before or after roasting, and when successive upgrading by square buddle and kieve are judged to be too expensive.

The 'shacking tyes' need no particular explanation here, and I believed that no useful purpose would be served by representing them as diagrams.

'Valves' At Polgooth, in 1855, I saw, following the main tyes, small 3" diameter valves on the boxes, given an alternating up and down movement via the stamps engine. They do not appear to have given very good results (I).

At Balleswidden, much was made of a valve worked in the same way, but of bigger diameter, and sufficient to clean all the 'true' roughs. The monthly expense, which was at first £7. 10s. on this part of the floors, was subsequently reduced to £1. 10s.

(I) However, in 1858, the floors at Levant had several analogous valves, working well. The pyramidal box was 3' deep, with a cross-section 3' square at the top and 8" square at the bottom. In a 3" opening was a 6" cylinder of 2½" diameter, with a raised, profiled head, receiving a 1½" lift, 10 times per minute. The discharge space thus made available each time was, thus, a ½" wide annulus.

The box valve at St. Day United is constructed on better principles. The discharge at the bottom of the box is alternately opened and closed by a ring-shaped disc, rotating horizontally, with a 120° cut-out sector. A vertical drive shaft, geared and connected to the stamps, gives it a rapid rotation, any deposit of 'roughs' passing out with each turn of the opening. There is neither disturbance of the mass of liquid slimes, nor inclusion of slimes with the sands, as there would be in the case of a vertically-operating valve.

At Polberro, there is a different arrangement, where a 4' diameter dipper wheel draws the roughs from the bottom of the box. The buckets are pierced on each side near the base by two holes, to allow muddy water to run back out into the box, while the roughs are discharged outside. Most of the slimes discharge themselves via a small overflow arrangement on the side of the box. The dipper wheel is driven by a small water wheel, mounted on the same shaft. The system treats marginally less than 70 tons per day.

§ VII. Paddle Trunks.

The main slimes pass to boxes and trunks in order to have any agglomerates broken up and for the slimes to be classified, while sands of a certain size are retained in the box, and the only material passing on to the trunks is a mixture of very dilute slimes and a small amount of very fine sands.

The trunks are each 12' long, 2' wide and 1' deep. The slope of the base is 1 : 48 (2.1%), and the necessary water is ⅔ - ⅝ of a gallon (3 – 4 litres) per minute.

The generation of material by successive washing is the only way of avoiding some sort of big problem, which will not fail to occur, to a greater or lesser depth, on the surface of the deposit if insufficient time is allowed for it to consolidate, and to lose in proportion some of the water that it holds to begin with.

The following results of analyses show how much this preparation of the slimes, necessary in order to create a suitable feed for the frames, leaves a lot to be desired as far as the relative tin distribution:

		Tin content	Comments
	Slime pit **K**	2.0%	Equal to the overall average
Box ***a***, roughs from the slimes		0.85%	Go to 'shacking'
Paddle trunks **L**	1.	1.73%	Go to frames **M**
	2.	1.30%	Go to paddle trunks **N**
Paddle trunks **N**	1.	0.90%	Go to frames **O**
	2.	-	Not taken, doubtless less than 0.7%, discarded to waste

These numbers show the relative values of samples taken for assay, yet they prove that the majority of the tin in the slimes is extremely fine, in the form of 'impalpable powder', and that a fraction of this tin 'floats away' and is not retained in the tail of the trunks. It is with good reason that Henwood (op. cit.) regards the operation of trunking as one of the main sources of tin losses.

One cannot pretend to minimise this loss. However much one would wish to treat this material as a thick slime, it would certainly be diluted and lost in the successive settlings in any suitably laid out pits.

§ VIII. Frames or 'racks'.

The work performed by frames, and their general layout, has been described above (page 37 ff.). It remains for me to give some details of the construction and operation of some of the various types of frames currently in use.

The Figs. below show a hand-operated frame. This older type is still in use on almost all the small floors where only one or two of them are employed, and they are still made use of on larger dressing floors for simple or less critical washings. I have included them especially as historical information, indicating the origin of frames.

Old hand frames

The machine frames at Wheal Vor are of recent construction under favourable circumstances (see Figs. below).

A frame is 8' long, 6' wide and slopes at 1½" per foot. There are 48 of them, in four groups, two of 16 and two of 8.

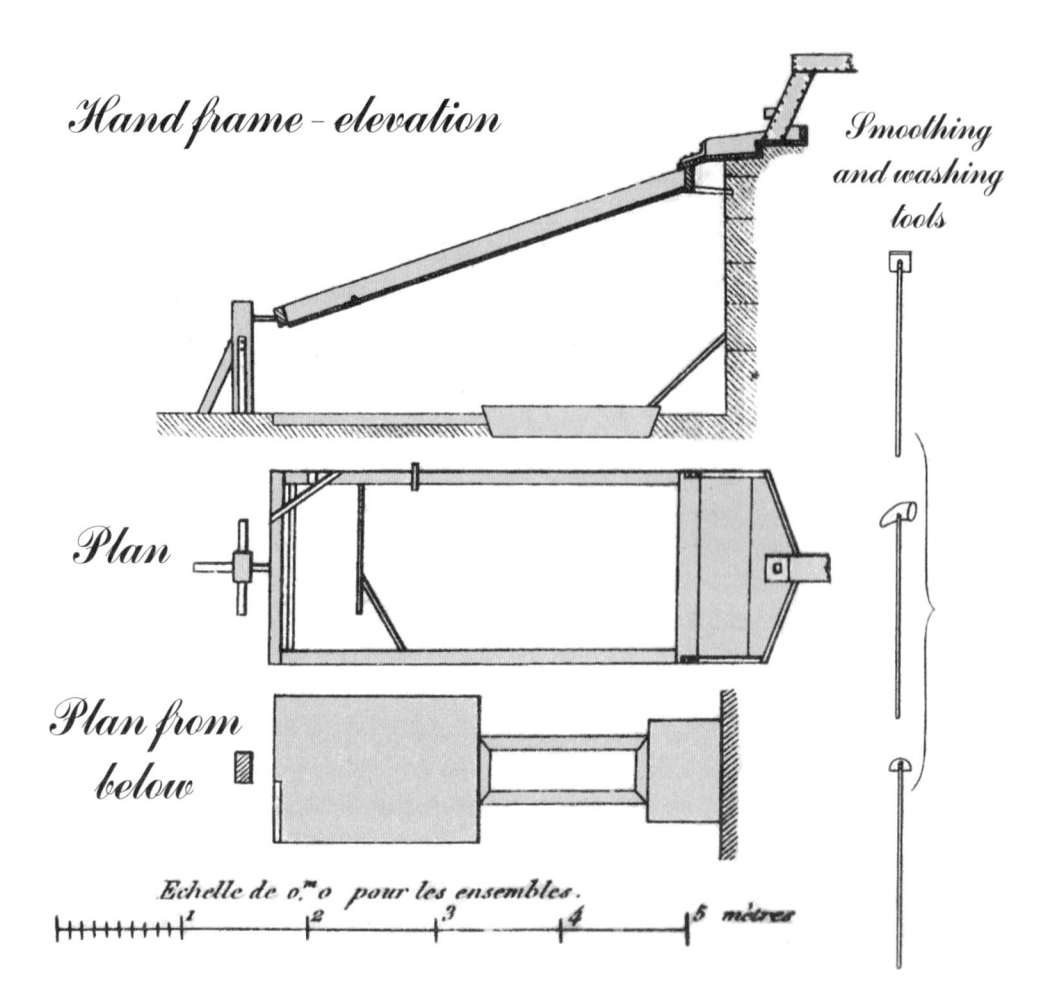

Hand frame - elevation

Smoothing and washing tools

Plan

Plan from below

Echelle de 0.ᵐ0 pour les ensembles.

Machine frames at Wheal Vor

A group of 16 frames (shown together on the floors plan) is laid out as two rows of 8, back to back, the whole arrangement having the same overall slope. At the head is a box, where the slimes are delivered as a suspension in water, and the roughs are recovered. The feed channel for the fine overflow material runs above and between the two lines of frames. Parallel, alongside and 8" away, is the clean water channel. An arrangement of slots allows the slimes feed to each frame to be shut off at a single stroke, the wash water opened, and vice-versa.

When the deck has been turned and washed by a directed water stream, lower channels take away the three classes of product. Those for the heads are 3' 8" wide and lead to three small pits, the second set takes the deposited tails to two pits, and, finally, a third set takes the slimy rejects to the lower secondary floors (*The 'Flow'*).

Side elevation

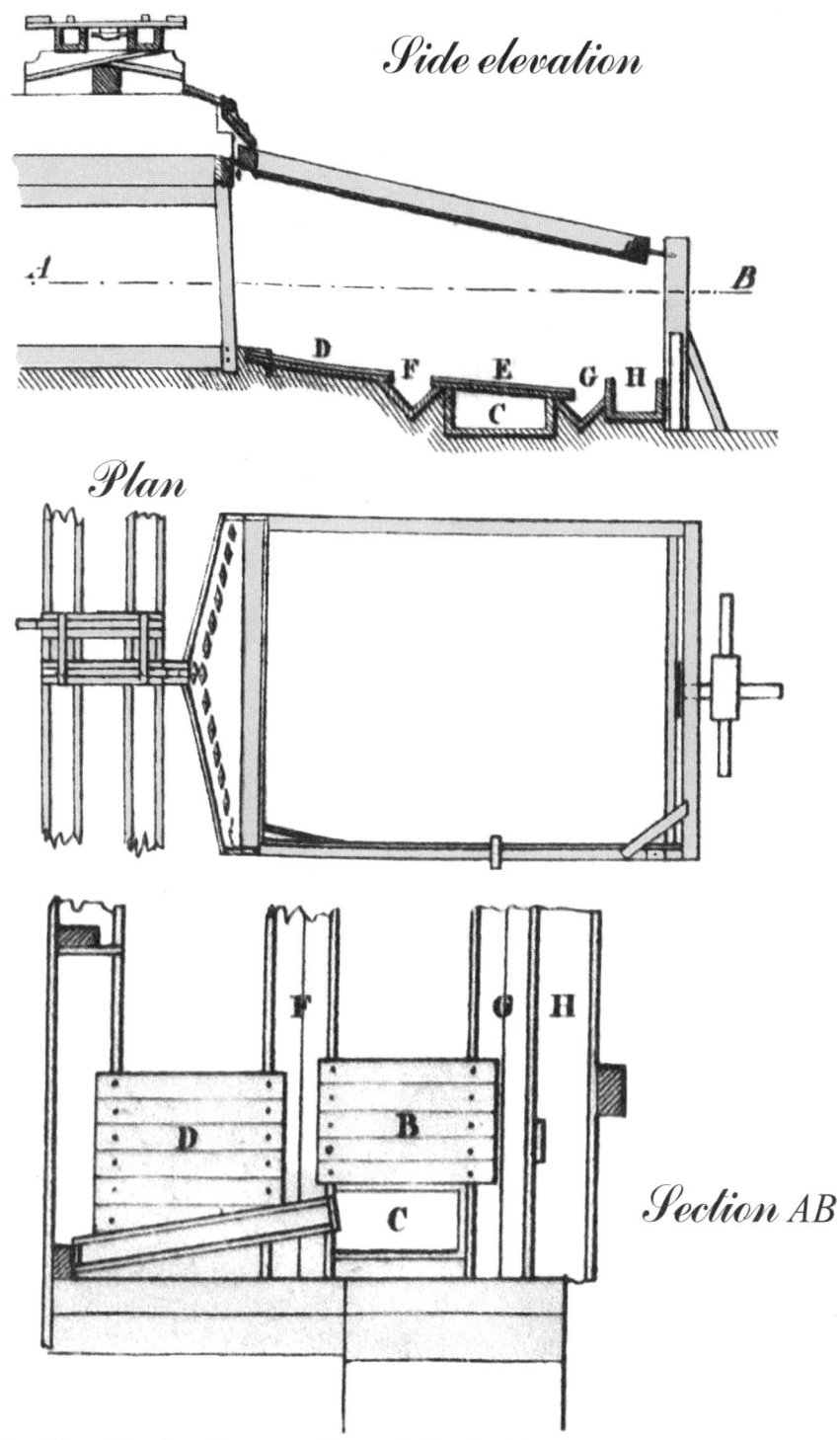

Plan

Section AB

The 30 self-acting frames at Tincroft (devised by Capt. Teague) are arranged in two rows with a passage down the middle, towards which the frames are inclined. Here and there down this passage there is a sort of balustrade or railing, supported at right angles to each frame by two

Self-acting frames at Tincroft and St. Day United

vertical pillars. This serves to support various parts of the mechanism controlling the operation, camshaft, catches etc. At the head of the rows of frames is the driving water wheel, 6′ x 8″ with 30 compartments. At the tail end are the pits to receive the three quantities of product.

On each side of the rows of frames runs a slimes distribution channel, **R**, whose base is pierced in front of the long axis of each frame. A conical rod, with an appropriately timed movement, alternately opens and closes the hole, **o**, by which the slimes fall into an individual feed

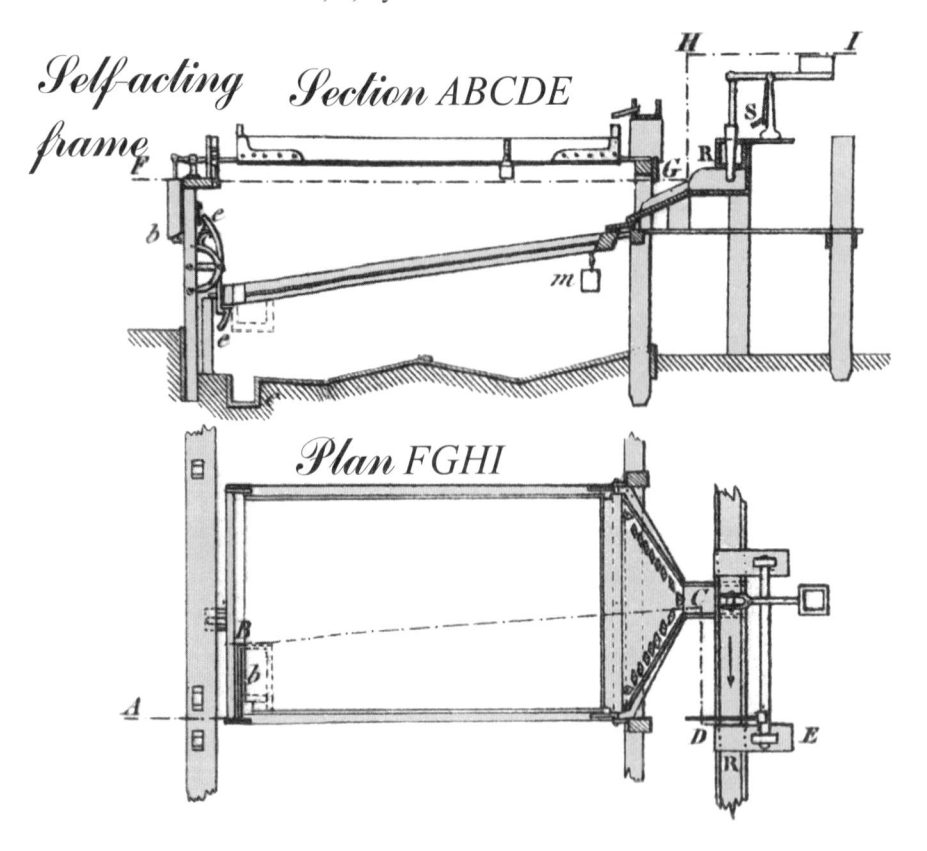

Self-acting frame   *Section ABCDE*

Plan FGHI

channel for each frame, taking them to a triangular headboard, with two lines of adjustable diamond-shaped feed distribution blocks, and a steep slope of 1 : 3 (33%).

The deck of the frame itself is 10′ long, 5′ 6″ wide and has a slope of 1¼″ per foot.

The operating cycle of movements is as follows:

1. The table is emptied and back in its normal position.

2. The feed hole, **o**, is opened by a counterweight, feeding slimes on to the deck.

3. Part of the slimes feed runs into the box, **b**.

4. The large lever, **l**, is pushed by the cam, **c**.

Mechanism, from the side

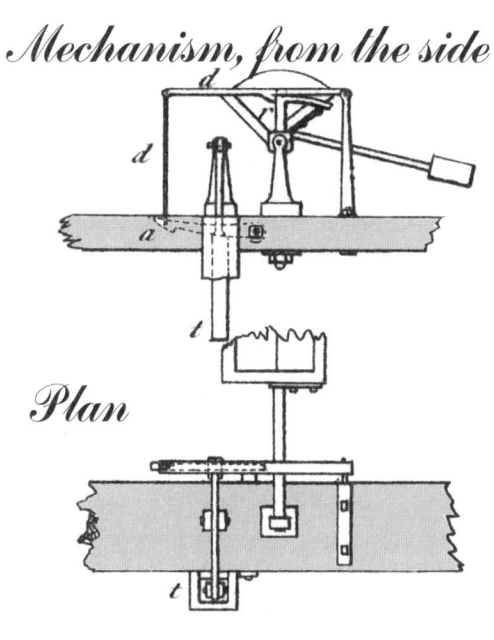

Plan

5. The table is now no longer supported and turns over because of the out of balance weight of the box, **b**.

6. During its rotation, it lifts up the latch, **a**, and by means of the transmission, **dd**, at the moment when it reaches a vertical position the clean water trough above escapes the catch **r**, and spills its contents down in an even flow carrying away the washings, while, during this, the counterweight box **b** at the foot of the frame empties itself.

7. The natural out-of-balance condition, due to the offset frame axis, and helped by the suspended mass **m**, hung near the head, tends to bring the frame back to its normal working position, where it is held only by the latch **a**, and as soon as a cam (not shown) presses on **t**, the table is freed and comes to rest on the lever **l**. During the washing-off the feed hole, **o**, is closed by the shaped rod **s** and the action of another cam (also not shown).

The drive shaft of each row of frames makes one turn every three minutes, and a single operating cycle for each frame lasts the same time. The various sets of cams are keyed on to the shaft so as to carry out the work evenly and regularly, and, as there are fifteen frames on the same line, the interval between two operations is only twelve seconds. (*In other words, the frames do not all move at the same time, but in sequence, down the line, at twelve-second intervals*).

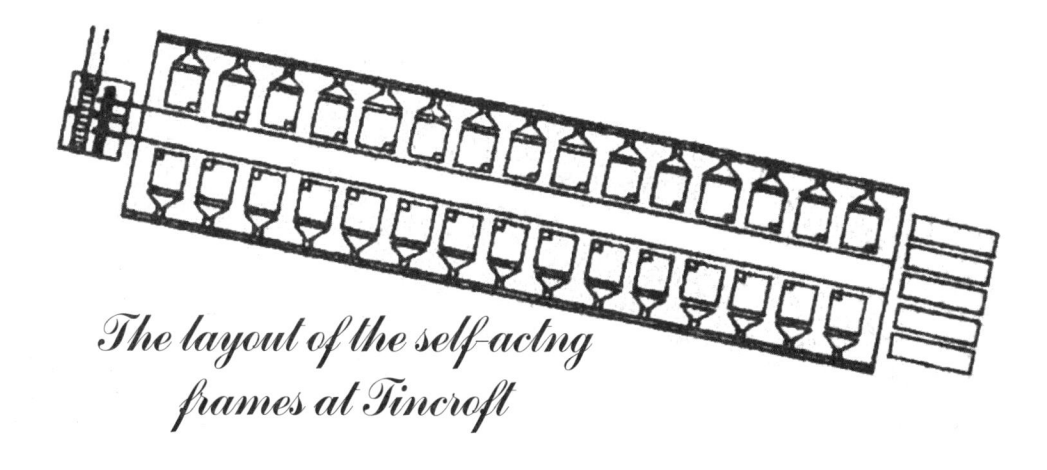

The layout of the self-acting frames at Tincroft

Hancock's large frame, at Polgooth and Par Consols

In 1855 I saw, at Polgooth, a new type of frame recently devised by Capt. Hancock, which was giving good results, and I found, in 1857, six of these large frames also at work on the dressing floors at Par Consols. They are intended to work on the 'top skimmings' from kieves and the enriched heads from other frames, either before or after calcining. These frames are not pictured here, but a short description of the frame and its operation follows:

The table is not less than 14 – 16 feet long, 6 feet wide, and has either two or three working decks with an equal number of collection boxes beneath. There is an abrupt short drop in height of 1¼" between the tail of one deck and the head of the next.

Feed material, as wet sand, such as that taken from kieves, is thrown into a wooden hopper whose length is equal to the width of the table, and whose volume is approximately 167 gallons (750 litres).

The base of the hopper is formed of a grille of iron bars, arranged in the direction of the long axis of the table and spaced 2" apart. Below this is a board that projects 15 or 16 inches in front of the hopper. The feed material, already somewhat broken up by passing through the grille, falls on to this board and is diluted by a flow of water that gradually carries it away. Below this first board is a second, which sticks forward a further 15 inches. The feed slurry runs over this and comes to a flap at the end, and from there on to the frame decks.

The operator works a rake over these two boards to break up any agglomerates of fine sands, and distribute them evenly. The table having been charged, by moving a handle that works levers controlling a subsidiary distribution board, a stream of clean water is fed on to the second board at the same time as it blocks off the first one.

The cleaning period having taken place, the operator tips the frame decks upwards on their transverse axes. Along the opposite long side runs a wooden channel pierced with holes on a level with the table. As the table decks tip, a tap is opened allowing water from an upper channel to spread rapidly into the lower one, and from there on to the table, washing any retained material into the collection boxes below each deck.

The spindle under these frames is carried on a bearing, free to move vertically by a rod with a threaded screw and nut, and by means of this the slope of the decks can be varied. At Polgooth this is 1" per foot (1 : 12), and at Par Consols 1½" per foot, a slope of (1 : 8).

Critical examination of various arrangements

The necessity of using stationary frames for the treatment of slimes is evident. A perfectly flat and uniform surface is essential, in order that particles can come to rest according to their relative 'mobility'. That is to say, they can only be successfully washed by a very thin water layer. Even under these conditions, very fine grains are easily entrained and can be carried away down the entire frame in a short time. Without a greatly elongated deck, such as the 30-ft. long German 'kehrherd', there is no option but to perform a series of very short operations.

Considering the requirements of quantity of material treated, grading and separation, and tin recovery, a frame of extended length is advantageous, but, unfortunately, this is incompatible with the tipping of the frame for product removal. Effectively, it is difficult to construct a framework, on just two bearings, more than about 15 feet long without fear of warping or buckling, and the immediately resulting irregular flow of water and feed leading to poor performance. Nevertheless, while maintaining the tipping capability of these frames, so necessary for product discharge, the dressing Captains have managed to more or less double their length from 8 – 10 feet to 14 – 16 feet (I).

Table length

Although the treatment capacity of a frame is obviously proportional to its width, in this regard the same danger of warping is even greater, and has not permitted an enlargement beyond about 6 feet (II).

Width

(I) A very simple arrangement, being tried out, I believe, at this moment (1858) would allow the construction of frames as long as desired. Instead of fixing bearings to the small corners of the frame, they need only be placed at either end of an 8″ square beam. This, then, forms the base of the table, and on to it transverse planks are nailed, and the frame itself is then no more than a simple rim or raised edge.

(II) An unsuccessful trial, made some years ago at Carvath United, proved that these fears were only too justified.

The main slimes and those from the small slime pits make up the major part of the fine material to be treated, and are relatively poor. Their treatment is delegated to mechanical frames laid out in rows, and the arrival of feed material as a suspension, and, likewise, the running off of the various products, enable a great saving in manpower. At the same time, the feed being in the form it is, in suspension and well disagglomerated, helps the apparatus to do its work much more efficiently. At St. Day United, each rank of 9 self-acting frames is looked after by a single boy, while at Tincroft, two boys superintend 30 frames.

With this system of operating frames, making the operating mechanism a little more complicated has dispensed with washing with clean water. This measure, which seems, at first sight, unsatisfactory, is still questionable.

Dispensing with washing by clean water

So, at Tincroft, where there are no de-sliming paddle trunks, the slimes contain very fine tin along with other fines. It is conceded that a flow of clean water, even very controlled, will carry off that part of the tin that would stay on the frame if there were no washing, and thus persuaded, the Captain at Tincroft has used up to now ordinary machine frames without washing. The work is a little more rapidly carried out, each operation taking four minutes as opposed to six, thus saving one-third of the time. But it is only by repeated tossing in kieves that the resultant insufficient cleaning can be made up for.

Now, the tossing of fine material is a lengthy and expensive business. Experiment and experience alone can indicate if the very fine tin that is thus retained, by the saving of time in framing, compensates advantageously for the extra work and effort by kieve. At St. Day United, the use of paddle trunks (and better de-sliming) lessens the chances of not using clean water having a useful or beneficial effect.

Wash water on the frame only really ceases to be sensible if the frame has been overloaded, allowing rich grains to reach the lower part of the frame. The general flow of water affects not only the movement of fine, light particles, but also that of a large proportion of the very finest tin grains, and those that would have arrived near the foot of the table by being naturally misplaced. I have stressed this point to emphasize the usefulness of lengthening the frame. A long frame would not have been overloaded in the case described above, and would have retained this fine tin, making a division that could be enriched separately.

Fitting frames with cloth

At Balleswidden, the heads of the frames have been fitted with 4-ft. long strips of linen, quite coarse and tightly stretched, which help significantly to retain fine tin.

The top skimmings from the kieve are generally already quite rich and well classified, retrieved from the kieve as wet sand, and almost always treated on hand frames. At Par Consols they are passed to Hancock frames, where, as usual, they are not put into suspension with water and the operator has to attend to their distribution. His time is already fully occupied without the manual work being added to, but the treatment is rendered imperfect by the necessity of breaking up agglomerates with a rake, as far as the table itself. The addition of the hopper with grille demonstrates this assertion, but it is only a partial improvement.

Preliminary suspension

It would be better to adopt, as in the German 'kehrherd', a paddle wheel working in a hopper, stirring the material into suspension with added water.

Following from the preceding observations, it can be seen that whenever the manual work of an operator has to be replaced by a mechanical arrangement, too much care cannot be taken in the construction of the apparatus, and strictly applied to the precision of its movements. It is only by getting very close to these identical conditions that one can hope for a good result. In addition, I believe that in spite of their simplicity, self-acting frames whose movements are governed solely by the filling of a subsidiary box should not be used.

Working slope

The working slopes of frames vary with the nature of the material to be treated, from 3″ to ¾″ per foot, or from 1 : 4 to 1 : 16. For example:

Floors	Type of frame	Slope	Material treated
Wheal Vor	Machine frames	1½″ per ft	Slimes from paddle trunks
Tincroft	Machine frames	1¼″ per ft.	Slimes from large
	Self-acting frames	1¼″ per ft.	slime pits
Par Consols	Hancock frames	1½″ per ft	Slimes. Top skimmings

Water used and solids treated

It is very difficult to evaluate the quantities of water used and material treated per minute by a frame.

According to Henwood, the old-fashioned hand frames receive, at each operation, about ½ to ¾ of a gallon (2 – 3.5 litres) of slimes on the jagging board. Water is fed from a ⅝″ diameter hole, under a 3″ head of pressure, delivering approximately 1¼ gallons (5½ litres) per minute.

At Par Consols, the 12 frames, **O**, treating the slimes from the second row of paddle trunks, work as follows:

They are superintended by three female operators, one to each four frames. Each frame operates on a six-minute cycle, that is, the feed comes on to the frame for 4½ minutes and the girl then devotes 1½ minutes to washing with clean water, regularising the deposit, turning the frame and washing-off.

Each operation treats about 2 gallons (9 litres) of slimes (taken as being in a dry and uncompacted state), plus 2½ times their volume of water. Over one day's work, close on 1 ton of slimes is treated per frame, along with a total water consumption reaching nearly 3 tons (3 cubic metres).

Hand frames and Hancock frames need one operator to each frame. With machine frames, according to whether the slimes are gritty (i.e. handled rapidly), or very fine (handled slowly), one girl manages 1, 2, 4 or even 6 frames. Women and older girls employed on frames do not earn less than £1 per month.

On several floors, poor slimes (main slimes and those from small pits) whose grade is fairly consistent are set 'on tribute'. The Captain is aware how far well-conducted work is capable of upgrading them to an approximately known value, and based on that, and the more or less favourable arrangement and layout of the frames, he sets the 'tribute' to be paid to the operator such that her earnings can, if she wishes, reach at least £1. 4s. by the end of the month. The 'tribute' is the sum paid for a fixed weight (I) of black tin, verified by vanning assay, in the batch of frame product.

This is how things are organised at Par Consols. The table below allows an assessment of the variations resulting from the nature of the material and the type of frame used. Depending on the skill of the girl or woman, and assuming that the tribute set is fair and equitable, it works out that she may earn, on average, £1. 6s. for the month.

(I) The fixed weight taken is 1 cwt. (50.8 Kg.) of black tin. (*In his original table, Moissenet sets out all the figures - weights, assays and remuneration - in metric notation, with payments in francs. Any student, or more experienced Mineral Processor, will be fully aware of how much simpler this makes any calculation, as opposed to weights in cwts., quarters, and lbs., and assays in lbs. per ton of black tin. So, I have left all weights and assays in Kg. and percentages, respectively, as originally stated, but I have taken the liberty of converting monetary values of tribute and earnings into pounds, shillings and pence for the benefit of U.K. readers). It may be of relevant interest here to record the fact that, some seven or eight years later, fairly strong proposals were being made on behalf of metrication, and its general introduction into Britain.*

Separation performance of frames

With regard to the separating performance of frames, below are figures I was given of the analysis of samples at Par Consols:

Frames	Tin content of divisions	Observations
M	1. 4.40%	Working on material with a head grade of about 2%,
	2. 1.40%	from the strip where L_1 is thrown.
I	1. 6.70%	Working on the middle, G_2, of the small slime pits
	2. 0.75%	at a head grade of 0.9 – 1.0%.
β	1. 48.0%	Hancock frames.
	2. 5.0%	

Comparing the performance of frames **M** and **I**, it can be seen how much easier it is to upgrade feed material that is a little coarser in nature.

The high tin content of product $β_2$ (the second division of the Hancock frames) shows that, despite the length of the frame, the tail, sent to the tributer's floors, still carries a high proportion of tin.

Hancock's new, large frame

Since 1856, Capt. Hancock has devised at Polgooth a new frame, which I saw working in September 1857, that is meant to avoid the main difficulties and drawbacks set out above. The only objection to make with regard to this apparatus is its fairly high price and the necessity of keeping it in perfect working condition. Experiment and experience alone will provide the answer, but however, having been installed in the open air for a year, it has remained in good condition and working order.

The table is 40′ long, 18′ wide, and has an overall slope of 4′ (1 : 10). It has four decks (Nos. 9 and 10 on the diagram) capable of movement on their transverse axes, and connected by the levers, **A**, to two lines of rods, whose ends can be pulled and operated by counterweight boxes (11) at the tail, and (13) at the head.

The slimes from the paddle trunks are fed via a launder that the operator

Table of work performed by 23 frames, superintended by 11 girls, at Par Consols during August 1857 - work set on tribute.

Frames on Par Consols floors plan	No.of frames Total	No.of frames Per girl	Number of girls	Weight of frame product (Kg.)	% black tin content by vanning assay	Weight of black tin (Kg.)	Tribute per 100 Kg. black tin	Monthly earnings	Observations
O	12	4	3	11,000	4.565	502	13s. 3½d.	£3. 6s. 8½d.	Machine frames, treating the heads from the second paddle trunks, N_1.
T	4	1	4	2,250	9.549	214	11s. 7½d.	£1. 4s. 10½d.	Treating slimes from slime pits, S, (tributer's floors) on 12' x 5' machine frames, self-washing.
				2,000	12.999	260	11s. 7½d.	£1. 10s. 2½d.	10' x 5' machine frame, washed by hand.
				1,350	12.200	164	14s. 0½d.	£1. 3s. 0d.	
				900	11.750	106	£1. 4s. 10¾d.	£1. 6s. 5d.	Old-fashioned hand frame.
									Machine frames, treating heads from first paddle trunks, L_1.
M	4	2	2	24,000	4.340	1,041	3s. 4d.	£1. 14s. 8½d.	2 treating heads from strip where L_1 is thrown.
				16,000	3.630	581	3s. 7½d.	£1. 1s. 2d.	2 treating tails from strip where L_1 is thrown.
									Machine frames, on slimes from small pits G.
I	3	1	1	8,150	6.386	520	5s. 0d.	£1. 6s. 0d.	Treating the middle, G_2.
		2	1	8,100	4.565	370	7s. 11½d.	£1. 9s. 5¾d.	Treating the tail, G_3.
Totals	23	-	11	83,750	-	3,758	-	£14. 5s. 9½d.	Average monthly earnings, £1. 5s. 10d.

123

opens and closes by means of connecting rods and the handle, **C**, and the feed is spread over the table by the two fan-shaped and battened distribution boards (6, 6).

Discarded slimes tails leave the table and fall into the counterweight trough (11). During the time this is being filled, a long trolley (23) moving on four rails (24) is given a reciprocating up-and-down movement by the rod (29), driven (*presumably by crank*) from a water wheel (not shown). This trolley carries four rows of brushes, to just touch the surface and lightly carry material back up the table during the upward part of their travel. When the trolley reaches the top of its run, the lever (26) butts up against a stop or buffer. The brooms are lifted up and held in this position (*i.e. above the table surface*) by a catch (27) until the trolley is back at the lower end of its travel, and at this point the lower stop (28), pressing on the tail of the catch (27), lowers the brushes, allowing them to retake their normal operating position. The run of the trolley is 7', and it makes two passes per minute.

At the end of 12 minutes the table is considered to be fully loaded. The operator then shuts off the feed, and, by means of the handle, **E**, allows on a flow of clean wash water from the trough (22), which washes on to an extension of the head of the table deck below the two triangular headboards. When this washing is completed, the trolley is returned to the top of its run by a hook (34), worked by means of handle, **B**. By working the lever, **D**, the operator, aided by the counterweights (11 and 13), rotates the four separate sections of the deck into a vertical position. This same movement opens the valves (16, 16) by means of the rod (15). Clean water now discharges from the launder (14) into four other channels (18, 18) and falls as a weak flow on to the four deck sections, whose contents are then washed into the four receiving troughs (19), which send them to four settling pits off to one side of the frame.

A complete operating cycle lasts 15 minutes, and 11 gallons (50 litres) per minute of water are used. The surface of the table having an area of 560 square feet, that is, about ten times larger than an ordinary frame, it is obvious that the water consumption is as very nearly the same per unit area as one could make it. The loading time of the table is extended by a factor of three, but the cleaning stage lasts no longer than ordinary.

From these various observations, it can be concluded that, in a given time, this large frame handles as much feed as 12 good, ordinary machine frames, and comparative experiments, in a long trial at Polgooth, showed a 30% reduction in manpower. In other words, a single operator is capable of replacing 3 girls each working 4 machine frames. It has been found besides, that the definitive products from the large Hancock frame recover 5% more tin than those of ordinary machine frames handling the same slimes feed.

125

The Figs. below show the new, large, Hancock frame, clearly with four decks, and are the same drawings as appear in Hancock's patent specification, No.2704, dated 30th November 1855 (sealed 16th May 1856)

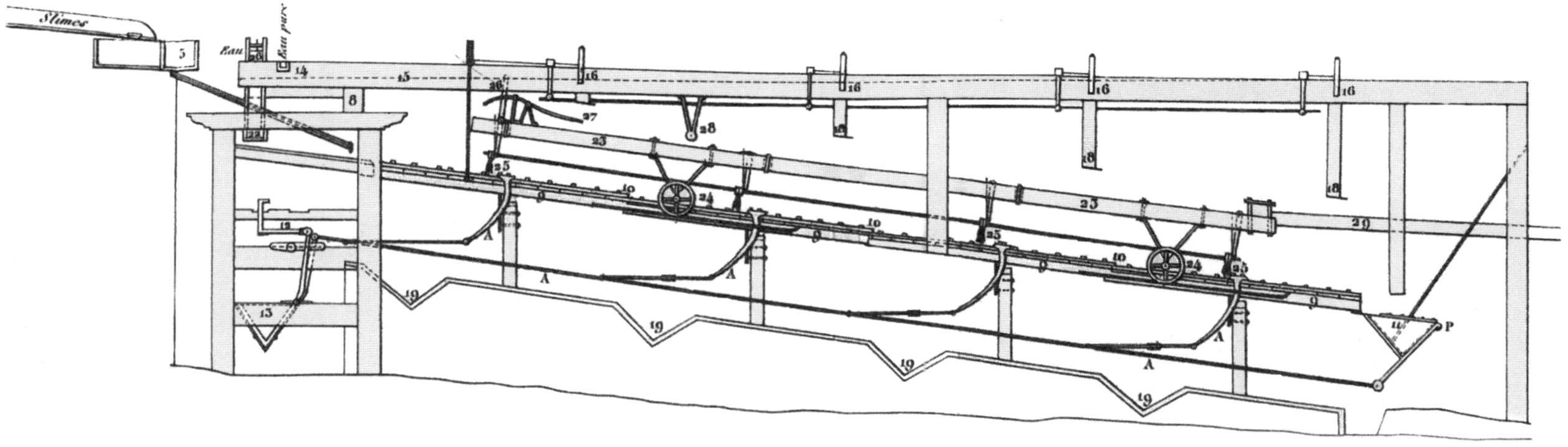

126

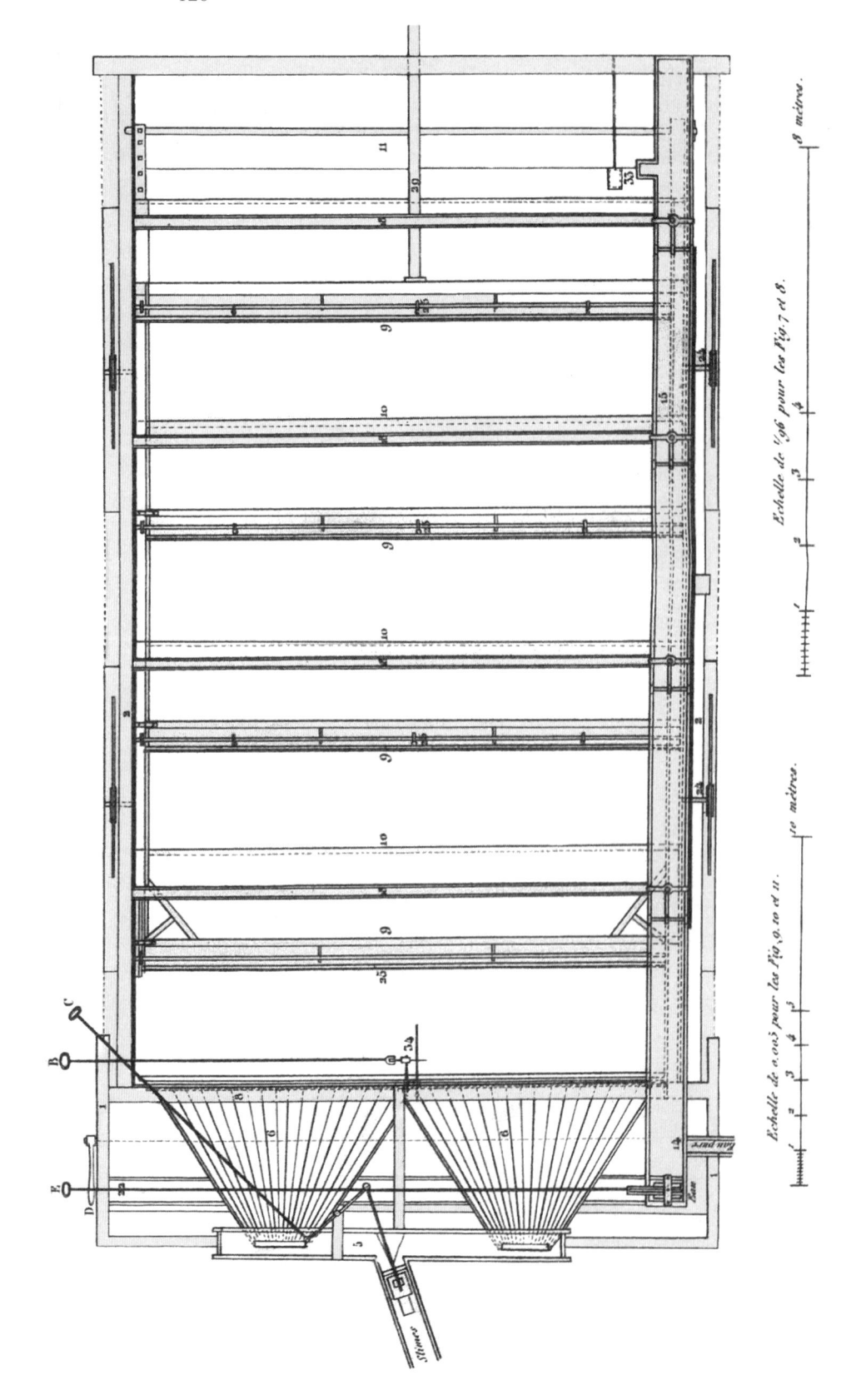

§ IX. Roasting, or calcining.

Roasting or calcining

The roasting of tin ores has to be carried right to completion, without at the same time producing partially fused agglomerates or 'frits' of material. It is this that characterises the operation, and makes it exceptionally difficult.

From a practical point of view, it is conducted under the same conditions as those used for antimony sulphide, that is, slowly and at relatively low temperature.

Ores carrying only iron pyrites are the easiest to roast. Copper pyrites is less easily decomposed, and mispickel (*iron/arsenic sulphide*), containing arsenic, needs still more care.

Straightforward reverbatory furnaces, or those with a revolving bedplate, as are used in Cornwall, have narrow and quite shallow fireboxes. The temperature is barely above deep red, if it is not entirely at the end of the operation.

At the start, the hearth being charged, the door is shut and minimal air allowed to enter. At this time, there is a first stage where sulphur and arsenic sulphide are sublimed off. Then, the temperature rises and oxidation begins, producing sulphur dioxide and arsenic trioxide. Ingress of air is always kept very low, because the combustion of pyritic materials, if too rapid, brings about an unwanted rise in temperature, whereby the sulphides are no longer properly decomposed, and quartz and chlorite gangue minerals can begin to react with the oxides. At this stage, 'rabbling' or stirring of the roasting charge is particularly necessary. It is important to prolong the period during which arsenic trioxide is driven off, and to avoid the formation of iron arsenates. Towards the end, iron and copper sulphates are produced, the former itself being subsequently decomposed.

The tin oxide does not entirely escape the sulphurous reactions at the start. The gases being slightly reducing, and the sulphur produced in abundance, lead to the formation of a small quantity of tin sulphide, later roasted, at least partially, and transformed into stannic and stannous sulphates.

I verified this partial attack on the tin oxide on a sample of roasted ore leaving the furnace at Par Consols. The tin witts before roasting contain about 30% iron pyrites. After roasting, the material, re-treated with hydrochloric acid, gave, in the soluble portion, 70% tin oxide, though simply re-treated with water, a noticeable quantity still dissolved.

It can be positively stated that all the portion of tin oxide thus attacked is subsequently lost in the after treatment, in that it is either dissolved in sulphuric acid, or lost during mechanical washing. Overall, this is a source of loss, which, although small by metallurgical standards, is by no means negligible, and can, certainly with very impure ores, account for more than 1.5% of the total tin oxide in the original tin witts. A second cause of loss is the carrying away of particles with the furnace exhaust gases, weak as this is, into the arsenic condensation chambers, where the tin is deposited mixed with arsenic.

The calcining ovens are stationed in the 'burning house', alongside the sheds where the treatment of the roasted ore is carried out. This close proximity is most useful of all when a large proportion of the products from a first washing are re-passed for a second roasting.

All the flues from the calciners pass into a masonry conduit leading to a tall chimney. When the ore carries much mispickel (*i.e. is highly arsenical*), this conduit may be over 100 feet long. Near the calciners, its internal section is 6' 6" high by 8' 3" wide. A series of partitions, alternating on each vertical side wall, effectively subdivides the long flue into chambers, and in this way the path of the exhaust gases is made longer by winding through this layout, helping the condensation of the sublimed arsenic trioxide. These chambers are emptied out every one or two months through openings in one side, ordinarily closed by iron doors sealed with clay.

Roasters at Par Consols

Simple batch reverbatory furnaces, with an elliptical hearth, and of variable size, are still much used. At Par Consols, this hearth is 7' long, 4' wide towards the head, 5' wide in the middle and 18" wide at the end, where the working port is located. The firebox is 10" wide, and stands 11" below the head of the hearth. The height of the arched roof is 8"above the head, 16" above the middle of the hearth and 10" towards the sides, because of the downward curve of the roof. The hot gases cross the whole length of the hearth and escape via a flue near the working port.

During the operation, the material to be fed is put to dry on a circular iron plate in the upper masonry chamber above the hearth arch. In the centre is a feed hopper, ordinarily closed by a plug with a handle. The roasted ore is moved by rabble (rake) to a rectangular opening at the very end of the hearth bed, and falls into a space below, opening on to the floors on the same side as the working port.

With the furnace empty, and the fire temperature properly at deep red, a new charge can be introduced. A boy loads the dried ore (I) into the hopper, while the calciner operator spreads it out over the furthest half of the hearth bed. During roasting, his work consists of rabbling or raking over the bed every 20 or 30 minutes, depending on the nature of the ore. Each time, material is spread out to form three mounds across the width of the hearth, exposing one side to the direct action of the hot gases. On several floors this system is varied by raking the mounds alternately along the long axis of the hearth. When several brilliantly bright points of light begin to appear, and there are no more white fumes being given off, the roasting is finished.

(I) If the ore has not been dried beforehand, it needs to lie in a heap on the hearth for an hour, in order to avoid the rapid evolution of steam carrying away fine tin.

The ore at Par Consols, depending on its origin, contains a fairly high proportion of iron pyrites, and always an appreciable amount of copper pyrites, therefore worthy of note, but no more than traces of mispickel.

Only the bottoms of the kieves on 'best work', and some on 'common work' need no more than a single roasting. The other sands and rich slimes are re-worked after a first roasting, and the washed products are re-passed to calcining for a second time.

The charge is always 10 cwts, half a ton. Each operation lasts 12 hours for the first roasting, using 287 lbs. of coal. A second roasting lasts 8 – 10 hours, and consumes 198 – 242 lbs. of coal. The 'burning house' is made up of four primary furnaces, looked after by just two operators, one by day and the other by night. Help in charging the furnaces is borrowed from among the washing operators on the floors.

In one month, to produce 50 tons of enriched, roasted products, some 85 tons of material is effectively passed through the calciners, and during the same time period, some 21 tons of coal are burnt. Leaving aside secondary expenses, the specific costs are:

   2 operators, at £2. 15s. 0d.   £5. 10s. 0d.
  21 tons of coal at 13s. per ton £13. 13s. 0d.
                                  £19. 3s. 0d.

Comparing the relative costs per ton of ore stamped and per ton of black tin produced, the specific costs of roasting are:

Per ton of ore stamped			Per ton of black tin	
0.42 days	9¼d.	Labour at 1s. 10d. per day	2.2 days	4s. 0½d.
31 lbs.	2¼d.	Coal at 13s. per ton	15 cwt. 7 lbs.	9s. 9½d.
Total	11½d.	-	Total	13s. 10d.

Comparing the relative natures of the products for roasting, below are the results of analysis of several samples:

Material for roasting	Pyrite	Gangue	Tin oxide	Total
1st quality: Bottom of 'best work' kieves, C_3	20%	10%	70%	100%
2nd: Bottom of 'common work' kieves, C'_3	25.66%	15%	59%	99.66%
3rd: Bottom of kieves working heads of square buddles fed with bottom skimmings	33%	10%	56%	99%
4th: Hopper of 'shacking tyes', B_4	36%	10%	53.5%	99.5%
5th: Heads of frames, β_1	29%	35%	35%	99%

After roasting, ore corresponding to '1st quality' above, and still damp, gave as follows on analysis:

Tin oxide	Iron oxide	Copper oxide	Gangue	Sulphuric acid	Water	Total
64.9%	16.0%	0.3%	10.0%	0.76%	8.0%	99.96

It can be seen that the average pyrite content at Par Consols is 30%. To successfully decompose this does not use an equivalent weight of coal less than 42% of the weight of the ore, or 140% of the weight of pyrite.

The sulphur expelled, that is, the loss in weight, is 16 – 17%. At mines where the ore is very pyritic, the tin content of products for roasting is, consequently, not high.

In the following table I have summarized the main information pertaining to several important dressing floors, which will allow an appreciation of the possible variations that the operation of roasting can present:

Floors	Hearth bed dimensions		Charge	Coal used per operation	Coal used as % of charge wt.	Duration of roasting	Costs per ton of black tin	
	Length	Width						
Par Consols	7'	5'	10 cwts	2.6 cwts	26%	12 hrs.	14s. 1d.	(a)
			10 cwts	1.8 - 2.2 cwts	18 - 22%	8 - 10 hrs.		
Polgooth	7'	5'	6 cwts	1.5 cwts	25%	12 - 14 hrs.	13s. 7¼d.	(b)
St. Day United	7'	5'	5 cwts	1.5 cwts	30%			
			6 cwts	1.5 cwts	25%	6 hrs.	£1. 0s. 0d.	(c)
			7 cwts	1.5 cwts	21.5%			
Balleswidden	12'	6'	20 cwts (1 ton)	1.5 cwts	7.5%	10 hrs.	4s. 0d.	(d)

(a) Iron pyrites and a little copper pyrites, 3 furnaces, generally 2 roastings.
(b) Ore similar to (a), 6 furnaces, generally 1 roasting.
(c) Much arsenical pyrites (mispickel), generally 2 roastings.
(d) Almost clean ore, very few impurities, 1 roasting.

Rotary calciners

Rotary calciners (*Brunton type*) and their continuous action can give good service on a large floor. Their installation is more expensive, and they need driving power.

The following figures represent one of the two such furnaces at Wheal Vor in 1855 (I).

(I) Since that time the number has been increased to three.

The bedplate is 12′ in diameter, and is a circular iron plate whose rim drops to form a very shallow cone, 9″ high, with a slope of 1 : 16 or 6.25%. At Wheal Vor, the bedplates carry four equidistant, annular iron rings. On this metallic framework are laid, successively, slates, a layer of clay and flat bricks. The fire port is 15″ wide and 6′ long, and the fire grille itself is 11″ below the head. The top of the furnace arch is a spherical vault, of thick brick, 10″ above the centre of the bedplate.

The ore is pre-dried on the floor of the chamber above this arch, and fed via a conical hopper such that it falls progressively down on to the bedplate to be spread by the action of one fixed set of rakes, whose blades are set obliquely to the drive shaft of the cone, and come to an end on the side opposite to the fire box.

By means of a type of shutter arrangement, the discharge port is connected alternately with two chambers, of which one receives the roasted material, while the previously roasted and cooled product is recovered from the other.

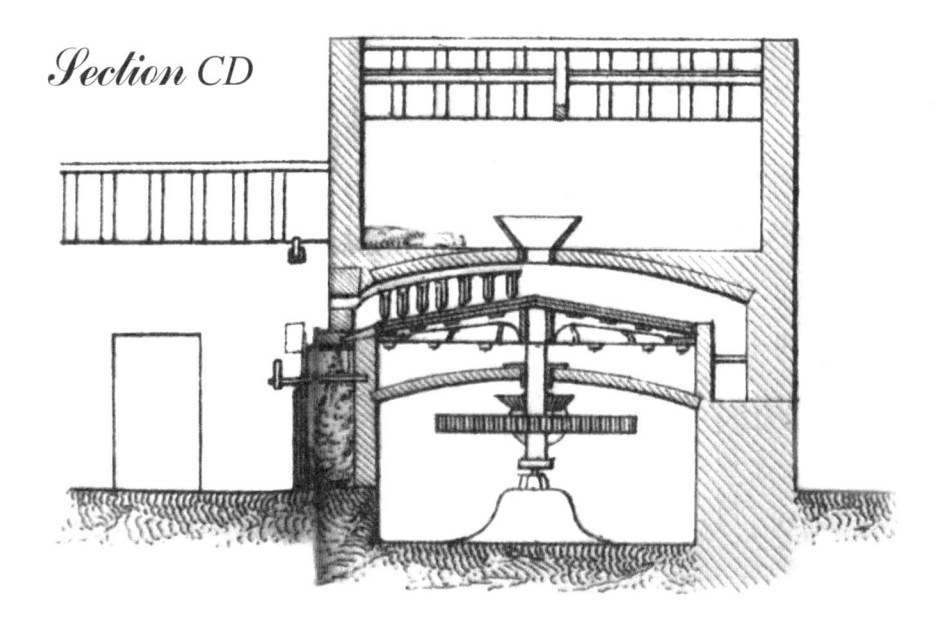

Section CD

The rake is cast iron, and its blades are prism-shaped and 8″ long, fixed on a common support by cotter pin, and assembled in a sort of swallow-tail arrangement. When, eventually, the action of the roasting sulphides has eaten them away, the equipment can be repaired by pulling out a removable part of the masonry structure that holds it by its end to the side of the chamber.

Plan

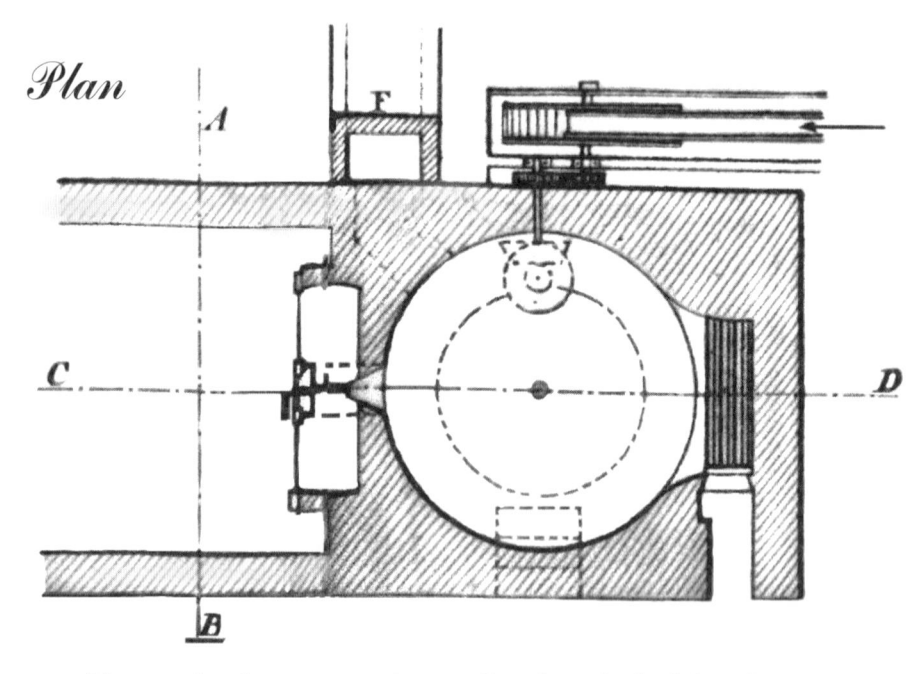

The rotational movement is transferred to the bedplate from a water wheel located outside the construction. Its dimensions are 6' diameter by 8" width and it makes, by observation, 10 r.p.m., whereas the bedplate makes a single revolution in 40 minutes, its speed being reduced by gearing with a ratio of 1 : 400.

The calciner at Tincroft shows several differences. It has two firebox doors, laid out on the same axis, opening in the solid masonry and with the ends of their working fire grilles 1' apart. Each is 20" wide and 2' 6" long. There are three sets of rakes, spaced at 120° angles and supported by iron rods that pass through the arch and are secured in the upper part of the building. Finally, there is a single discharge port, where the roasted material falls directly from the furnace into water (see p. 44).

The nature of the ore at Tincroft makes for very difficult roasting, as it carries a lot of iron/arsenic sulphide (mispickel), appreciable copper pyrites and a high proportion of iron pyrites, with most of the primary concentration products having to be roasted twice. In addition to the calciner used for crop tin witts, there are at Tincroft four other furnaces for slimes products. The charge held on the bedplate is 1 ton.

For the first roasting of very impure ore, 2 tons are treated in 24 hours, i.e. they have a 12-hour long treatment. For the second roasting, 3 tons can be handled over 24 hours, so 8 hours per treatment is sufficient. Over each 1 or 1½ hours, about 2 – 3 cwts. (100 – 150 Kg.) are charged. The minimum and maximum rotation speeds of the bedplate are 1 and 3 revolutions per hour.

Over a month, some 20 tons of coal are burnt at Tincroft, or 1.428 tons per ton of black tin produced. It will be noted that this coal consumption

Rotary calciner.
Elevation AB

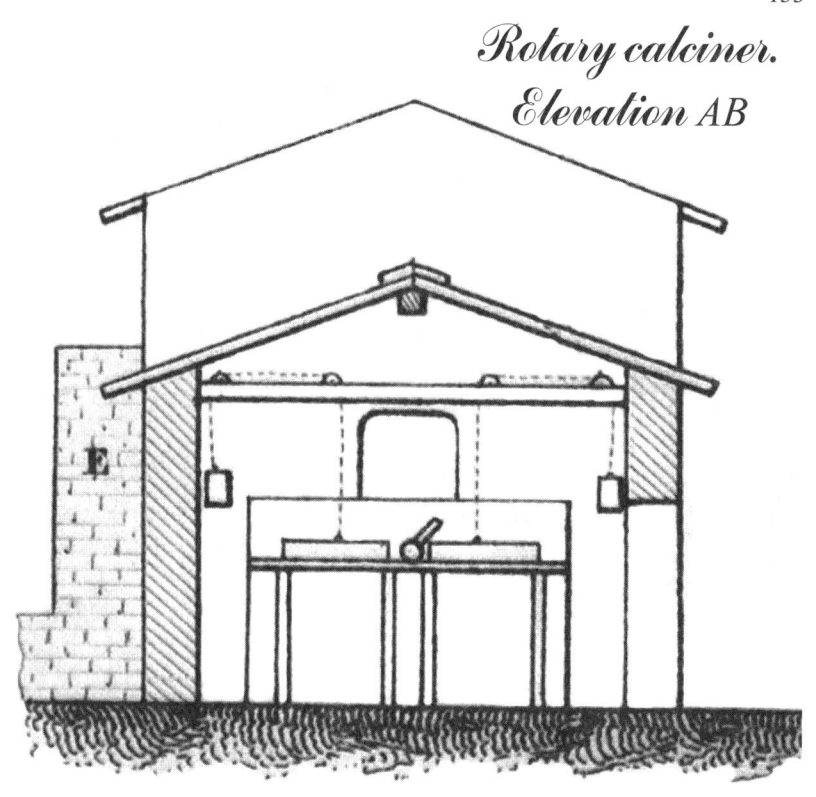

is almost double that of Par Consols.

A single operator per shift manages the calciner. He has to charge the ore, superintend the firebox, control the water to the drive wheel, and grease the gearing.

Having said this, his time is far from being fully occupied, and it is perfectly possible for him to look after two furnaces, as at Wheal Vor, or even three. Here, the operator works two of the other four reverbatory furnaces (for slimes) at the same time, all four of them not being in constant use.

I do not have all the necessary information to make a rigorous comparison between revolving and reverbatory furnaces; this is not possible unless they are both working on the same ore. Nevertheless, it is not without some interest to compare the facts laid out above.

Comparison of the two types of furnaces

From a technical point of view, the rotation of the bedplate is an excellent solution of the particular difficulties in the roasting of tin ore. Fresh ore arrives at the centre and, at first, is subjected to only moderate heat. After this, the temperature rises progressively the nearer it gets to the circumference and the source of heat. The circular movement submits it alternatively to more and more intense heat as it approaches the firebox, followed by periods of relative cooling as it moves away, ideal conditions to avoid agglomeration and 'fritting' (*partial fusing of particles*). The action of the fixed rakes above the bedplate is extremely regular, and their oblique alignment gives a complete turning over of the material, slow enough to avoid fines being stirred up and carried away by the flow of gases.

As far as the actual work of the operator is concerned, this ceases to be so unhealthy. As to manpower, significant economies can be made on large dressing floors employing several calciners. Effectively, we can see that the three reverberatory furnaces at Par Consols handle little more than the single calciner at Tincroft, that is, about 3 tons in 24 hours. Now, if it is acknowledged (as appears evident) that the fuel is no less efficiently used in the rotary calciner than in the reverberatory furnace, the roasting at Tincroft, consuming double the fuel, would need 6 reverberatory furnaces at work, at double the manpower. Actually, the use of the rotary calciner at Tincroft makes for a saving of 50% on manpower, and this could be raised to 75% if, as at Wheal Vor, there were two adjacent calciners (I).

Per ton of black tin produced, the specific costs of roasting at Tincroft are:

Manpower	4.28 days at 1s. 10d. per day	7s. 10¼d.
Coal	1.428 tons at 13s. 6¼d. per ton	19s. 3½d.
	Total	27s. 1¾d.

I think that this can be regarded as almost a maximum for Cornwall. The costs on the principal floors, with averagely pyritic ore, can be estimated, including wear and tear on tools and maintenance of the calciners, at about £1 per ton of black tin (II).

(I) At Carnbrea (1858) there are 2 calciners and 6 reverberatory furnaces, handled by 4 operators, 2 by day and 2 by night, each man working 1 calciner and 3 furnaces at the same time. The calciners work only on 'crop' ore. One handles the first roasting, passing 4 tons per 24 hours (6 hours per treatment), with the bedplate making 1 revolution every 35 minutes. The other, on the second roasting, treats 2 tons 16 cwts. per 24 hours, making 1 revolution every 70 minutes. Each calciner has rakes with 10 blades.

The slimes tin goes to the reverberatory furnaces, with a charge of 8 cwts. The treatment is occasionally prolonged up to 18 hours.

For a monthly production in the region of 40 tons of black tin, about 160 tons of material are roasted, averaging 25% black tin.

Overall, some 250 tons are roasted, using 60 tons of coal, or, per ton of black tin:

Manpower	3 days at 1s. 10d. per day	5s. 6d.
Coal	1.5 tons at 15s. 6¼d. per ton	23s. 3¼d.
	Total	28s. 9¼d.

Addtionally, some 17 tons of arsenic are produced each month.

(II) At Altenburg, in Saxony, using a reverberatory furnace, the costs are much higher:

Manpower	5 days at 8¼d. per day	3s. 7¼d.
Wood	4.17 tons at 9s. 7¼d. per ton	£2. 0s. 0¼d.
Sundries	-	1s. 7¼d.
	Total	£2. 5s. 2¾d.

To the cost of roasting must be added the value of tin lost. Even by assuming no more than a 1% loss of the treated ore, this cost is actually doubled, i.e. it rises to about £2.

On mines where the roasting operations are more difficult, due to an abundance of arsenical sulphides, a considerable compensation is often obtained from the sale of the dry arsenic trioxide recovered from the condensation chambers. So, at Tincroft during 1856, 150 tons 14 cwts. of black tin were produced along with 81 tons of arsenic sold for £178. 4s. 4¾d. This sum, related per ton of black tin, gives £1. 3s. 2½d. to be deducted from the cost of roasting, greatly reducing this to about 4s.

Finally, the precipitated copper recovered on scrap iron from leached copper solution is a further source of profit, though very variable compared with others.

§ X. General work over the entire floors.

Personnel – Water consumption – Cost of equipment and apparatus.

After having looked at the successive pieces of apparatus for ore treatment, we are led to take account of how they combine in the overall set-up of the dressing floors.

Handling of 'crop ore' from the 'common work' at Tincroft

First, I will examine the moving about of materials on that part of the Tincroft floors treating the crop from the 'common work' ore. Referring back to a previous table (pp.52-3), and the lengths of the various product divisions marked out in the strips and in the round and square buddles, it is possible, on the one hand, to calculate the cubic volume of each of these divisions, and on the other, to determine how many cubic metres of material each piece of apparatus has to treat per day, according to the procedure laid out in the table. The results of this calculation are shown.

Assuming intensive and very active work, the 28 heads of stamps on 'common work' ore fill 14 strips, and we have:

14 strips, **A**	1. 1.30m³	Round buddle, **B**	1. 3.50m³
	2. 3.80m³		2. 1.50m³
	3. 9.90m³		3. 7.00m³
Total	15.00m³	Total	12.00m³

Square buddle, **C**	1. 0.47m³	Round buddle, **B′**	1. 3.65m³
	2. 0.38m³		2. 8.35m³
	3. 0.37m³	Total	12.00m³
	4. 0.66m³		
Total	1.88m³		

Square buddle, **C₃**	1. 0.30m³	Square buddle, **E** and Kieves, **D**
	2. 1.00m³	to be borne
	3. 0.70m³	in mind
Total	2.00m³	

Apparatus	m³ handled per day	Personnel	Total earnings per day	Labour cost per m³	Ratio to ore received in the strips
14 strips, **A,A**	15.0	3, boys	2s	1.6d.	100%
2 round buddles, **B,B′**	20.0	4, boys	2s. 8d.	1.6d.	133%
2 square buddles, **C,C₃**	6.0	4, girls and boys	2s.	4d.	60%
1 square buddle, **E**	3.0	2, girls and boys	1s.	4d.	
3 kieves, **C**	1.50	3 girls, 1 boy	2s. 4d.	18.67d.	10%
Totals	45.50	17 workers	10s. 0d.		303%

From which it can be seen that the total amount of material handled each day as 'crop' work is three times the new feed that arrives in the strips during the same time.

Each day's work produces:

Tin witts, at 50% black tin	400 litres
Top skimmings, at 7 – 10% black tin	200 litres
Crazes, from buddle **C₃**	500 litres
(being 7.33% of the total volume)	1,100 litres
Rejected roughs and slimes carried to pits	13,900 litres
	15 m³

Since this part of the floors receives some 600 tons of sand each month, and that 9 tons of black tin are recovered:

Costs of manpower

Apparatus	Per month	Per ton of ore	Per ton of black tin
Strips	£3. 0s. 0d	1.2d.	6s. 8d.
Round buddles	£4. 0s. 0d.	1.6d.	8s. 10¾d.

Square buddles	£4. 10s. 0d	1.8d	10s. 0d.
Kieves	£3. 10s. 0d	1.4d.	7s. 9d.
Totals	£15. 0s. 0d	6d.	£1. 13s. 3¾d.

In making comparable calculations for the four large square buddles at Wheal Vor, we find that the 4 divisions, a, a', b and b', of the strips total 9 m³, or 20 m³ of moving material, and are treated for about 4s.

Operation o the 4 large square buddles at Wheal Vor

For 15 m³ of sand, as at Tincroft, the equivalent cost (*of treatment by square buddle*) would thus be 6s. 8d. as opposed to 2s. 8d. for the present treatment by round buddles. The increase in cost per day would, therefore, be 4s., in other words, raise it from 10s. to 14s. The sand obtained from large square buddles is better enriched than that of round buddles. Nevertheless, operation of the smaller 'tin cases' at Wheal Vor costs as much as that of the small square buddles at Tincroft.

The manpower needed at Tincroft to handle the 'crop' product would have to be raised by 40% if the round buddles there were replaced by large square buddles. An inverse change of apparatus at Wheal Vor could reduce their current manpower costs by 28.6%.

Taking only that portion of the total work whereby strip sands are rendered good enough for treatment by kieve, and considering the associated finishing 'tin cases' as either part of the large square buddle work or part of that of the round buddles, it is clear that the introduction of round buddles has generally reduced the working costs by more than half, in fact at Tincroft by two-and-a-half times.

Savings by the use of round buddles

Here is a résumé, from the same point of view, of the whole of the work on the floors of Par Consols. The following figures, very liable to variation, are by no means absolute values, and are not to be taken as an average indicator. For this purpose, the main and tributers' floors are combined.

Summary of the whole floor at Par Consols

Each day, about 50 tons of material are handled, of which 35 tons can be regarded as sands and 15 tons as slimes:

Before roasting

					\multicolumn{3}{c}{Cost per ton of material Received}
Divisions	No. of operators	Tons per day	Average tons per operator	Cost per day	Handled	On the floors	On the divisions
Crop	26	104	4.0	17s. 3½d	1.92d.	4.13d.	5.95d.
Roughs	30	150	5.0	15s. 0d.	1.25d.	3.84d.	5.47d.
Slimes	64	160	2.5	£1. 16s. 0d.	2.69d.	8.64d.	2s. 4.8d
Totals / averages	120	414	3.45	£3. 9s. 3½d.	-	1s. 4.61d.	-

Handling of material before roasting at Par Consols.

The various columns of the table show the relative importance of the divisions (or sections of work), and the difficulty and cost of work on each of them. I would point out the great expense involved with the slimes, whose contribution to the total black tin produced does not exceed one quarter.

Among the 64 operators on slimes, there are 28 girls on frames. Each of these handles barely 1 ton per day, the 'average' figure quoted being raised to 2.5 by the work of the boys at the slime pits, boxes and paddle trunks.

While 1 ton of crop material involves 3 tons in movement around the dressing floors, 1 ton of enriched slimes represents more than 10, the general average being 8.3 : 1, calculated by taking everything coming on to the floors as one single feed material.

After roasting The washing operations after roasting at Par Consols need:

1 Master dresser	£3 per month.
10 boys	15s. per month.
1 girl on a frame	£1 per month.
12 workers	£4. 15s. per month.

Per ton of black tin produced, the labour costs are from 8s. 5½d. up. If we take into consideration the need for repeated roasting, some 2 tons 8 cwts. has to come on to this part of the floors to yield 18 cwts. of black tin.

These figures give an indication of the multiplicity and care needed for effective treatment of roasted material, given that 2 tons 8cwts. demands the attention of 12 people.

Staff on the floors In September 1857, the staff on the dressing floors at Par Consols comprised 143 individuals, made up as follows:

12 men	5 at the stamps.
	2 on roasting furnaces.
	1 Master dresser, after roasting.
	1 Captain.
	2 Foremen / superintendents.
	1 Joiner / carpenter.
102	Girls and boys.
29	Women and girls on frames.
143	

On all other dressing floors with steam stamps the number of workers to supervise them could not be smaller than here, which can be taken as the minimum for tin production. The number of boys needed varies according to circumstances, and that of the girls working on frames to the overall proportion of slimes and the types of frames employed. The necessary staff after roasting depends on the pyritic content of the ore, and can, in fact, vary from day to day on any floor, according to the nature and quantity of the roasted products.

Formerly, on the floors at Polgooth, out of 110 workers, 7 were normally occupied in the 'dressing house' – 2 men, 2 women and 3 boys.

Consumption of water

We have already looked at the water consumption of various individual pieces of equipment; here are the figures relating to overall consumption <u>per minute</u>.

Apparatus	Water, per minute	Average
Square buddles (all types)	4 – 36 litres (0.9 – 8 gallons)	16 litres (3½ gallons)
Round buddles	"	30 litres (6⅔ gallons)
Tyes	"	48 litres (10⅔ gallons)
Paddle trunks (per trunk)		3 – 4 litres (⅔ - 0.9 gallons)
Frames (machine frames)		5 – 6 litres (1.1 - 1⅔ gallons)

Total water consumption per minute:

Par Consols	2,724 litres	605 gallons (**2¾ tons**)
Tincroft	1,943 litres	432 gallons (**2 tons**)
Balleswidden	1,716 litres	381 gallons (**1¾ tons**)

Water is almost everywhere a significant cause of expense, but one difficult to evaluate numerically. Most often, it involves extra work on the part of the pumping engine (as at Par Consols and Balleswidden) in raising water from adit level to the surface reservoir for dressing purposes, not forgetting the stamps engine, which also pumps clean water back from the lower parts of the floors in similar fashion. At Tincroft, this amounts to £100 per year.

Cost of apparatus

The main items of equipment, either of wood or masonry construction, cost:

Buddles	Large square buddles	£2. 10s. 0d.
	Ordinary square buddles	£2. 0s. 0d.
	Round buddles	£4. 0s. 0d.
Frames	Hand frames	£2. 0s. 0d.
	Self-acting (as Tincroft)	£2. 10s. 0d.
	Hancock frames	£10. 0s. 0d.
	New, long Hancock frames	£60. 0s. 0d.

Kieves	1s. per inch diameter	£2. 0s. 0d. (average price)
Roasting furnaces	Reverbatory type	£30. 0s. 0d.
(complete)	Revolving type	£250. 0s. 0d.

The total wooden apparatus on a large dressing floor such as Par Consols costs £400 - £500. Well-maintained, and looked after with light expense on materials by a single joiner / carpenter paid £3 per month, they can have a working life of up to 20 years, and depreciation is reckoned as not more than £40 - £50 per year.

Total costs The total cost of setting up a complete dressing floor, with 60 or 70 heads of stamps, is £2,800 - £3,200. To this must be added the cost of acquiring, adapting and setting out the site, which can be significant if many large terraces have to be constructed along with necessary light wooden buildings.

The maintenance and depreciation costs for the whole floor, assuming active, effective working and an ore carrying 2% black tin, come to no more than £1 per ton of black tin produced.

Section 4.

Economic considerations.

In this final part of the work I intend to bring together the economic information spread over sections 1 – 3, and to complete it such as to obtain the total costs of dressing. Included will be every major expense incurred in order to be able to produce tin metal, and I have added here some statistical information on tin production in Cornwall, along with the relative value of the metal at various times.

§ I. Costs of preparation.

The two preliminary operations, breakage of coarse, raw ore and weighing, sampling and assaying, constitute the transition from mining to mechanical preparation on the dressing floor, to which it is necessary to return first of all.

The cost of rock breaking The cost of rock breaking obviously varies with the relative hardness of the ore, and the size of the pieces judged appropriate to be fed to the stamps. The three following examples will provide an appreciation of these possible variations.

Par Consols demonstrates a more or less average situation. Each month 1,443 tons are sent for stamping. The proportion of barren, rejected material is small, and at least 1,500 tons of ore has to be broken.

The breakage of the largest lumps, or 'ragging', is done by 3 men, each paid £3 per month. The further breaking of smaller fragments, 'spalling', employs 20 women or older girls on piecework, paid according to their capability. The work can pay up to 1s. 2½d. per day for, at the most, 3 tons broken during that time. The overall costs of rock breaking are reckoned at 9d. per ton of ore ready for stamping (I).

(I) It is really 10½d., but there is reason to reduce this by one-eighth because of the mode of weighing the ore. (See below).

At Tincroft, the ore is hard but the breakage is coarse. A payment of 5s. is made per 100 'sacks' broken (this being equivalent here to 5.45 m^3, weighing 10 tons), or 6d. per ton. A day's pay for 'spallers' varies from 8¾d. to 10d.

At Balleswidden, the rock is not very hard but the necessary breakage is fine. Here, the payment is 8s. per 100 sacks, weighing 9 tons, or 10½d. per ton.

Converted to the relative costs per ton of black tin produced at each of these mines, the figures become:

> **Tincroft** £1. 13s. 7¼d.
> **Par Consols** £1. 18s. 11½
> **Balleswidden** £2. 10s. 0d.

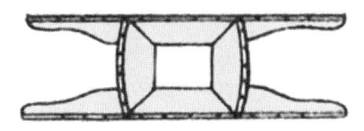

Weighing and measuring

A miner's batch of ore is sorted at the same time as it is broken. The 'best work' is separated, normally as a small quantity, and is weighed or measured as one lot. The 'common work' (*or normal grade ore, in a much greater quantity*) is divided into equal heaps, each built up successively by wheelbarrow loads. Several piles are made, each containing about 1 ton.

Sampling for assay

The Captain 'Assay Master' chooses any two of these piles, which are then opened down the middle. A barrowful of ore is taken from each, mixed, and from this mixture a large box is filled, holding about 1 cwt. This is then sent for assay.

He then designates one of the untouched piles and this is then measured, either by weight or by volume (if the ore is to be assessed by the number of sacks of a stated volume). The whole batch of ore is then evaluated by multiplying the result by the number of piles.

The system of weighing, infinitely more exact, tends to be preferred. However, some older miners keep to the use of volume measurement.

At Tincroft, a device known as a 'measuring barrow' is used, whose capacity is 1½ 'sacks', in this case 18 gallons. Below, are reproduced two lines from the 'measuring notebook':

15th August	Th. Trevillean	No. of sacks per pile	Total sacks
5 heaps	1 1 1 1 1 1 (6 measures)	9	45

At Par Consols, each pile is weighed in portions in a barrow, tared on a large set of scales. The weighing plate takes 2¼ cwts., that is, one-eighth over and above, which is discounted. The register of weights then indicates an official weight less one-ninth part (or 11.1%), which is reckoned as:

$$\begin{array}{rl} \textbf{Water} & 6.25\% \\ \textbf{Surplus} & \underline{4.86\%} \\ & 11.11\% \end{array}$$

This mode of evaluation serves no purpose other than that of wrongly depriving the miner directly. It allows the assayer, by adding to the loss on vanning by shovel, to arrive at a figure for a total black tin content of the batch of ore that is noticeably below that recovered on the dressing floor. The 'spallers' are paid by weight. The Master Assayer has two helpers, either girls or boys.

Returning charges

In Cornwall, work done underground in the mines, with enterprise always encouraged, is divided into two classes, 'tutwork' and 'tribute'. The 'tutwork men' drive levels and sink shafts, and are paid for progress achieved to specified dimensions by direct measurement of the work. They break down ground on lode and are paid, in general, by measurement on the plane of the lode, or in a small number of mines by the ton of ore broken.

The 'tributer' receives what is, in effect, a temporary concession (normally for one month) within assigned bounds in the mine workings. It is then up to him and his workmates to make the best of their 'pitch'. The value of ore broken is decided according to three rules:

1. The amount of 'tribute'. That is, the amount in shillings and pence, per pound sterling, of the absolute value, that is mutually agreed.
2. The 'standard', or fixed value of 1 ton of black tin agreed at the mine where he works.
3. The black tin content of his ore, as determined by assay.

The following describes how a tributer's ore is assessed, and how the 'returning charges' are calculated for the mechanical processing of his ore. I will assume assessment by weighing of the ore.

Register of assays

The master assayer keeps a book known as the 'sampling book', where he records the detailed results of his assays of all the parcels of ore. Each month, a summary shows the ore ready for stamping and its black tin content. For each batch of ore broken by a 'pare' (*or working group*) of tributers he records:

1. The date.
2. The name of the head of the pare.
3. The weight of each ore parcel (this information being drawn from the 'notebook' on the weighing site).
4. The black tin content per ton of ore.
5. The number of tons, cwts., qrs. and lbs. of black tin in each ore parcel.
6. The total of these amounts for each batch of ore.

Here are shown the main entry columns in the 'pay book' (I): *The 'pay book'*

  (a) The number of men (or boys) in the pare.
  (b) The name of the bargain taker (head of the group).
  (c) The weight of ore sent to the stamps.
  (d) The weight of black tin, by assay.
  (e) The fixed 'standard' per ton of black tin, as agreed for the floors.
  (f) The dry weight of black tin in the ore.
  (g) The 'returning charge', i.e. the overall cost of recovery of (f).
  (h) The net value of the black tin, after deduction of (g).
  (i) The 'tribute'. (Shillings and pence per £ to be paid on the tin value, agreed at the time of 'setting' the bargain, and variable according to (e) and (g) on each floor).
  (k) The product (h) x (i).
  (l) Deductions. Any advance payments made during the month, materials supplied – gunpowder, candles etc., sickness benefit contributions, medical aid, barber, any outstanding debts.
  (m) The balance. To either pay to the tributer, or enter as a continuing debt.

  So, we have the result: m = (d x e - g) x i - l

(I) Besides the 'sampling book', which provides (c) and (d), two other books are held on the mine. The 'setting book', which records the tribute conditions accepted by the taker of the bargain, and includes (a), (b) and (i), and one other that lists materials supplied and any advances in pay made during the month. This is the 'materials ledger', which provides (l).

On almost every mine the so-called 'returning charges' are decided in a different way. The following, however, explains three general methods: *Three ways of fixing 'returning charges'*

1. A returning charge in shillings per 100 sacks of ore sent to the stamps.

Examples: **Wheal Vor** and **Carnbrea**, at 40s. per 100 sacks, or about 4s. per ton, and **Tincroft**, at 50s., or about 5s. per ton.

2. A sliding scale, based on black tin content:

Dolcoath		Levant	
Black tin content	**Returning charge per ton**	**Black tin content**	**Returning charge per ton**
Up to 1.25%	2s.	Less than 5%	5s.
1.25 – 2.50%	3s.	5.00 – 8.00%	7s.
2.50 – 3.75%	3s. 6d.	8.00 – 12.00%	10s
3.75 – 5.00%	4s.	12.00 – 25.00%	12s. 6d.
5.00 – 6.25%	5s.	25% and above	20s
6.25 – 7.50%	6s.	**Wendron Consols**	
7.50 – 10.00%	7s.	Up to 1.85%	2s. 8d.
Above 10.00%	10s.	Above 1.85%	3s. 6d

3. Returning charges paid in kind. The Co. deducts a fraction either of the weight, or of ore ready for stamping, or of black tin.

Examples: **Par Consols**, where $\frac{1}{7}$ of the weight of the raw ore is retained, and **Polberro**, taking $\frac{1}{8}$ of the black tin, plus 1s. per ton of raw ore. It cannot be expected that the returning charges represent exactly the treatment costs, which, themselves, vary with the frequent changes made on the floors. (*On copper mines, the total costs of the treatment of tributers' ores were always deducted from their payment*).

This is only one of the elements aiding the management in determining the value of (m) sufficient to provide for the miner, and advantageous to themselves. The variations in (e) and (i) in the formula are predominant. It is, therefore, good, even for the Co., that the value of (g) approaches that of the true costs, in order for the quantities (e) and (i) to keep to common sense values. The so-called 'standard' (e), adopted by the mine, has an effect on *all* tributes, but this number, once fixed, means that the determination of (i), in every particular case, is subject to the judgement of the underground Captain, and must depend solely on the nature of the lode. These standards are set below the market value of black tin, and in general remain fixed on each dressing floor for quite long periods.

However, when the price of black tin takes a strong drop the value of (e) is reduced, avoiding changing the tributes, which makes for difficult relations between the tributers and the mine agents (I).

It must be appreciated that the tributers remain charged for the cost of breaking and sorting their ore, that is, they are only supposed to pay those dressing expenses associated with preparation for stamping.

The rules and conditions set out above will result in the following costs for average grade ores:

	Per ton of black tin	
Carnbrea	£9. 16s. 5d.	The true cost is £10. 8s. 10d.
Tincroft	£17. 12s. 0d.	
Dolcoath	£6. 0s. 0d.	
Levant	£10. 9s. 7d.	
Wendron Consols	£4. 18s. 5d.	
Par Consols (II)	£13. 12s. 0d.	Approximately. It varies with the price of black tin (breakage included).

(I) The 'standards' were:

	Per ton of black tin
Par Consols	£50 (1857)
Polberro	£56 (1858)
Wheal Vor	£60 (1855)
Tincroft	£60 (1857)
Wendron Consols	£60 (1858)
Dolcoath	£60 (1857)

(II) At Par Consols, $1/7$ of 1 ton of black tin, at a standard of £50, gives only £7. 2s. 10d. However, the surplus yield on the stated assay value being about 10%, it is necessary to add to the tributers' charges (and to the gain of the management) 2 cwts. (100 Kg.) of black tin at market value. This being, on average, £68 per ton, the returning charges are therefore augmented by £6. 16s. bringing the total to between £13. 12s. and £14.

A. Costs of mechanical preparation for 1 month on the dressing floors of Par Consols.

| Type of expenses |||| Number of workers ||| Totals ||
General		Specific		Men	Boys or girls	Women on frames	Partial	General
Labour	On the ore	Breakage	Ragging	3			£9. 0s.	£52. 19s.
			Spalling		20		£43. 19s	£61. 4s
		Assay	1 master	1			£6. 5s.	£8. 5s.
			2 helpers		2		£2. 0s.	
	On the floors	Stamping		5			£16. 0s.	
		Before roasting	Crop & roughs		42		£34. 0s.	£100. 0s
			Slimes		26	14	£34. 0s.	
			Tributers' floors		24	14	£32. 0s.	£152 0s.
		Roasting		2			£5. 10s.	
		After roasting		1	10	1	£11. 10s	
		Supervision	Captain	1			£6. 5s.	£16. 0s.
			Foreman	1			£3. 15s.	
			Supervisor of tributers	1			£6. 0s.	
		Joiner / carpenter		1			£3. 0s.	
	Totals			16	124	29	Workforce 169	
Coal	Stamping – 67 tons			88 tons			£57. 4s. 0d	
	Roasting – 21 tons							
Cast iron, wrought iron, grease for the stamps								£31. 17s. 10d
Sundry expenses, tools, furnace maintenance, washing apparatus, interest and depreciation								£27. 3s. 6d.
Total expenses on the ore and dressing floors (transport not included)								£329. 9s. 4d
Expenses on the dressing floor alone								£268. 5s. 4d.

B. Cost of mechanical preparation on the dressing floor of Par Consols.

	Per ton of sorted ore			Per ton of black tin ready for sale			
Labour	3.513 days		3s. 0d.	Men	17.6 days	186.57 days	£7. 16s. 11d
				Boys and girls	136.88 days		
				Women on frames	32.09 days		
Coal	Stamps	0.046 t.	0.06 tons	0s. 9½d.	2.469 tons	3.234 tons	£2. 1s. 3½d.
	Roasting	0.014 t.			0.765 tons		
Cast & wrought iron, grease for stamps			0s. 5½d.				£1. 3s. 11¾d.
Sundry expenses			0s. 4d.				£1. 0s. 3½d.
Total costs (transport not included)			4s. 7d.				£12. 2s. 5¾d.

Reducing the principal costs to rounded percentages of the total gives us the following split:

Breakage of ore	16%	
Stamping	27%	(43%)
Labour before roasting	30%	
Roasting	6%	
Labour after roasting	3%	
Supervision and assay	8%	
Sundries	10%	
Total	100%	

The labour before roasting accounts for 30% of the total costs, and is almost equally split between the washing of sands and washing of slimes on the main floors, and treatment of the residues by the tributers.

These latter recover each month material as crazes and enriched slimes that carry marginally over 2 tons 3 cwts. of black tin, or ⅛ of the total production. The tribute agreed is 9s. in the £, on a 'standard' determined in such a way that the earnings of the head of the tributers' group do not exceed £6 for the month.

Labour on this part of the floors is worth about £38 per month, or more than one-third of the costs after stamping and before roasting. Per ton of black tin content, these expenses rise to £17. 16s. In recognising that in achieving the preparation of these types of materials, the expense is from £4 - £6 more, it can be seen that some £22 - £24 will have to be dedicated to the recovery of 1 ton of black tin from the mixture of about ⅔ coarse sands and ⅓ slimes leaving the main floors (I).

If, instead of thinking of two separate parts of the floors, they are considered in their entirety, the natural divisions into 'crop', 'roughs' and 'slimes' are instantly seen to carry respectively about ½, ¼ and ¼ of the total black tin. The costs of labour before roasting, per ton of black tin ultimately recovered, are split as:

Crop	£1. 18s. 5d.	Per ton of mixed	**Crop**	£0. 19s. 2½d.
Roughs	£3. 10s. 5d.	black tin ready for	**Roughs**	£0. 17s. 7¼d.
Slimes	£8. 0s. 0d.	sale, they become	**Slimes**	£2. 0s. 0d.

(I) The content of this mixture seems to me to be able to be evaluated at 0.6% black tin, or 12 – 15 lbs. per ton.

The cost of labour on a single floor

According to the method of accounting followed in Cornwall, the payments for labour paid each month to the workers employed on a single floor are made up to a number divided by the number of tons of black tin produced. Decided in this way, the costs take no account of rock breaking, assaying, the stamps mechanics, the carpenter or the Captain.

Elsewhere, the labour is the principal variable part of the total costs of preparation, and for a given ore, depend on the work being well organized and directed, while operations on the raw ore, the consumption of coal by the stamps, and various materials involve an expenditure that remains almost constant. It is not a question of reducing the labour, but obviously of using it on each floor to recover as much black tin as possible.

The table below shows the approximate costs, as judged suitable to make, on several large dressing floors, according to the nature of the ore and the system of work, and I take complete responsibility for any errors that might be found in the figures.

It appeared to me, even looked at individually, that considerable differences would stand out, such as necessarily exist from one mine to another. Any discussion of these figures, which I shall not enter into, could only be done with complete knowledge of the individual system of working.

This is particularly so for those floors where the expenditure already seems very high, yet there is a reason to suggest that it be increased. Or another where it does not need to be as low as it is, or yet another where, with less expenditure, but better methods, more black tin would be recovered.

I have combined in the same table various appropriate pieces of information that characterise the importance of the floors – the number of heads of stamps, the tonnage stamped each month, the black tin prepared, and finally the workforce.

Table of costs from the point of view of labour on a single floor, per ton of black tin.

Mine	Heads of stamps	Tons Stamped per month	Tons of black tin produced	Yield of black tin	Workforce, as 1 floor Men	Girls & boys	Total	Labour per ton of black tin	
Levant	48+16 = 64	666	16.0	2.401%	26	143	169	£10. 1s. 7d.	(a)
Botallack	Water stamps	400	16.8	4.10%	17	55	72	£5. 12s. 0d.	(b)
Wheal Bal	16	100	8.0	8.00%	3	20	23	£3. 12s. 0d.	
Providence	30+16 = 46	320	32.0	10.00%	10	86	96	£3. 3s. 2d	(c)
Wendron Consols	24+18+6+3 = 51 Water stamps	642	22.5	3.505%	3	81	84	£3. 8s. 10d.	
Dolcoath	64+48 = 112 (88 effective)	2,000	50.0	2.50%	65	375	440	£7. 7s. 2d.	(d)
Carnbrea	96	1,914	36.1	1.886%	38	220	258	£7. 2s. 5d.	(e)
Par Consols	68	1,443	27.2	1.883%	11	131	142	£4. 17s. 7d	(f)

(a) Two-thirds of the black tin is slime tin. The stamps are 'flashers'.
(b) One-half of the black tin is slime tin. The stamps are 'flashers'.
(c) One third of the black tin is slime tin.
(d) Workers whose salary exceeds £2 per month are counted as 'men'.
(e) Only one-eighth of the black tin is slime tin. Spalling costs included, as are supervision and assaying.
(f) One-quarter of the black tin is slime tin.

Black tin content

Below is a table of recoverable black tin content, as determined by assay at certain mines:

Providence	10.00%	
Wheal Bal	8.00%	
Botallack	4.10%	
Wendron Consols	3.505%	
Dolcoath	2.50%	
Charlestown (abandoned)	2.50%	
Levant	2.40%	
St. Day United	2.03%	
Carnbrea	1.886%	
Balleswidden	1.830%	
Par Consols	1.827%	
Tincroft	1.42%	
Great Polgooth (viewed on the mine)	0.90%	
Polberro (viewed on the mine)	0.777%	
Carclaze (stockwork)	0.40%	'Best' 0.625% 'Common' 0.30%

Cost of preparation of an average ore

The yield from the average tin ore treated in Cornwall can be estimated fairly exactly at 2% by weight, that is, some 50 tons of ore have to be stamped to produce 1 ton of black tin.

Considering the example of Par Consols, one can say that with an ore of average hardness, with quite fine tin and a yield that varies either side of about 2%, it is advisable to look at a sum of £12 - £13 per ton of black tin produced by mechanical treatment, or around 4s. 10d. per ton of broken and sorted ore.

Minimum tin content for viable working

In taking for black tin a minimum value of £60 per ton, or about 6½d. per lb., the costs of treatment will be covered by 8½ - 9 lbs. recovered from 1 ton of ore, or 0.4% as an average recoverable tin content (I).

(I) At a price of £80 per ton (as in 1857), the costs are covered by a 0.3% recovery, or 6¾ lbs. per ton.

Adding on the mining costs, the following types of lodes may still be advantageously worked:

Lodes

According to Captain	Minimum tin content, by assay	Type of lode and ore
Puckey	28 lbs. per ton – 1.25%	Par Consols, a large mine
Ch. Thomas	22 lbs. per ton – 1.00%	Dolcoath, a large mine
Hancock	16 lbs. per ton – 0.71%	Polgooth, above adit
Baratt (sic)	14 – 15 lbs. per ton – 0.63%	Soft ore and coarse tin

At Carclaze the tin content is far less, but the extraction of the ore is very cheap. Most of it falls of its own account, in winter, from the steep faces of the excavation, which also produces kaolin or 'china clay' by washing. Several very rich veinlets are followed individually amongst the irregular workings of the clay extraction, where the tin is present as coarse grains. The purity and cleanliness of the tin ore makes roasting unnecessary, and assures a high price for the black tin concentrate. Water powered stamps, with coarse screens, work very well, and I believe the treatment costs can be calculated at:

Carclaze stockwork

Breakage by hammer	1s.	However, per ton of black tin produced, the cost rises to at least £29.
Stamping	4d.	
Washing and cleaning	1s.	
Treatment cost per ton of ore	2s. 4d.	

With the sands from stream works there is no raw breakage, only partial stamping of any coarser pebbles, very few slimes and no roasting. At £60 per ton for black tin, the treatment costs of 1 ton of sands are covered by a recovery of 0.1% of black tin, or 2¼ lbs. per ton. The possibilities of working such sands therefore rest almost entirely on the mass of excavations that have to be made and the removal of water, either by running away or pumping, but the mechanical treatment of the ore is relatively easy compared to that of other tin deposits.

Stream work

As is the case with all metallurgical operations, it is impossible to evaluate exactly the tin losses occurring during treatment. However well the assays are performed, this never provides sufficient guarantee. On the other hand, the assay samples that I have been provided with, and which I have analysed comparatively by wet method, were not numerous enough to enable me to ascertain with any certainty the losses in vanning.

Possible tin losses during treatment

The difficulty of making an assay is made still greater when it comes to assessing the tin in the discarded material. Nevertheless, the importance of keeping account, however approximate, of these losses, leads me to give, with reservations, the figures that I have obtained for the dressing floors at Par Consols.

1. On analysis, the losses during vanning would be:

'Best work', carrying 20 – 25%,	5 – 10% of the black tin content
'Common work', carrying 2 – 3%,	20 – 25% of the black tin content
The probable average on 2.5%,	20% of the black tin content

It is normally necessary to add 4.86% to the weight of black tin on the shovel.

The assay register will therefore indicate only about 75% of the black tin content, or a loss of about 25%. The ore at Par, assumed in dry condition, gives 2% black tin recovered on the floors. The tin content indicated by vanning assay is 1.827%, so the recovery exceeds this by 10%, and the actual vanning loss is 17.5%.

2. The slimes leaving the paddle trunks (N_2 and Q_2) make up one-third of the material, with a black tin content of 0.7% (15.68 lbs. per ton).

The sands leaving the tributers' floors make up the remaining two-thirds, and have a black tin content of 0.4% (8.96 lbs. per ton).

0.7 x 0.33 = 0.233
0.4 x 0.67 = 0.266

Indicating an overall loss of 0.5% on a recovery of 2%, giving:
Recovered black tin – 25% loss.
Indicated black tin content – 20% loss.

From these two points of view the loss at Par Consols would be about one-fifth, or 20% of the black tin content.

Value of the combined cost and losses

If we take V as the value of 1 ton of black tin recovered, and D as the total expense of metal lost and the treatment costs, then:

D = 0.25 V + £13.

If V = £60, then D = £28, and if V = £80, then D = £33.

Comparison of sands and slimes

Taking my given figures regarding labour costs before roasting, and, by observation, that the loss of black tin is split, like the labour costs, almost equally between slimes and sands, it can be seen that, while the mass of the slimes is only half that of the sands, for equal weights of these materials, the slimes contribute double the loss, and cost twice as much in labour on this part of the floors.

At Tincroft, where there is no treatment of 'roughs', it is likely that on a yield of 1.6% of black tin recovered, the losses reach 33% of the actual black tin sold.

Comparison of costs of mechanical

Here is not the place to go into the methods of tin metallurgy practised in Cornwall, but it is interesting to compare the expenditure incurred on dressing floors to that of a smelting plant.

During the long and elaborate processing that the ore undergoes in order to arrive in a metallic state, it will be noted that the smelter has only a few things to do to complete the work of ore dressing.

Black tin is sold to smelters by private contract. Around 1837 public 'ticketings' were tried, as conducted for copper ores, but it was not long before this was dropped. The mining companies transport their ore in sacks to the smelter, generally by wagon or by rail. When the ore is purchased by the smelter nearest to the mine, the transport is the responsibility of the latter. In every other case the smelter reimburses any additional expense, known as 'extra carriage'. At the smelter, a definitive assay, attended by both parties, allows the fixing of the purchase price, which is decided on the basis of:

1. The current price of metallic tin.
2. The tin content and 'quality' of the parcel (*i.e. presence of impurities etc.*)(I).

The smelter deducts as his 'returning charges' 1¼ parts of tin metal in 20 parts of ore (equivalent to a reduction of the agreed assay value by 6.25%), or 137.8 lbs. of metal in 1 ton of black tin, or, with ore of an average content of 66.5%, 9.36% of the weight of the black tin.

Besides this, he also deducts 3 lbs. per cwt. under the heading of 'wastage':

$3/112$ = 2.68%, bringing the total deductions to 12.04%.

(I) At Par Consols, the black tin sold between 10th of March and the 27th of August 1857:

	Tons	Cwts	Qrs	Lbs	Black tin content	Price per ton
1st parcel	145	4	3	10	68.75%	£80
2nd parcel	4	4	0	14	57.50%	£50

Here, in addition, is a table resulting from assays performed by Mr. Johnson, and showing how rapidly the price given by the smelter decreases with black tin content.

Black tin content (deduction of 6.25% made as 'returning charge')	Price paid per ton of black tin	Price paid per ton of metal (deduction made of 'returning charge')
56.75%	£42. 5s. 0d.	£74. 10s. 0d.
47.75%	£32. 15s. 0d.	£68. 12s. 0d.
41.75%	£27. 10s. 0d.	£65. 12s. 0d.
35.75%	£18. 10s. 0d.	£51. 16s. 0d.
32.75%	£15. 0s. 0d.	£46. 0s. 0d.

These figures appear to relate to the year 1848, and to an average value of £78. 10s. per ton of tin metal.

The relative treatment costs per ton of black tin are:

Par Consols dressing floors			Smelting plant	
186.57 days	£7. 16s. 11d	Labour	0.6545 days	1s. 7d.
Stamping, 2.469 tons			Coal	
Roasting, 0.765 tons		Fuel	Anthracite	16s. 3d
3.234 tons	£2. 1s. 3½d.		Wood	½d.
Materials & sundries	£2. 4s. 3½d.	Extras	Stamping, washing slag	4d.
			Various, tools, repairs	9½d
	£12. 2s. 6d.	Totals		19s. 0d.

Total expense. Costs and probable losses

Losses at the smelter are equally difficult to evaluate. I will state that the average black tin actually contains 73% metallic tin. The smelting yield being 66.5%, the loss is 6.5%, mainly left as tin silicate in the slag. A comparison of the figures above shows that labour costs are 100 times greater for dressing. The consumption of fuel is triple, just for stamping, and more or less the same value for the average roasting conducted on various dressing floors.

As to losses per ton of black tin in smelting, these are:

	Losses per ton of black tin	
	Recovered	**Stated content**
Dressing	551 lbs.	441 lbs.
Smelting	216 lbs.	236 lbs.
	767 lbs.	677 lbs.

In taking the average prices in 1855 (see later) of £68 per ton for black tin, and £120 per ton for the metal, the costs will be:

Cost of preparation and smelting (round numbers)	£14. 0s. 0d.
Losses – 767 lbs @ 7.4d. per lb.	£23. 13s. 3d.
	£37. 13s. 3d.

to produce 1,473 lbs. of metal at 12.875d. per lb. worth £78. 18s. 0d. In other words, the total production cost is almost half that of the metal obtained.

§ II. Statistics. (I)

De la Bêche gives a complete table relating to the production of metallic tin in Cornwall from 1750 to 1838, and the prices of the metal from 1780 to 1838. From this, I have taken the following figures showing maxima and minima for both production and price. Conversion from English values has involved some approximation.

Year	Tons of tin metal produced	Price per ton
1750	3,179	-
1751	2,400	-
1772	3,400	-
1780	3,230	£67. 10s.
1793	3,400	£101. 10s.
1801	2,400	£104. 10s.
1810	2,100	£157. 0s. (Napoleonic War)
1817	4,000	£113. 0s.
1820	2,890	£73. 0s.
1838	5,130	£82. 0s.

(I) Most of the information in this section is taken, for older times, from the work of de la Bêche, and after 1853 from the published Mining Records, produced annually by Robert Hunt, in the Memoirs of the Geological Survey of Great Britain, along with extracts from the 'Annales des mines', the work of M. Delesse.

Since 1853, Mr. Robert Hunt, in his annual statistics of mineral production for Great Britain, has provided exact and detailed information, including the following:

		Year			
		1853	1854	1855	1856
Cornwall & Devon	Black tin (tons)	8,866	8,747	8,947	9,350
	Tin metal (tons)	5,763	5,947	6,000	6,177
	Smelters' yield	65%	67.5%	68.86%	66.05%
Average price	Per ton of black tin	£68	£64	£68	£71
	Per ton of tin metal	-	£115. 10s	£120	£133
Imports (tons)	Dutch Indies, Banca etc. Straits Australia, Peru, France, etc.	2,449	2,251	1,612	3,464 & 749 regulus
Exports (tons)		1,277 1,073	1,406 669	1,338 280	1,874 200

During the year 1857 tin metal rose to a very high value, and black tin was selling at £80 per ton. In September, when the great commercial crisis in America came to affect European markets, the black tin price fell to £60 per ton from November, and in December the price of 1 ton of the metal was:

Variations in the black tin price

English £115
Banca £104
Straits £102

The great variations in the price paid for black tin are very injurious to the general prosperity of the mines. When it is high there is increased activity everywhere, and new enterprises are set up with unwise confidence, only to be abandoned at the next fall, and downright loss results from a stoppage of work in any mine.

In contrast, these variations in the black tin price are one of the main sources of profit to the smelters, for whom, as with all English industries, a good head for business has far more important consequences than a thorough understanding of how to operate the plant. This is easy to appreciate by comparing the average price of 1 ton of tin metal to that paid for an equivalent quantity in the concentrated ore.

	1855	1856
Price of 1 ton of metal	£120	£133
Price for 1 ton of tin in black tin	£98. 15s.	£107. 8s. 10d.
Difference	£21. 5s.	£25. 11s. 2d.
Difference per ton of black tin	£14. 12s. 6d.	£16. 17s. 10d.

These differences reflect the costs and elevated profit of the smelters. The antagonism between the interests of the smelters and the mines is extremely disturbing to the latter, and has an effect on the situation of the miners, whose pay, already not over generous, is sometimes obliged to be reduced, under the possibility of stopping work entirely.

The large mines protest against this and put up some resistance. In the winter of 1858 the Directors of Par Consols announced their intention of withholding in store their black tin for sale ('stocking') until the price paid for it by the smelters was raised, and even to look at smelting it themselves at the nearby Par lead smelter, which they also owned.

The effect of concentrate 'quality'

At any given time, the various mines can expect to receive different prices for their black tin product, as a result of differences in its 'quality'. I have already mentioned the influence of the presence of wolfram, which can lower the price paid by £20 or £30 per ton.

Very pure black tin commands a price notably above the average. Thus, at Carclaze in 1857, it reached £83 per ton.

Some years ago a Frenchman, M. Duclos, introduced into Cornwall a method of purification that entailed digesting the prepared black tin concentrate in hydrochloric acid. Although this method has given good results, its usage is not widespread.

Production of the principal mines in 1856

In the following table I have combined the production of the principal mines in 1856, leaving aside those selling less than 100 tons. They are in order of revenue (not included), and I have omitted any fractional tons. The relative importance of the tin districts can be judged, and it will be seen how much the former source of tin mineral riches, the Stream Works, seem worked out today:

Relative importance of the tin districts

Western district		Central district		Eastern district	
Mines	**Tons**	**Mines**	**Tons**	**Mines**	**Tons**
Boscean	284	Dolcoath	417	Par Consols	316
Balleswidden	268	Great Wheal Vor	425	Drake Walls	232
Huel Owles	232	Carnbrea	294	Great Polgooth	209
Reeth Consols	264	Polberro Mines	262	Boscundle	139
Providence Mines	242	Porkellis	236	Great Beam	115
Ding Dong	212	Great Work	188	17 mines	1,395
Huel Margaret	245	Trumpet Consols	168		
Levant	218	Huel Kitty (St. Agnes)	174		
St. Ives Consols	212	Pednandrea	141		
Botallack	149	Tincroft	151		
Huel Kitty (Lelant)	149	Great Wheal Fortune	127		
Huel Mary	121	Huel Tremayne	118		
West Wheal Providence	101	Wendron Consols	130		
Carnyorth	101	St. Day United	140		
26 mines	3,278	79 mines	4,367		
Various mines, numbered at 18, most of which are worked for copper					66 tons
4 Stream Works					10 tons
Devonshire, 6 mines					137 tons
Total weight of tin ore on which duty has been paid					9,243 tons

The tin mines also produce arsenic trioxide as an accessory mineral. The raw arsenic recovered from the condensation chambers sells for £2 per ton. Refined, it fetches £8 - £12 per ton.

Arsenic trioxide

A sample of the former, taken at St. Day United, gave the following analysis:

Arsenic trioxide	68.25%
Tin oxide	1.40%
Iron oxide	2.86%
Antimony	Trace
Sulphur	0.40%
Sulphuric acid	5.50%
Killas and quartz	7.20%
Calcium carbonate	1.00%
Carbon	2.00%
Water	11.00%
	99.61%

In 1856 the Cornish mines sold 513 tons 14 cwts. of raw arsenic for £1,011.

Shipped from the port of Truro	1855	660 tons
	1856	406 tons

§ III. Observations and conclusions.

For all metals, mechanical treatment of the ore and the metallurgical stage are intimately linked. The demands of the smelting plant make the rules for the dressing floor, and nowhere is this more the case than with tin. If galena (*lead ore*) needs to be raised to a higher grade, the treatment costs do not rise proportionally, and the value of the material lost is small. Should there be silver present to raise the value of the ore, then one settles for a lower yield, which more than compensates. For copper ores, whose value is nowhere near that of tin, it is recognized that very impure and poor ores are still saleable and can be smelted.

The enormous costs and losses imposed on tin dressing floors are the result of three principal causes:

1. The extreme difficulty of obtaining really pure tin concentrate.

2. The general differences of interest between the mines and the smelters.

3. And, especially, the power of tradition.

There is no disguising the importance of the first of the above, the 'nuisance' minerals such as copper, lead, zinc, tungsten, sulphur, arsenic, antimony, iron and the gangue are more than sufficient to make the point.

However the temperature is kept during the reduction of tin oxide by smelting, there is a tendency for the metal to combine chemically with iron, reduced at the same time. The ease of formation of fusible silicates of tin and iron ensures that quite a lot of tin ends up in the slag. Any reduction of metals in the slag needs a very high temperature, and only results in producing 'irony tin', or, rather, 'tinny iron'.

Is one then to conclude that any change in actual methods is impracticable? I do not think so. On the contrary, I believe that there is reason to attempt radical reform of both dressing and metallurgy at the same time. In other words, look for a way of directly treating poor ores and concentrates. As I have shown, the true costs and losses, which I do not believe I have exaggerated, leave a large margin available. Even continuing to rely on physical properties – low melting point and high density – could one not, among the chemical properties of tin, find and use others just as easy for its reduction? The man who has great mineral riches at his disposal and always lets a large part of it go to waste despite being able to remedy it, is truly guilty in the eyes of posterity.

From another point of view, there is reason to propose, from now on, use of the progress in modern day chemistry, and the chance of profiting by so doing.

In my opinion, in spite of the considerable progress in mechanical methods of treatment over the past thirty years, and in spite of what is still possible in that direction, the greatest improvement would be to replace this by looking at one particular part of treatment costs created, carried forward and accumulated on the dressing floors. The production of a high proportion of slimes is never avoided, and the excessive dilution of this material always militates against the reduction of any losses in washing.

Apart from these observations, and considering the actual operating circumstances governing treatment, it can be considered as well conducted. For stamping, only the fine detail of the layout can be improved. As to the manipulation of material:

1. Treatment of the 'crop' material is good, and the introduction of round buddles leaves little room for improvement.
2. For the 'roughs', the use of well-designed and efficient valves on the boxes ahead of paddle trunks is most advantageous. At present restricted to a few mines, I believe there is a need for their coming into general use.

In these two sections of the work, as in the case of the slimes, it would be beneficial, before sending them to washing operations, to concentrate on achieving perfect homogeneity. This could be easily done by increasing the number of small paddle wheels on the floors, to serve as mixers. In the special case of cleaning coarse sands, the attrition (*or rubbing together*) of the grains against each other would help greatly to detach any adhering slimes. A wheel of this type would be advantageously placed a few metres above the valve regulating the discharge of roughs.

3. For some years, every effort on the part of the more intelligent dressing Captains has been directed towards the slimes. The new, large Hancock Frame is the most improved apparatus of its type in Britain today, but nothing equivalent to the round buddle for sands has been found for slimes treatment.

I have been fairly insistent on the size classification to be looked for on the various classes of slimes. The main slimes pass to the 'roughs box', then to two stages of paddle trunks. Those from the small, secondary slime pits are kept separate, and in the case where (as at Par Consols) the pit contents are recombined in a single, slightly elongated, single trough, three product divisions are again made, for separate treatment. For more than ten years now, German floors have used a series of pyramidal boxes, known as 'spitzkasten apparatus', for the classification of their slimes (I). Nothing would be simpler than to first of all substitute these for the small slime pits. Experiment, whose success on 'gritty' slimes seems to me to be beyond question, would serve as a guide to trials that could be made on particularly fine main slimes.

(I) Rivot, 'Mechanical treatment of lead ores in the Upper Harz', *Annales des mines*, Vol. XIX, 1858.

A few years ago, German dressers devised rotating tables for washing slimes, seemingly giving good results. I have seen nothing of this apparatus, and the information given to me in this regard is insufficient to recommend these ingeniously laid-out tables being brought into use for the treatment of tin slimes, particularly in view of the excessive fineness of the latter.

(It is my opinion that the above statement refers to the piece of apparatus that came to be referred to in Britain as the 'Zenner buddle', a convex, revolving, continuously-operating table. Patented in Germany in the early 1850's, this device was later installed on the dressing floors at both Botallack and Levant in the early 1860's, and remained in use there for a number of years, not necessarily on slimes – A.J.C.)

NOTE:

On the methods of assaying tin ores, and the examination of samples.

Assay by 'vanning shovel' for black tin

The chosen 1 cwt. (50 Kg.) assay sample of raw ore is taken to the Master Assayer's laboratory, where his helpers first break the whole of the material down to a finer size, mixing this first product by shovel and taking out a small quantity, which they then pulverise and pass through an iron wire mesh sieve. The powdered sub-sample is then thoroughly dried on a shovel over a low charcoal fire. The assayer receives it and, depending on which system of raw ore quantity assessment is in use at the mine, he either measures or weighs about 2 ozs.

The assayer's tools

His tools are:
- A large, slightly concave, round-ended shovel, about 15" wide at the socket end, and approximately the same length. The handle is about 4' long and fixed underneath the blade.
- A large kieve, almost full of water. An upright pack or pile of wood, to one side, serves as a rest for the shovel, which is maintained in place by a hook, under which the front edge of the blade is pushed.
- A double-ended hammer head, or mass of iron, to break or grind coarser material on the shovel.
- Finally, a crucible.

The powdered sample is diluted in suspension on the blade of the shovel with a little water taken from the kieve. The subsequent manipulation of the shovel by the assayer, which is very difficult to describe, may be summed up in two main actions:

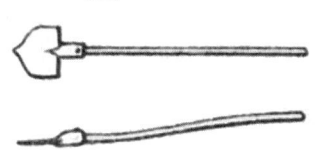

1. 'Cleaning' of the sample by rapid agitation, which washes out slimy water as material is swirled in the water on the shovel.
2. Separation and enrichment of the sample by a series of small up-and-down and back-and-forth jerks of the shovel, which causes the heavier or denser material to be propelled diagonally up the blade of the shovel, away from the main mass. The poorer sands are washed down to the back of the deposit, where material judged to be barren is carried to the opposite rear edge and discarded by a flick of the shovel. The enriched ore contains 'crazes' (*coarser grains with some 'locked' tin*). The assayer rests the shovel on the wooden pile, and, with one end of the hammer head vigorously grinds the sands. He then repeats the tin separation and washing process, finishing with a product equivalent to tin 'witts', which needs a more or less extended roasting, depending on the content of pyritic material (I), performing this in his earthenware crucible of about 3" diameter, on a grille above an ordinary, hot coal fire. In order to get the tin witts into the crucible, he first quickly dries them over the fire on the shovel blade, and then brushes them into the crucible with a fine, hare's-foot brush. When the ore is seen to be completely roasted (*no more white fumes etc.*), it is returned to the shovel, washed, ground, re-washed, dried and finally weighed.

(I) At Tincroft, this roasting lasts maybe 15 or 20 minutes.

Here, now, is the way in which the black tin content of a batch of raw ore is assessed and calculated:

1. The parcel of raw ore is measured in 'sacks' of, say, 12 gallons (II).

Calculation of black tin content of a batch of ore

(II) The 'sack' is a purely local measurement. At Tincroft and Carnbrea etc. it is 12 gallons, At Levant, 14 gallons, and at Wendron Consols, 11 gallons, and so on. Everywhere, however, the assay is reported as the weight of black tin 'per ½ - noggin' of ore, the various calculation tables employed working to different mathematical bases.

The assayer first measures out his sample of the dry, pulverised ore taken from the original 1 cwt. sample in a small, cylinder holding '¼ of a noggin', that is 2.166 cubic inches (or 32.333 cc.). In doing this, he tips the first contents of the measure out on to a small blade with edges, and refills the small measure a second time, levelling it off with a sort of trowel and being careful not to impart any little knocks or jerks, the degree of packing down of the material in the measure being only the same if identical precautions are taken each time.

The small weight of black tin concentrate obtained is determined on the 'Troy weight' system (I), especially reserved for assaying, with the weight being expressed in 'grains' and 'pennyweights'. The assayer has a conversion table, assuming the assay to have been made on a ½ - noggin of sample. For the purposes of this hypothesis, it is taken (at Tincroft) that each 9 grains recovered on assay represents 1 cwt., 0 quarters, 0 lbs. of black tin per 100 sacks of ore (i.e. 112 lbs. per 10 tons, or 11.2 lbs. per ton, or 0.5%). The rest of the table gives in quarters (28 lbs.) and lbs. the quantities corresponding to 8, 7, 6 down to 1 grain, enabling the assessment of a wide range of ores both above and below this value.

It is of no use to show here the actual end of the calculation, but I would make the observation that the principle of this evaluation consists of assuming the complete equality of the ratio:

One ½ - noggin of dry sand per 100 sacks of damp ore fragments = 9 grains per cwt.

Whereas, careful comparison actually gives:

One ½ - noggin per 100 sacks = $1/7.680$

but 9 grains per cwt. = $1/7.168$

It is natural that the original assumption should be less accurate and reliable, since the bulk density of ore broken and ready for stamping is greater than that of the sand in the small assay measure.

Experience leads to the adoption of the figures in the table, so as to allow for water in the sorted ore, and that there is still a financial advantage for the management.

(I) A comparison of Troy and Avoirdupoids weight systems:

'Troy' weight, for assays	Avoirdupoids weight system
24 grains 1 pennyweight	16 drams 1 oz. (= 437½ grains)
20 pennyweights 1 Troy oz. = 480 grains	16 ozs. 1 lb. (= 7,000 grains)
12 Troy ozs. 1 Troy lb. = 5,760 grains	28 lbs 1 quarter (of 1 cwt.)
	20 cwts 1 ton (= 2,240 lbs.)

(In the above, the 'grain' is the same for both weight systems, their basic relation being that 5,760 grains = 1 lb. Troy, and 7,000 grains = 1 lb. Avoirdupoids).

2. The parcel of ore has been weighed.

The assay is conducted on the basis of 2 ozs. (Avoirdupoids) of sample, with the recovered black tin still being weighed in grains etc. The assay conversion table is calculated on the following observation:

If 2 ozs. of sample give 1 grain of black tin:

1 ton = 2,240 lbs. = 2,240 x 8 lots of 2ozs. = 17,920.

So, 1 ton of ore will give 17,920 grains of black tin.

17,920 grains = 2 lbs. 8 ozs. 15 drms. and 10 $\tfrac{5}{32}$ grains.

So, each grain of black tin recovered per 2 oz. assay is equivalent to 2.56 lbs. per ton (or 0.114%) black tin per ton.

The table is continued, with each 1 grain recovered regarded as 2½ lbs. per ton, up to 25 pennyweights, corresponding to 13 cwts. 2 qrs. 24 lbs. per ton, or 1,536 lbs. per ton (68.57%).

In this case, the imposed deduction for water content and management 'bonus' is made equivalent to that in example 1.

I thought it necessary to enter into these details because this is the practice of Cornish assayers for <u>all</u> tin ores handled by them. Also, with the deplorable weights and measures system still in use in England, almost mysterious complications are introduced where a simple 'rule of three' (things to remember) would suffice.

The assay of black tin concentrate for tin metal is performed by a metallurgical method (I), (*in effect, a miniature smelting*). Graphite crucibles are used, of 3" diameter and 4" tall. Two at a time can be put into a small kiln, whose main dimensions are 10" wide, 7" depth to the chimney, 15" depth to the fire and with the cross-section of the arch 10" by 3".

The assay of black tin for tin metal

The charge is 20 pennyweights (= 1 oz. Troy) of black tin, mixed with 5 pennyweights of powdered anthracite, sometimes adding 4 pennyweights of borax or a little fluorspar (*to aid slag formation*).

The crucibles are placed on the hot coke fire, and the reaction and fusion lasts 20 or 25 minutes. The metal is poured out into a cast iron mould and the slag, heavily charged with globules of metal, is put to one side and combined with everything that can be detached from the crucible. It is pulverised and then put into a tin-plate bowl with holes, which retains the largest metal blobs flattened by the pulverisation, those that pass the holes being recovered on a vanning shovel. Finally, all the separated metal is recombined and weighed, the ingot plus the large and small metal globules.

(I) It will be noticed that the Cornish assay procedures for black tin and tin and copper metal, as defective as they are as a system of metallurgical account-keeping, are excellent from the practical point of view, as their results are entirely comparable and compatible with the various operations as a whole, which they limit.

The 'quality' of the tin metal is judged by a supplementary procedure. The tin is melted in a small iron dish, and poured out into a marble mould. The impurities from this 'refining' stay sticking to the dish, from where they are detached by tapping before cooling. I shall not stress here the necessary aspects of producing a good tin ingot.

The examination of samples on the floors at Par Consols

The dressing Captain on his floor is engaged practically all the time in examining the slimes and sands in course of treatment. The vanning shovel is his only instrument, and one may say that it is enough for him, thanks to an extraordinary practical ability that experience in vanning gives.

On the dressing floor of Par Consols I have collected sixty or so samples, chosen from the most important phases of treatment, and I have had, in the course of this work, to indicate the black tin content and the degree of fineness and classification of most of them. I shall only return here to clarify what is meant by the terms 'large', 'middle' and 'fine', used above, or 'sand' and 'slimes', at least as far as the large floors (such as Par Consols, Polgooth, Tincroft and Wheal Vor etc.) are concerned, where the tin is disseminated in the gangue.

I thought it necessary to add a table (see later) of the bulk densities of the various sand products, and to set out in summary the method of investigating them, which, after numerous attempts, seemed to me the one, exact way to characterise them.

Physical examination of the materials is much the more important, and this can only be done meticulously by microscope. For most of the samples a magnification of 125 diameters is needed.

(At this point, I should state that Moissenet defines the particle sizes he found and discussed in terms of units of 0.01mm., or $1/100$ of a millimetre, possibly because that was a reasonable standard at the time, and the $1/1000$ of a millimetre unit – the micrometre, or 'micron' as it is nowadays known, and often abbreviated to the Greek letter, µ - was not due for many years to become the internationally agreed standard that it now is. Consequently, I have multiplied Moissenet's quoted numerical sizes by a factor of 10, to convert them to microns for easier interpretation by today's mineral processors and students. With a little patience this is not hard to come to terms with, 1mm. thus being equal to 1,000 microns, bringing all the quoted particle sizes to the modern standard. With apologies to purists, A.J.C.).

Returning to Moissenet's text:

The measurement of the grains can be achieved either by spreading a tiny quantity on to a glass plate engraved with millimetres divided into 100 equal parts, or, more easily, by introducing into the microscope eyepiece, a similarly engraved device, which can then look directly at particles on any part of the slide at any given magnification. This way, even the finest dust can be examined.

With a little practice, a room in daylight serves well, and it is easy to measure at leisure the outlines of the particles observed.

- The coarse sands at Par Consols, those retained in the 'roughs box', **F**, are not more than 1mm. (1,000 microns) in diameter.
- By far the major proportion of the main slimes, **K**, is reduced to what may be termed 'impalpable powder', that is, to sizes that cannot be estimated at a magnification of 125 times, many of these particles being smaller than 10 microns in diameter ($^{10}/_{1,000}$ of a millimetre). Comparing these extremes, it can be appreciated that their relative particle volume is 1 million to one.
- The 'crop' tin reaches 200, 300, 400 or 500 microns (½ a millimetre) for the coarsest grains, while those of the 'top skimmings' from kieves barely exceed 40 – 70 microns, i.e. generally about ⅕ of the size.
- In the slimes, the particles that can be seen *distinctly* are 20 and 30 microns in size.

In well-classified materials, the gangue is noticeably coarser than the tin. It will be easy to appreciate this by means of the following figures, where I have reproduced several grains of the main constituent minerals for each of the product divisions of kieve, **C**. (See p. 111).

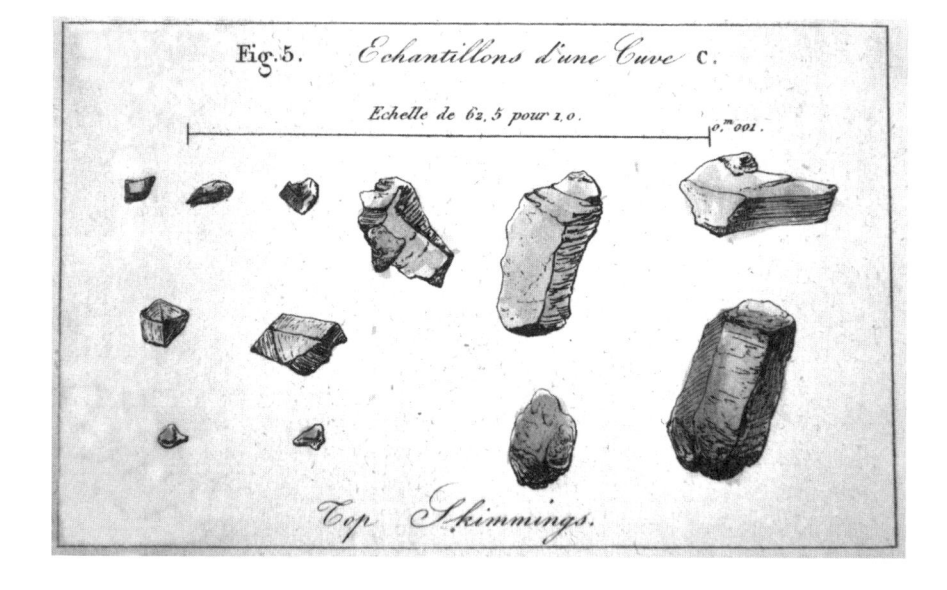

Fig. 5. *Echantillons d'une Cuve* c.

Echelle de 62,5 pour 1,0. $0,^m001$.

Top Skimmings.

Bottom Skimmings.

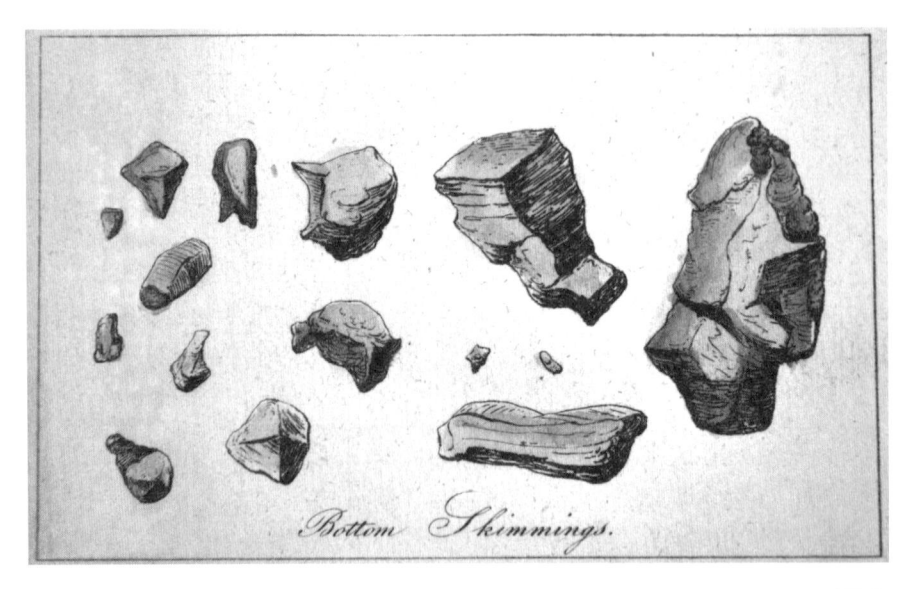

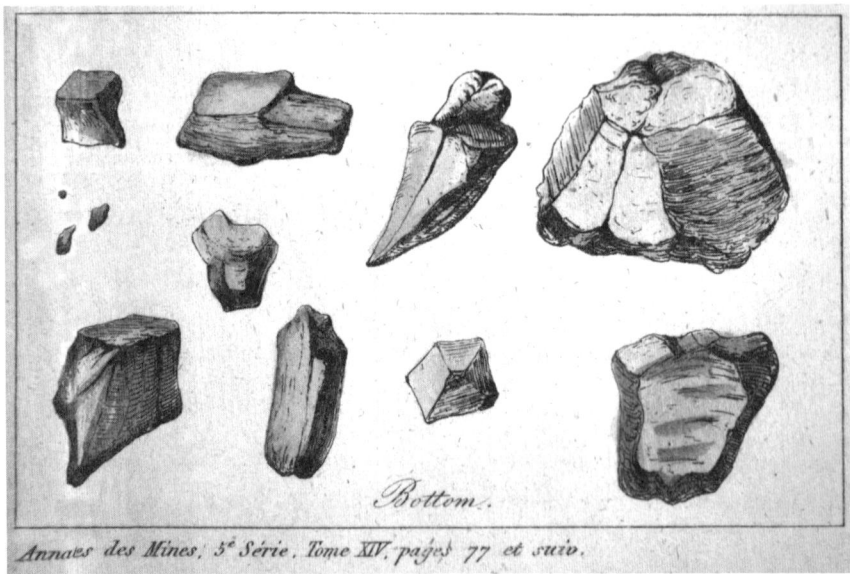

Bottom.

Annales des Mines, 5ᵉ Série, Tome XIV, pages 77 et suiv.

If space had allowed me to present similar drawings for the other samples, then most of the subtle points that I discussed in dealing with the work of various pieces of apparatus would become evident.

The effect of the paddle trunks, **L**, is one of the most remarkable to examine. In the head, with a small quantity of powder, are concentrated grains of 100, 200 and 250 microns (up to ¼ of a millimetre). The majority are 40, 50, 60 and 70 microns in size. In the tail, in contrast, there are some grains of 100 and 200 microns, spread amongst a mass of particles of 10 and 20 microns, and smaller. The immediate rejection of some of this fraction from the main floors (*via second paddle trunks, N, to the beach*) is thus easily explained, despite its still appreciable tin content.

Below are the particle dimensions of several species relating to the divisions of a large square buddle, **B'**, on 'common work':

Division	Species	Sizes (μ)	Average (μ)
Head	Tin	30, 40, 70, 100	40
	Gangue	Fine, up to 100	50
Middle	Tin	As in the head	40
	Gangue	Now coarser	100 - 150
Tail	Much coarse material	200, 250, 500	
	Some very fine	20, 30	

The general fineness of material when, as at Par Consols, the gangue carries a significant proportion of chlorite, has a connection with intensity of colour. The chlorite, not as hard as quartz, tends to be more prevalent in the slimes than in the sands, but the most pronounced hue in the former has, above all, to be attributed to the play of light on fine dust. The products on the floors, when becoming enriched, take on a yellow-brown colour, as much due to pyrite as to tin oxide.

The tin, looked at under the microscope by transmitted light, is, prior to roasting, honey-yellow, greenish and generally reddish. After roasting, the surface is brown and ceases to be uniform, many small roughnesses appearing to reflect the chemical action of sulphides, as mentioned earlier (*see 'roasting'*).

The washed black tin is sparkling, but by transmitted light many of the grains appear to have gone brown.

Another characteristic, by which one can confirm that slimes are really very fine, is their solidification en masse on drying. The main slimes, the tails from paddle trunks, become astonishingly hard, considering their somewhat 'gritty' nature.

The damp ores ready for stamping weigh from 9 to 10 tons 'per 100 sacks', or, put another way, they have a bulk density of 1.670 – 1.860 Kg. per litre (*also the same numerical value in tonnes per cubic metre*). At Par Consols, it is the lower of these two figures.

Bulk densities of solids, and of materials settled in water

Treatment products have to be well dried for their relative weights to have a fixed basis for comparison, one cause of important variations being settling and compaction. Personally, in evaluating this, I am happy to introduce dry material into a tared (*i.e. pre-weighed*) measuring cylinder, which serves to measure both the volume of the settled solids and their weight, with settlement without tapping as an extra inducement to compaction. The 'natural compaction' resulting from this type of experiment is then a characteristic of the degree of fineness and classification of the various products.

After weighing the dry sand, I used to add water to achieve complete wetting and mixing, and then let the water fill the vessel, when the slimy material would settle over time. This compaction under the influence of water was especially pronounced for fine and poorly classified material.

The difference (column 4) between the 'wet density', as determined above, and the dry, bulk density, represents the cube of the volume of voids left between grains of material in the dry state.

The interpretation of the figures is easy. One can recognise the influences of:

1. The density of tin oxide on the rich products.
2. Predominant particle size.
3. A mixture of slimes and sands.

They will always be found in accordance with their significance both in established, practical characteristics of products, or under the microscope.

I would remind readers not to confuse the weights in column 3 with the densities of sand samples taken and measured while still in the wet state, as the latter would be much higher. Thus, for N_1, instead of 128 one would have 178.

Analysis for tin by the wet chemical method

The procedure set out by M. Rivot for the analysis of tin ores, and which is based on chemical reduction of tin oxide by hydrogen, is the only one that has given me good results.

It is not that, for most of the samples indicated above, a rigorously exact figure for the quantitative determination of tin metal content proves indispensable, as the approximate figure (*by vanning*) is unlikely to exceed this, but, when it is a question of a metal like tin, an incorrect analysis can have significant consequences. There are no small errors.

The use of Rivot's method, so simple for rich ore, becomes far more delicate and laborious when the tin content falls below 4 – 5%.

To be able to guarantee the quantitative determination of tin, it is necessary to arrive at a final weight of 0.5 – 0.6 grammes of material (*tin oxide*), so that for sands or slimes whose tin content is assumed at 1%, less than 50 grammes cannot be used to start with.

Below, is a summary of the series of operations:

1. Preliminary drying of material on a sand bath at about 100° C.
2. Weighing of the sample.
3. Very careful 'porphyrisation'. Chemical attack by 'aqua regia' (*a mixture of nitric and hydrochloric acids*) to get rid of iron pyrites. At this stage, chlorite will be partially attacked if the aqua regia is too concentrated, and gelatinous silica in solution makes the subsequent filtration prolonged and difficult. It is better to use very weak aqua regia, and especially not to apply heat.
4. The unattacked part of the sample, tin oxide and gangue, is filtered off, roasted, weighed, and chemically reduced by hydrogen in a small boat in a porcelain tube at red heat. It is re-weighed, which gives the weight of oxygen removed.

Material origin on the floors		Product	1. Black tin content, %	2. Dry (g)	3. Wet (g)	4. Voids (wet – dry)
Best work	Strips, **A**	1	24.00	152	194	42
		2	8.00	142	191	49
		3	2.00	144	188	44
	Square buddle, **B**	1	42.00	222	277	55
		2 & 3	10.00	147	205	52
		4	3.00	142	200	58
	Shacking tye hopper	41	53.50	170	227	55
	Kieve, **C**	1	11.00	142	194	52
		2	20.00	152	202	50
		3	70.00	264	307	43
Common work	Strips, **A'**	1	18.00	150	191	41
		2	0.80	135	185	50
		3	0.85	126	164	38
	Round buddle, **R**	1	18.50	157	191	44
		2	2.00	114	151	37
		3	0.68	121	161	40
	Round buddle, **R'**	2	2.80	121	168	47
		3	0.30	128	171	43
	Round buddle, **R"**	1	11.50	128	175	47
		2	1.70	128	178	50
	Kieve, **C**	1	7.00	121	168	47
		2	18.00	143	187	44
		3	59.00	218	262	44
Roughs box, **F**		1	0.80	121	160	39
Slimes	Small pits, **G**	1	1.20	121	161	40
		2 & 3	0.85	114	160	46
	Frame, **I**	1	6.70	125	169	44
		2	0.75	114	157	43
	Slime pits, **K**	1	2.00	100	147	47
	Paddle trunks, **L**	1	1.73	100	143	43
		2	1.30	98	147	49
	Paddle trunks, **N**	1	0.90	93	128	35
	Frame, **M**	1	4.40	121	168	47
		2	1.40	108	150	42
	Large frame, **β**	1	48.00	200	243	43
		2	5.00	121	165	44

5. The chemically reduced material is disagglomerated, if needed, attacked by cold, concentrated hydrochloric acid with a few drops of nitric acid added.
6. The liquor is diluted, filtered, and the tin precipitated as tin sulphide by the prolonged passage through the solution of hydrogen sulphide gas.
7. The tin sulphide is filtered off, dried slowly, and separated as far as possible from the filter paper (which can be burnt off in part). It is then returned to the state of tin oxide by heating in a muffle furnace.

The complete analysis of black tin ready for sale gave me the following results:

Tin oxide	92.00% }	Oxidised tin	93.66%
Iron oxide (combined)	1.66%		
(free)	2.66% }	Gangue	4.32%
Gritty gangue	1.66%		
Water	2.00%	Water	2.00%
	99.98%		99.98%

The metallic tin content reported at 72.312% be weight.

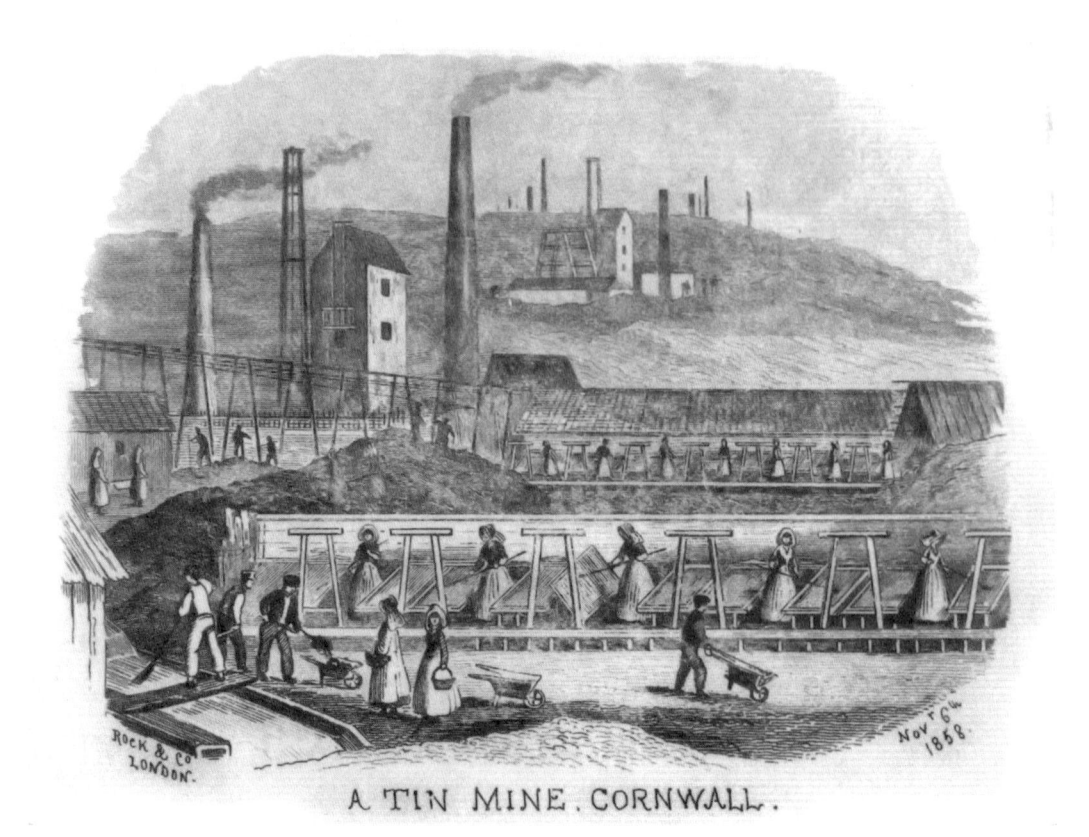

A TIN MINE, CORNWALL.

Index

arsenic 13, 23, 24, 55, 63

arsenical pyrites. *See under* Tin dressing, treatment, operations and equipment

assaying 160, 170
   black tin in ores, by vanning 25, 88, 89, 96, 121, 123, 142, 151, 152, 160
   black tin in ores, wet chemical 168
   tin metal in black tin 160
   tributers' ore parcels 141, 163

authors, references to 9, 11, 16, 31, 37, 38, 66, 71, 92, 155, 160

black tin 23, 24, 150, 167
   carriage, to smelters 14, 153
   cleaning by acid 156
   coarse and fine, as dresed product 23
   losses during treatment 129, 133, 134, 151
   price of 10, 64, 156, 157
   recoverable 150
   'small' tin 23, 26, 42
   yield 19, 150

coal consumption, general 13
   during roasting 132, 134
   during stamping 70, 71, 86

copper ore, in tin lodes 18
   recovery of, during tin dressing 23, 24

copper ores, in tin lodes
   recovery of, during tin dressing 44, 135

dressing of tin ores
   different ore types
     at Great Wheal Vor 48
     at Par Consols 55
     at St. Day United 54
     at stream works 151
     at Tincroft 50
     Drakewalls 63

dressing operations. *See* tin dressing, treatment, operations and equipment

foundries 15

geology, Cornwall, general 15
   granite 16, 18
   sedimentary rocks 16

labour
   costs of 86, 96, 108, 134, 135, 147, 149
   earnings 15, 86, 103, 121, 123, 135, 138, 141, 146, 147
   personnel 135
   workforce 15, 86, 103, 108, 111, 121, 129, 136, 138, 141, 146

mineral production in Cornwall 12

mines and stream works
   Balleswidden 10, 19, 22, 24, 26, 66, 67, 73, 80, 85, 88, 112, 130, 139, 141, 150, 157
   Beam 19
   Boscean 157
   Boscundle 157
   Botallack 149, 150, 157, 160
   Carclaze 10, 17, 19, 25, 88, 150, 151, 156
   Carnbrea 11, 18, 39, 66, 67, 70, 79, 84, 88, 90, 134, 144, 145, 149, 150, 157
   Carnyorth 157
   Carvath United 10, 81, 91, 106, 119
   Charlestown Consols 150
   Ding Dong 157
   Dolcoath 11, 18, 21, 55, 66, 67, 70, 71, 145, 149, 150, 151, 157
   Drakewalls 10, 19, 20, 23, 48, 63, 64, 95, 157
   Grat Polgooth 24
   Great Beam 157
   Great Hewas 71
   Great Polgooth 26, 43, 66, 67, 73, 81, 83, 85, 88, 112, 117, 118, 122, 130, 139, 150, 151, 157, 164
   Great Wheal Fortune 157
   Great Wheal Vor 10, 12, 19, 22, 28, 38, 40, 43, 47, 48, 53, 55, 57, 66, 67, 68, 71, 72, 73, 74, 76, 83, 94, 97, 98, 99, 100, 103, 106, 108, 110, 114, 121, 130, 131, 133, 134, 137, 144, 145, 157, 164
   Great Work 19, 157
   Huel Kitty (St Agnes) 157
   Huel Margaret 157
   Huel Mary 157
   Huel Owles 157
   Huel Tremayne 157
   Levant 11, 88, 112, 145, 149, 150, 157, 160, 161
   Old Budnick 19
   Par Consols 10, 18, 19, 22, 24, 26, 29, 33, 35, 40, 42, 43, 48, 55, 57, 58, 59, 60, 61, 62, 66, 67, 68, 70, 73, 81, 82, 84, 85, 86, 88, 89, 90, 91, 94, 97, 102, 103, 105, 108,

111, 117, 118, 120, 121, 122, 123, 127, 128, 129, 130, 133, 134, 137, 138, 139, 140, 141, 144, 145, 146, 149, 150, 151, 152, 154, 156, 157, 159, 164, 165, 167
Pednandrea 91, 157
Pentuan 10, 43
Polberro 11, 19, 20, 88, 90, 144, 145, 150, 157
Poldice. See St. Day United
Polgooth 10, 19, 71
Porkellis 157
Providence Mines 10, 88, 150, 157
Reeth Consols 157
St. Day United 10, 20, 22, 24, 39, 48, 53, 54, 55, 64, 71, 72, 74, 85, 108, 112, 116, 119, 120, 130, 150, 157
St. Ives Consols 157
Tincroft 10, 18, 19, 21, 22, 24, 29, 39, 43, 44, 48, 50, 51, 52, 53, 66, 67, 69, 70, 72, 73, 75, 76, 83, 85, 86, 88, 94, 95, 96, 99, 101, 103, 104, 105, 106, 108, 110, 115, 118, 119, 120, 121, 132, 134, 135, 137, 139, 141, 142, 144, 145, 150, 164
Trumpet Consols 157
Wendron Consols 11, 25, 144, 145, 149, 150, 157
West Wheal Providence 157
Wheal Bal 25, 149, 150
Wheal Kitty (Lelant) 157
Wheal Providence 149

mining districts 17, 55, 157

mispickel. See arsenical pyrites

Oxland Process, for wolfram removal 23, 63

particle behaviour in water 92, 93, 94, 101, 105

ports in Cornwall 14

railways and tramways 14

sampling tin ore for assay 141, 142

slimes. See under Frames

smelting works 14

stamping 25–26, 65
  coal consumption 70, 71, 86
  costs 90, 91
  operation 82, 86, 87, 88
  water consumption 85

stamps
  axles and cams 77, 78, 79, 86
  coffer boxes 73, 75, 76, 77, 80, 82, 83, 84, 85

construction and layout 79
duty 69, 70, 71
engines 66
feed 72, 74
'flashers' 88
guides and bearings 72, 76, 77, 79, 81, 86, 87, 89
improvements 71, 72
power needed 68
purchase price 91
speed 69
steam-powered 21, 66, 67
tallow, oil, grease and hemp consumption 86
tappets 70, 77, 78, 81, 83, 87, 89
water-powered 20, 90

strips 26–27, 91–97, 135–136

surface captains 10, 15, 28, 29, 52, 88, 96, 102, 107, 119, 120, 121, 138, 141, 146, 148, 151, 159, 164

tin dressing floors
  arrangement and layout 20, 21, 95
  arrangment and layout 96
  economics and costs 140–156
  topography and siting of 20

tin dressing, treatment, operations and equipment
  associated minerals 130
    arsenical pyrites 19, 30, 31, 55, 63, 93, 103, 127, 128, 129, 130, 132
    copper pyrites 23, 30, 93, 127, 129, 132
    iron pyrites 93, 127, 129, 130, 132
    wolfram 18, 19, 20, 23, 55, 63, 64, 65
  best work, treatment of 20, 22, 48, 56, 169
  boxes 33
  breaking of ore 20, 140
  buddles, round 26–29, 53, 56–63, 104–109, 135–139
  buddles, square 26–29, 39, 48, 53, 56–63, 97–104, 136–139
  chimming, in kieves 31
  classification 26, 27, 32, 33, 34, 36, 39, 40–42, 50, 53, 91, 110–112, 159, 167
    spitzkasten 159
  common work, treatment of 22, 48, 52, 56, 169
  comparison with copper and lead ores 10, 20
  cost of various apparatus 89
  costs of ore breaking 140–141
  costs of various apparatus 139, 140

costs, per ton of black tin produced 64, 89, 130, 134, 136–138, 141, 146–151, 153
costs, per ton of ore treated 89–91, 103, 108, 111, 129–130, 136–137, 141, 147, 151
costs, total 146–147, 154
crazes 22–24, 46, 52, 55, 56, 84, 102
crop tin 22–24, 52, 56, 148
cropt tin 135–138
developments in since 1828 9–10
dressing of tin ores
  equipment maintenance and working life 139
  final cleaning 43–45, 138–139
    'dressing' (or 'burning') house 43–44, 50, 128
  general 20–24, 31–32, 44, 135, 160–162
  historical 9, 10
  losses during treatment 129, 134, 151
  kieves 26, 28–30, 42, 46, 49, 53, 109–111, 136, 137
    chimming 30
  products of, under the microscope 165–166
  maintenance of equipment, and working life 139–140
  ore breaking
    ragging 20, 141
    spalling 20, 141
  ore character, ease of treatment 26
  paddle trunks 36, 37, 41, 56, 57, 112–113, 166
  products, examination by microscope 164–166
    bulk density, assessment of 163, 164–165
  recent progress and improvements 9
  roasting 25, 31, 41–44, 127–135
    by reverbatory furnace 127
    by rotary calciner 127–134
    coal consumption 132, 134
  roughs 22, 28, 29, 31–35, 49, 53, 56, 148, 169
    boxes 36
    boxes, valves 33
  shacking, for recovery of roughs 34
  sieving and dilluing, secondary treatment 45
  slimes, handling, apparatus and treatment 22–23, 36, 50, 55–57, 113–126, 148, 165, 169
    frames 36–39, 50, 53–57, 113–126
      effect of length 119
      effect of width 119
      Hancock 117–118, 122–126
      hand 113–114
      machine 114–116
      performance 122–123
      self-acting 116–118
    tyes 33, 34, 37, 43, 44, 45, 46, 49, 56, 57, 63
      working slope 120–121
    tailings to waste 43
    tin 'witts' 23, 30, 31, 34, 43, 45, 52, 63
    treatment according to particle size 22
    tyes 33
    tables, German rotating 160
tin metal and black tin value 155
tin ore
  associated and gangue minerals 11, 18, 19, 90, 93, 101, 129
  best work, treatment of 20, 22, 48, 56, 169
  character and ease of treatment 26
  common work, treatment of 22, 48, 52, 56, 169
  deposits 17, 18
  lodes in granite 18
  lodes in killas 19
  lodes with copper ore 18
  lode types 18, 19, 150, 151
  sorting 20
  yield of black tin on dressing 150, 151
  yield of black tin ore dressing 20
tin trade, historical background 11
tramways 14
tributers, ore and payment 140
water, consumption during dressing 82, 85, 101, 121, 135–139
  provision for dressing 21
wolfram 18, 19, 20, 23, 55, 63, 64, 65